Activity Theory in Education

Activity Theory in Education

Research and Practice

Foreword by Yrjö Engeström

Edited by

Dilani S. P. Gedera and P. John Williams

SENSE PUBLISHERS
ROTTERDAM/BOSTON/TAIPEI

A C.I.P. record for this book is available from the Library of Congress.

ISBN: 978-94-6300-385-8 (paperback)
ISBN: 978-94-6300-386-5 (hardback)
ISBN: 978-94-6300-387-2 (e-book)

Published by: Sense Publishers,
P.O. Box 21858,
3001 AW Rotterdam,
The Netherlands
https://www.sensepublishers.com/

All chapters in this book have undergone peer review.

Printed on acid-free paper

TABLE OF CONTENTS

YRJÖ ENGESTRÖM

FOREWORD

Making Use of Activity Theory in Educational Research

Cultural-Historical Activity Theory is applied around the world in various disciplines and domains of practice. However, its historical roots since the pioneering work of Vygotsky and Leont'ev are closely intertwined with transformations in education. In spite of the widespread and rapidly increasing use of Activity Theory in educational research, few collections of this work are available. *Activity Theory in Education: Research and Practice* is such a much needed collection of practical experiences, theoretical insights and empirical research findings on the use of Activity Theory in educational settings.

Activity Theory is probably most commonly used in educational investigations as a conceptual lens through which data are interpreted. The well known triangular model of an activity system (Engeström, 2015, p. 63) is frequently applied as a graphic model and lens for such interpretive data analyses. The chapters of the first part of the present volume are to a large extent examples of this type of study. In such analyses, the model of an activity system makes visible the context of the educational processes under investigation. Context is represented as a systemic formation within which specific components and their relations can be identified and examined in detail. Extending the unit of analysis beyond a single activity system to encompass multiple interconnected activities – i.e., third generation Activity Theory – will become an important challenge as educational processes become increasingly distributed and networked.

Qualitative change and development in activity systems, including schools and other educational organisations, is driven by contradictions. The chapters of the second part of the present volume focus on contradictions and tensions in educational contexts. Contradictions are historically accumulating systemic tensions that cannot be observed directly. Only their manifestations, such as disturbances and conflicts, are observable in the daily flow of actions. That is why the examination of contradictions requires historical analysis. Hypotheses generated by historical analysis can then be tested and enriched with data on disturbances and conflicts experienced and articulated by practitioners.

Applying Activity Theory in concrete research typically requires intermediate theoretical concepts. Such intermediate concepts connect general theoretical concepts such as activity system and contradiction to the specific context and data under investigation. Chapters in the third and fourth parts of the present volume employ several intermediate theoretical concepts. These include emotion, cognition and action as an interconnected triad, organisational culture, community education and sustainability, and pedagogical content knowledge. These chapters contain fruitful questions and challenges. For example, what is the relationship between psychological tools and organisational culture? Or, How to integrate emotions in the study of human activity?

In its developed form, research based on Activity Theory develops and applies a methodology of its own. Here methodology is understood as the bridge between theory and data. In other words, methodology is more than a collection of specific methods or techniques. It puts forward and implements a theory-driven set of principles, or "an argumentative grammar" (Kelly, 2004), upon which the choice of specific methods is based, starting from data collection and reaching all the way to conceptual interpretation of the findings. The present volume contains interesting examples of methodologically informed choices of methods. For instance, think aloud and stimulated recall as methods of data elicitation were clearly chosen because they corresponded to both the specific context of the study and to the concerns generated by the basic Activity-Theoretical ideas guiding the study.

We may think of an ideal-typical design of an Activity-Theoretical study with the help of Figure 1.

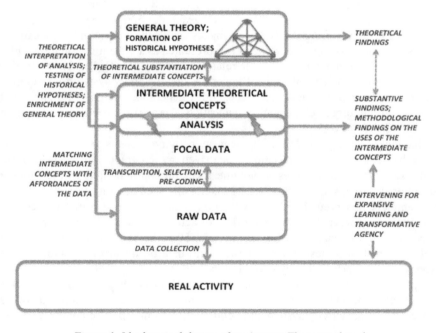

Figure 1. Ideal-typical design of an Activity-Theoretical study

The lightning-shaped arrows in the analysis box in Figure 1 indicate that the meeting between intermediate theoretical concepts and focal data is a creative field of surprises. It is a tension-laden encounter in which the intended concepts will be questioned, modified and occasionally discarded.

The text on the right-hand side of Figure 1 indicates that Activity-Theoretical studies lead to interventions aimed at enhancing expansive learning and transformative agency (Engeström, Sannino, & Virkkunen, 2014; Sannino, Engeström, & Lemos, 2016). Several chapters in the present volume anticipate and provide building blocks of this kind of formative intervention. Examples of such openings include community education for sustainability and teachers designing their classroom curriculum. Perhaps these openings may be read as markers of an emerging zone of proximal development for making use of Activity Theory in educational research.

REFERENCES

Engeström, Y. (2015). *Learning by expanding: An activity-theoretical approach to developmental research* (2nd ed.). Cambridge, UK: Cambridge University Press.

Engeström, Y., Sannino, A., & Virkkunen, J. (2014). On the methodological demands of formative interventions. *Mind, Culture, and Activity, 21*, 118–128.

Kelly, A. E. (2004). Design research in education: Yes, but is it methodological? *The Journal of the Learning Sciences, 13*, 115–128.

Sannino, A., Engeström, Y., & Lermos, M. (2016). Formative interventions for expansive learning and transformative agency. *Journal of the Learning Sciences* (in press).

Yrjö Engeström
CRADLE
University of Helsinki

PREFACE

Cultural Historical Activity Theory (Activity Theory), as a multi-disciplinary research framework has gained increasing popularity in recent years. Activity Theory is rooted in the works of Vygotsky, Leont'ev and Engeström and offers analytical as well as conceptual tools to examine human practices. *Activity Theory in Education: Research and practice* focuses on a variety of perspectives on the application of Activity Theory in Educational contexts. It provides methodological guidance/theoretical aspects and also moves beyond the theoretical realm and offers perspectives on the pragmatic use of Activity Theory framework in contemporary learning contexts.

The book stems from our insights and knowledge accumulated through the experience of a number of substantial research projects which were carried out between 2011 to 2014. The quest for a better understanding of Activity Theory involved discussions, scholarly debates, and many hours of reading which inspired us to initiate this book.

We are very grateful to the authors, who each contributed a chapter to this book. We are particularly pleased that Professor Engeström agreed to write the Foreword to the book after reading the drafts of all the chapters. We would also like to thank several people who have been supportive in one way or another in the course of this journey; Jenny Mangan, Arezou Zalipour and Noeline Wright. It is our hope that the various experiences recounted in this book will develop deeper understandings of Activity Theory to enable more effective use of such frameworks in educational research.

MARILYN FLEER

1. THE VYGOTSKY PROJECT IN EDUCATION – THE THEORETICAL FOUNDATIONS FOR ANALYSING THE RELATIONS BETWEEN THE PERSONAL, INSTITUTIONAL AND SOCIETAL CONDITIONS FOR STUDYING DEVELOPMENT

INTRODUCTION

In 1984 Yrjö Engeström, Pentti Hakkarainen and Mariane Hedgaard wrote that:

> For the self-conscious development of any science – including didactics [education] – it is essential to work out the basic inner relationship of its object system. This bare generality, the initial 'germ cell', is the original contradiction that has given birth to the concrete system under investigation. The mental reproduction of this germ cell is the first step in the process of understanding and shaping practically the rich forms of the totality, of the 'unity of the manifold', in their lawful inner determination and development, i.e. of ascending from the abstract to the concrete. (p. 127)

Key for Engeström, Hakkarainen and Hedgaard is the germ cell or unit as the basic inner relationship of the object system. Vygotsky (1987) and those that have followed have sought to identify what makes up the smallest unit or germ cell of a system. What is the essence or basic unit that shows all the relations of that system? What might be the contradiction or tension that acts as the catalyst for the development of that system? These were central questions in 1984 for Engeström, Hakkarainen and Hedgaard, as they were for Vygotsky, and as will be shown in this chapter, are still relevant questions today.

A "self-conscious development" of educational research that draws upon a non-classical methodology to progress understandings (see Robbins & Stetsenko, 2002) is still much needed. Mainstream research methodologies have not yet institutionalised a cultural-historical approach as a key methodological paradigm for engaging in research. Yet, a growing body of empirical research is being undertaken which seeks to examine the contradictions that exist within a concrete system of education for specific fields of inquiry. As such, an interesting tension exists between the research needs of educators, empirical studies being formulated, and what is promoted in the mainstream methodological literature.

D. S. P. Gedera & P. J. Williams (Eds.), Activity Theory in Education, 1–15.

Consequently, there now exists a general mix of concepts and theories that draw their inspiration from Vygotsky, but where the integrity of the original theory may have been lost. To test this out, an analysis of a sample of 11 chapters that draw upon a mix of theoretical concepts, but which fit loosely under the Vygotskian suite of studies, will be examined. The concept of a germ cell or unit will be applied to these studies in order to determine if and what might be the unique features that characterise the whole Vygotsky project. In this chapter the term Cultural-Historical Theory is used to name the original theory set out by Vygotsky. The Vygotsky project names the collection of theories that have since emerged (Stetsenko & Arievitch, 2010). Insights from this investigation will be used in this chapter to inform a theoretical discussion on the Vygotsky project for the context of education, giving new theoretical understandings and methodological integrity to what constitutes the essence of the Vygotsky project. Therefore, the focus of this chapter is a theoretical discussion on the methodological tensions inherent in existing empirical research that draws upon Activity Theory, Sociocultural Theory, Cultural Historical Activity Theory (CHAT), and Cultural-Historical Theory for the context of education. The outcomes contribute back into mainstream theory on the place and integrity of cultural-historical research as a key methodology for understanding development.

This chapter begins by drawing out the central methodological dimensions originally proposed by Vygotsky, where the historical and dynamic processes of development are unearthed. Key concepts from Vygotsky's (1997) methodology and those who have followed, are used to determine the unit or essence of the relations found within each empirical study analysed. It will be argued that the societal, institutional and personal motives and demands that are constantly interacting in these educational settings still require further interrogation, if we are to fully understand the relations between the learning of the participants and development of the system as a whole, with methodological integrity. In order to undertake this methodological analysis and theoretical discussion, this chapter begins by foregrounding the key concepts of the *Vygotsky project*.

THE VYGOTSKY PROJECT

Stetsenko and Arievitch (2010) refer to the Vygotsky project to capture the original foundations from which many new directions have been formulated. As is well known, Vygotsky's seminal ideas were launched in the 1920–30s with a range of scholars, including Leontiev and Luria. After Vygotsky's untimely death in 1934, the Vygotsky school, as it became known, continued to develop its methodological approach against a backdrop of classical reductionist research methods driven by behavioursim. According to Stetsenko and Arievitch (2010), the hotspot of intellectual activity included D. Elkonin, P. Galperi, A. Zaporozhets, L. Bozhovich, L. Lisina, P. Zinchenko, and V. Davydov who together shaped Russian research from that period. Cultural-Historical Theory later influenced Western thinking through the translation of Vygotsky's original texts and the above mentioned authors' papers (and others) that were published in the Journal of Russia and East European Psychology – thus making their ideas accessible to English readers.

Kozulin (1990) names the original three thinkers as the now famous "troika" (A. Luria, A. N. Leontiev & L. S. Vygotsky) and later the "magnificent eight" (including Lidia Bozhovich, Roza Levina, Natalya Morozova, Liya Slavina & Alexander Zaporozhets). Together, these constitute the original Vygotsky project.

The Vygotsky project has grown in the West, with foundational concepts being researched and elaborated by scholars such as Hedgaard, Rogoff, Elhammoumi, Karpov, Moll, Wells, Robbins, Stetensko, and many more. It is suggested by Stetsenko and Arievitch (2010) that the works of these scholars have supported the progression of concepts and expansion of models as noted in the important publications of Bruner, Scribner, Wertsch, Cole, John-Steiner and Engeström. The latter work being particularly pronounced in this publication, where some have linked the concepts central to Activity Theory to Engeström (e.g. Lockley, 2016; Li, 2016) but also back to Leontiev (e.g. Li, 2016; Mwalongo, 2016).

The Vygotsky project as first named by Stetsenko and Arievitch (2010), can also capture the collective nature of developing methodological concepts in cultural-historical research. The collective nature of formulating and developing theoretical concepts has been noted by both Wertsch (1995) and Kozulin (1998), and can be best understood through the common expression of: – *we stand upon the shoulders of the past intellectual giants, who have together generated the methodological tools now available to us in education.* Wertsch (1995) has shown through examining the concept of copyright and patents in the context of inventions, how Western individualism has invited us to conceptualise new ideas and tools as being the property of an individual or group of individuals (as we might see when the Nobel prize is awarded to a group of scientists) not something that has emerged historically and collectively. It can be argued that this collective conception of concept development can also apply to the development of a cultural-historical methodology.

The concept of the Vygotsky project in this chapter is used to signal the contributions made across time in Cultural-Historical Theory and Activity Theory, and as is shown below, as a collective rather than individual activity. It is proposed that the Vygotsky project best illustrates how researchers in education invariably draw upon a range of concepts and tools from across Cultural-Historical Theory, Activity Theory, CHAT and Sociocultural Theory, where a vast array of methodological similarities and differences are evident. To test out this new theoretical claim a sample of 11 chapters were analysed that all drew upon a common theoretical approach to guide their empirical study.

SAMPLE

To achieve the theoretical goal of this chapter, an analysis of chapters drawn from three specific contexts was undertaken: 1) learning and teaching in online learning environments, 2) historical and systemic tensions in educational contexts, and

3) the relations between learning and development of individuals and collectives. In Table 1.1 below is a summary of the sources used and the theoretical positions that are named in each chapter.

Table 1.1. Theories guiding research

Sample	Source	Theoretical position named
Mwalongo, 2016	Leontiev Engeström Vygotsky	Activity Theory
Otrel-Cass, Andreasen and Bang, 2016	Leontiev Vygotsky Bakhtin Engeström	Activity Theory CHAT
Gedera, 2016	Leontiev Vygotsky Engeström	Activity Theory
Harness and Yamagata-Lynch, 2016	Wertsch Cole	CHAT
Li, 2016	Engeström Leontiev Vygotsky	CHAT
Tay and Lim, 2016	Engeström	Sociocultural Historical Activity Theory
Ramanair, 2016	Wertsch Lave and Wenger Leontiev Engeström Cole	Activity Theory
Aguayo, 2016	Engeström	Constructivism Activity Theory
Pohio, 2016	Engeström Vygotsky Wertsch Kozulin	Activity Theory
Eames, 2016	Wenger Engeström	Activity Theory Sociocultural Theory
Lockley, 2016	Engeström	Activity Theory CHAT

Table 1.1 gives a snapshot of how research that loosely draws from the original cultural-historical tradition plays out in both the naming of the theory guiding the research, but also the key sources drawn upon to frame the studies.

What is immediately evident is whilst the work of Engeström is common to almost all studies being analysed, the researchers have named their framing differently because they go beyond the work of Engeström in building their theoretical case. Activity Theory, CHAT, and Sociocultural Theory are commonly used, sometimes within the same chapter. This reflects a broader issue noted across many journals where a range of theoretical pathways are given by researchers when foregrounding their cultural-historical study designs. The theoretical labels mostly used reflect the theoretical pathways of what now constitutes the Vygotsky project, strengthening the case for the need to name the family of theories commonly used. Table 1.1 shows this need.

Further, the analysis of the 11 chapters where authors sought to draw upon a common conceptual tool (Engeström's triangles), have also enriched the theoretical presentation given because they draw back to Leontiev and Vygotsky, but also project forward when discussing the works of other scholars such as, Wertsch, Lave and Wenger, and Cole (see Column 2). Once again, the citations that go back to the original source and forward to contemporary works, reflect the diversity that now exists in the Vygotsky project.

The findings of the theoretical analysis as presented in Table 1.1 support the use of the term the *Vygotsky project* to capture the use of the theoretical mix of names used in the literature (e.g. CHAT, Sociocultural) and the diversity of sources used to build study designs (e.g. Engeström, Vygotsky). Scholars who stay primarily within one tradition, such as when citing Vygotsky as the original source and only using one label to describe their theoretical stance (as opposed to a mix), would sit outside of this analysis as they do not illustrate a mix of sources and theoretical labels. The analysis and theoretical points made here give a different reading to that of Stetsenko and Arievitch (2010). Using the term the *Vygotsky project* is supportive of the increasing mix of diverse theoretical sources and names used, but it also makes clear a new category of theoretical framing that is increasingly prevalent in the current literature.

METHODOLOGICAL CONCEPTS IN EDUCATIONAL RESEARCH

The Cultural-Historical Theory of Vygotsky and Activity Theory of Leontiev can be viewed as providing a methodological foundation from which to examine the relations between societal, institutional and personal dimensions of human development (Hedegaard, 2012). This perspective allows for the identification of a number of key methodological principles that will be discussed in this section in the context of an analysis of the empirical work presented in the sample of chapters shown in Table 1.1. To achieve this methodological analysis, the key ideas from Vygotsky of holistic research, the concept of development, the unit as the basis for analysis, and the embedded role of the researcher, are each discussed in this section and used for the analysis of the sample of chapters.

Development

Vygotsky (1997) stated that, "Before studying development, we must explain *what* is developing" (p. 44). Veresov (2014) suggests that there are two dimensions to answering the 'what is developing' question. First, what might be the psychological process to be investigated and what is the role of the researcher in this process. Veresov (2014) suggests that paired with the "what question" is a "how question". The question is how to set up the study so that what is being studied can be revealed. For example, we see in Table 1.2 below an analysis of the 11 chapters in the context of the paired questions of what is developing and how the researchers have set up their research to investigate the development of the system they are investigating.

Vygotsky (1987) suggested that everyday life provided the conditions for development through transition points and accidental moments of tension or crisis. Many studies seek to examine the naturalistic conditions that generate contradictions or crises, as noted in Table 1.2, where what is being developed forms the central research question of the empirical studies. Studies that fall under the name of Vygotsky project must focus on development. In a more detailed analysis of the chapters we can show how the researchers sought to examine the development of the system they were studying. For example, Li (2016) examined assessment practices where natural contractions were evident between tutors' emotional reactions to contextual factors and students emotional responses to assessment feedback. Development of a system has also been central for Eames (2016) who noted:

> The juxtaposition of at least three distinct activity systems, the works the planning of a unit, and the delivery of a unit, each of which exist alongside and in connection with other activity systems, allowed the exploration of how the implicit content and pedagogical knowledge of experts could be shared through the mediation of the CoRe tool.

What each of the sample of studies sought to do, was make visible the contradiction or tension that acts as the catalyst for development of that system. However, what is different from Vygotsky's original conception is that the development being studied is not the person, but rather the development of the activity system. This is an interesting point of distinction noted across the chapters analysed.

Holistic Conception of Research

What we also notice in Table 1.2 is a holistic conception of research in each of the studies presented, suggesting that the theoretical tools used in the Vygotsky project support this basic methodological principle originally outlined by Vygotsky (1987). Important to progressing scholarship in human development has been examining the relation between person, institution and society holistically, rather than drawing upon Cartesian logic which separated mind and body, and reduced and separated the

Table 1.2. Methodological framing of research questions

Sample	What is developing?	How can we investigate this?
Mwalongo, 2016	What are students' perceptions of the use of critical thinking skills in synchronous discussion forums?	Surveys, interviews
Otrel-Cass, Andreasen and Bang, 2016	What is the relationship between standardised testing and the formation of self	Ethnographic study: Interviews Observations Document analysis
Gedera, 2016	What were the contradictions that affected students' engagement in a university blended learning course?	Interviews, observations, questionnaires and document analysis
Harness and Yamagata-Lynch, 2016	What are the systemic tensions associated with teacher unions within the United States, and what entities have been perpetuating these tensions?	Content analysis of three key newspaper articles published about the teachers' union
Li, 2016	What are the relations between the contextual factors and cognitive process of tutors when engaged in assessing undergraduate written work, and what is the role of emotions in this activity system?	Online questionnaire, interview, think-aloud, stimulated recall and focus group
Tay and Lim, 2016	What are the actions of the school teaching community during one-to-one computing?	Ethnographic study: observations, field notes, document analysis of planning documents, publications and reports
Ramanair, 2016	How was Moodle used in classroom English language learning and what were the challenges experienced?	Ethnographic study: interviews of teachers and students
Aguayo, 2016	Can the use of ICT assist with the non-formal education for community understanding and action for sustainability?	Pre, post and follow up surveys after a Web-based intervention
Pohio, 2016	An investigation of the communication tools used to facilitate home-school community	Case study – interviews
Eames, 2016	How can experts in content and pedagogy work together with early career secondary teachers to develop one science topic CoRe and one technology topic CoRe to support the development of the latter's PCK?	3 activity systems: 1) observations/field notes of workshops, 2) reflective journal and discussions on planning, 3) classroom observations
Lockley, 2016	What are the ways that secondary teachers in NZ develop local curriculum for sustainability?	Teacher interviews, classroom observations, focus groups

research context from the lived experience of the person(s). Stetsenko and Arievitch (2010) argue that the Vygotsky project:

>...offers a dialectical and nonreductionistist, yet consistently materialistic (i.e., nondualist), vision of human nature and development as rooted in, derivative of, and instrumental in the material collaborative social practices of people (i.e., human goal-directed, purposeful, collaborative activities) aimed at transforming their world. (pp. 231–232)

The holistic method of Vygotsky (1987) and transformative stance of Stetsenko and Arievitch (2010), focus our attention on the holistic nature of research. That is, we must examine not just an individual, but also the social relations and the material conditions that societies and institutions create, which in turn afford (or not) opportunities for a person's development or the development of the system. Holistic research allows for not only the analysis of the system, but gives the possibility to examine the genesis of development. In research, Vygotsky sought to create the research conditions that allowed for the genesis of development to be made visible. As Vygotsky (1997) wrote, the "Analysis provides us with the initial point of their genesis as well as the initial point of the whole method" (p. 41). In the sample of chapters analysed, most of the studies do not specially seek to examine the beginnings of particular forms of development, because they were interested in particular systems as they were currently operating – yet the methodological principles actually allowed for this. For instance, Gedera (2016) focused on determining the contradictions that affected students' engagement in a university blended learning course. These systems were already in operation. However, through examining the systems in place holistically, it became possible to notice the contradictions, and these contradictions in turn represented the original contradictions that gave birth to the concrete system under investigation – that is, their genesis.

Unit

Vygotsky (1987) stated that we must "identify those units in which the characteristics of the whole are present, even though they may be manifested in altered form. Using this model of analysis, it must attempt to resolve the concrete problems that face us" (p. 47). This idea was introduced in the introduction where Engeström, Hakkarainen and Hedgaard reference the germ cell or unit as the basic inner relationship of the object system. The unit is a key concept in Cultural-Historical Theory, and when discussed as the basic inner relationship of the object system as referenced by Engeström, Hakkarainen and Hedgaard, we see it is also important in Activity Theory.

Determining what is the essence or basic unit of relations was first discussed by Vygotsky (1987) in the context of research method. Specifically, Vygotsky's (1987) methodology encompassed two methods of analysis. One approach he argued was designed to examine the elements, whereby an atomistic approach was adopted where the whole is broken down into the simplest components or elements. He suggested that this approach lost the properties of the whole. He cites the example of breaking down water (whole) into its elements (hydrogen and oxygen atoms). Vygotsky (1987) suggested that in this approach the analysis is flawed because the properties of the whole no longer exist in each of the elements, and therefore the results (elements) cannot help explain the relationship between concrete form and the concrete diversity encountered in everyday life. It is not possible to fully research the initial and final forms or examine the dynamic processes in motion (or the process of developing). Vygotsky said that this type of conceptualisation did not "help us untangle completely the whole thread of which they are the end" (Vygotsky, 1997, pp. 41–42) and it "causes the researcher to ignore the unified and integral nature of the process being studied" (Vygotsky, 1987, p. 46).

In contrast, Vygotsky's (1987) second method focused on units, whereby the researcher breaks down the whole into units that retain the properties of the whole. He argued that the latter method retained the dynamic and relational nature of the whole. He showed "…how the great is revealed in the small" (Vygotsky, 1997, p. 41). Vygotsky (1987) stated that "the term "unit" designates a product of analysis that possesses *all the basic characteristics of the whole*. The unit is a vital and irreducible part of the whole" (p. 46).

The research that constitutes the Vygotsky project also focuses on determining the internal relations. That is, the germ cell or unit of the system that is being studied. We see this in most of the 11 chapters where an activity system is presented and the relations between the constituting characteristics is explicitly shown so that insights into the development of that system (or otherwise) can be determined. In each of the 11 studies, the researchers have kept the whole system together, and have sought to examine the characteristics of that system as relationships – thus constituting a unit of analysis that reveals the object of the system, and as is discussed in the next section, the basic contradictions that develop that system (or not).

Historical Development

The concept of unit on its own was not enough to fully appreciate the complexity of whole systems that are in the process of change. Vygotsky (1997) suggested that, "To study something historically means to study it in motion" (p. 43). The historical dimensions of a cultural-historical methodology foregrounds dynamic motion across time and across generations, whereby the past is present in the moment – as we might see in the teacher union movement where the analysis of previously published material in the public domain about the teachers' union were examined from the perspective of teachers, parents, politicians and society in general (Harness & Yamagata-Lynch, 2016). We also see this in the work of Otrel-Cass, Andreasen and Bang (2016) who state that Activity Theory allowed them to take note of the history of standardised testing in Denmark, where their research was located, and to situate and shape their interpretations based on this understanding. Vygotsky (1997) argued that, "the past and present are inseparably merged" (p. 41). This causes many challenges for the researcher interested to examine institutional, societal and the human condition as a system. Many institutionalised practices have become fossilised, and unearthing their origins or the process of their development is challenging. This methodological challenge was first noted by Vygotsky (1997) when he said:

> …something might be said about human behavior by these weathered, historical scraps which have lost their meaning, these psychological survivors of a remote past that enter into the common tissue of behavior in an alien body, so atypical, impersonal, having lost almost all meaning in the mental adaption of modern [hu]man. (p. 40)

Tables 1.1 and 1.2 show how the weathered, historical and routinised dimensions of human practices are framed through the methods of CHAT, Activity Theory, and Sociocultural Theory, and in so doing reveal their inner contradictions. For instance, when the perspectives of teachers, the students, and the curriculum (as societal expectation) are brought together through interview data, document analysis and focus group sessions (see Table 1.2) contradictions emerge. Harness and Yamagata-Lynch (2016) found that although the public domain sources they examined, which on the surface appeared to be harmless presentations of figures, the analysis undertaken revealed a politicised and one-sided presentation of information about the activities of the teachers' union. They argue that "Teacher unions seem to be in tension with everyone from parents, politicians, government officials, political factions, teachers not associated with the unions, and even those within their own ranks, neoliberalism, and the very ideas purported democratic principles themselves these tensions within and outside the teachers' union contribute to create a hostile environment for all involved". This weathered and routinised perception of teachers' unions cemented in the public domain in newspaper articles is commonplace in many fields of research, requiring different kinds of research tools.

Vygotsky introduced the metaphor of the fossil to explain the fossilisation process and the need for methods that would support better understanding of systems. He gives the following examples to demonstrate how researchers have dealt with this problem:

> The zoologist reconstructs a whole skeleton from an insignificant fragment of bone of some excavated animal and seen as a picture of its life. An ancient coin, which has no value as a coin, frequently reveals to the archeologist a complex historical problem. The historian deciphering hieroglyphics scratched into stone, penetrates into the depths of vanished ages. The doctor diagnoses illness from insignificant symptoms. (Vygotsky, 1997, p. 40)

In analysing newspaper articles to find their contradictions in the objects of the differing groups, Harness and Yamagata-Lynch (2016) were able to see how skewed reporting took place and reinforced publically endorsed perceptions of teachers' unions. We also see examples of how researchers have tackled the fossilisation problem methodologically in the new research context of online learning. For instance, Li (2016) noted that when examining the activity system of tutors responding to assessment of written work, that emotional reactions to contextual factors became evident. Li also noted how tutors recognised and regulated the emotional reactions of students to feedback, where contradiction in relation to contextual factors had become evident. The convergences and divergences of teacher beliefs and practices were possible to discern when Activity Theory was used to gather and analyse data about the online activity system. Without examining emotions in the context of a predominantly cognitive activity, it would have been difficult to find the contradictions and to unpick the beliefs about practices that were guiding the assessment feedback. Finding the right methods to make visible the historical dimensions of large quantities of empirical data gathered was discussed by Pohio (2016), who showed how Activity Theory gave a useful visual framework for understanding the organisational culture that stakeholders could better understand, giving the possibilities for examining contradictions within remnants of historically formed practices.

In each of these studies, a holistic conception of the research was achieved, as the net was cast to include how the researcher set up the context for the identification and analysis of the contradictions inherent in the system. We now turn to the special role the researcher has in Cultural-Historical Theory.

Theoretical Robustness

The role and position of the researcher is always included in the generation of data in cultural-historical research. This holistic perspective supports both the validity and reliability of the data being gathered. We see this when the researcher makes visible the theoretical concepts used for the interpretation of the results, including her or his conception of development and the themes emerging from the study (Hedegaard, 2008). This establishes and increases *validity*. For example, Otrel-Cass, Andreasen and Bang (2016) explain that through the theoretical lens of Activity Theory the researchers adopted a reflexive position in order to better understand how the societal need for national testing, institutionalised and operationalised testing into practice, and what this meant for the personal motives and new demands made by the assessment practice that was currently being experienced by students. Because Activity Theory was predominantly used across the data sets, this ensured that valid data true to the theoretical framework of the research was being generated and interpreted.

Reliability in cultural-historical research is fostered when the researcher is clear about the object of the research (Hedegaard, 2008). For instance, Aguayo (2016) in examining how an online community supports education for sustainability explicitly examined student motivation in relation to the context of the participants. He noted that, "it appeared that these motivations were related to participants' particular socio-cultural context and individual backgrounds, making motivated actions relevant and meaningful within their own milieu, linked to their individual historical, socio-cultural, technological, educational and ecological realities". Important here is how Aguayo (2016) clearly stated the study goals (what development is being considered) and used methods (how to study that development) to examine the activity system under study, increasing reliability of the data being gathered. Table 1.2 shows how this was achieved across all the studies analysed.

Role of the Researcher

In Vygotsky's genetic approach where he sought to determine the genesis of development, he was careful to include the researcher in the fullness of the data gathering, critiquing approaches that did not do so. For instance,

> ...the experimenter creates the required attitude in the subject, elicits the process to be observed and establishes connections, but here, the psychological role of the instruction itself is usually ignored. The researcher then deals with the associations, processes, etc. created and elicited by the instruction just as if they appeared in the natural course in themselves without the instruction. (Vygotsky, 1997, p. 36)

Vygotsky (1997) argued that just when the data gathering commences, researchers often exclude valuable data, as we might see during the process of transitioning into a study site in naturalistic settings. The data gathered at these times is important for gaining a fuller picture, one that needs to be included to ensure validity in the analysis. Studying how the research context is established and the ongoing role of the researcher during the data gathering process gives greater insights into the process of development. Including the researcher as part of the data gathering process is exemplified by Tay and Lim (2016) when examining one-to-one computing, and Ramanair (2016) when examining if Moodle supported the development of English expression. How the researcher was embedded and what role they assumed or the conditions they created in the 11 studies, were not always made as visible as a cultural-historical methodology would suggest is needed.

CONCLUSION

In this chapter the relations between learning and development have been examined through an analysis of the content of 11 research chapters, where *what is developing* and *how this development can be studied* was undertaken. These studies examined continuous change and development through contradiction within an activity system. By noting the contradictions or tensions of the activity system, it becomes possible to make conscious the relations between the characteristics of that system, and through this begin to determine the germ cell or unit that reflects the basic inner relationship of the object system.

The broad range of theoretical concepts drawn upon by the 11 research groups that undertook the research that formed the basis of the analysis presented in this chapter, have a family connection, and these were collectively named as the Vygotsky project. What is foundational to each is the search for a unit that determines the inner core relationships that are reflective of the whole activity system. Determining what is to develop and how the unit of development should be analysed, are also foundational to the theories discussed under the Vygotsky project.

The 11 chapters have primarily drawn upon Activity Theory, CHAT, and/or Sociocultural Theory. The researchers have mostly referenced their theoretical framework back to either Leontiev or Vygotsky or have discussed their theoretical stance in the context of Engeström and other contemporary scholars. This theoretical breadth reflects the diversity that now exists in the literature and represents a new form of theoretical integrity, where there is an urgent need to categorise and name this approach to theoretically framing study designs. Using the name of the Vygotsky project for this purpose (although not originally its intention) captures the tendency to blend theoretical concepts across a broader range of scholarly works in educational research. Using the term the Vygotsky project identifies a place in the theoretical context of cultural-historical research for this theoretical blending of concepts. The point here is not to make judgments, but rather to notice this approach and because of its prevalence, to categorise and name this way of working. It will always be at the behest of the reviewers to determine the value of blending theoretical concepts for specific study designs, where broader conceptual tools may be needed.

Educational research that draws upon the theories coming from the collectively named Vygotsky project features the concept of contradictions, or crisis or some form of tension or transition. Studies of this kind look for the "original contradiction that has given birth to the concrete system under investigation" (Engeström, Hakkarainen, & Hedgaard, 1984, p. 160) so that the basic inner relationship of its object system can be revealed. Davydov (2008) said that, "Practical, object-oriented productive activity – labor – is the basis of all human cognition" (p. 85) thus linking labour with education. The most important dimension that separates one type of activity from another is the object of the activity. In the context of education, it can be argued that the goal of the learning activity is to produce citizens who have knowledge and skills to be part of society. It can be argued that in the early childhood period that the object of play activity is action in an imaginary situation, and in the world of work the "object of work activity is the result of labour process". For schools then, the object of the "learning activity must be the learning subject" as they develop through education (Engeström, Hakkarainen, & Hedgaard, 1984, p. 160). Understanding the object of each educational setting across the 11 chapters through a process of identifying the smallest unit that is characteristic of the whole system was exemplified through the identification of the contradictions.

The methodological foundations for studying education from a cultural-historical perspective, as originally conceptualised by Vygotsky, have provided a strong basis for the emergence of the Vygotsky project. In the self-conscious development of educational research from within this tradition, tools that study 1) the whole system of development, 2) that embed the researcher as part of the conditions of the research, 3) that look for the unit that characterises the whole, 4) that use the concept of contradiction or tension, and 5) where historically institutionalised practices lived in the moment are studied, collectively constitute the essence of what is the Vygotsky project. How the methods that sit under this are named and practiced will be variable, but these five dimensions characterise the essence of the whole Vygotsky project, extending the original concept from that of Stetsenko and Arievitch (2010) who introduced the idea of the family connections but who did not analyse what might constitute this connection. These five characteristics are unique to the work originally put forward by Vygotsky, and which have been further developed or used for educational research by the myriad of scholars who have followed since Vygotsky's death. Collectively, when these works (empirical and theoretical) are framed by these five characteristics, they constitute the essence of the Vygotsky project. This unit or germ cell that characterises the methodology of the Vygotsky project for educational research gives new directions and methodological integrity for scholars seeking to use a mix of concepts from across Activity Theory, Sociocultural Theory, CHAT and Cultural-Historical Theory.

REFERENCES

Davydov, V. V. (2008). *Problems of developmental instruction: A theoretical and experimental psychological study.* New York, NY: Nova Science Publishers.
Engeström, Y., Hakkarainen, P., & Hedegaard, M. (1984). On the methodological basis of research in teaching and learning. In M. Hedegaard, P. Hakkarainen, & Y. Engeström (Eds.), *Learning and teaching on a scientific basis: Methodological and epistemological aspects of the Activity Theory of learning and teaching* (pp. 119–189). Aarhus, Denmark: Psykologisk Institut, Aarhus Universitet.
Hedegaard, M. (2008). The role of the researcher. In M. Hedegaard & M. Fleer (Eds.), *Studying children. A cultural-historical approach* (pp. 202–207), Berkshire, England: Open University Press.
Hedegaard, M. (2012). Analyzing children's learning and development in everyday settings from a cultural-historical wholeness approach. *Mind, Culture, and Activity, 19*(2), 127–138. Retrieved from http://doi.org/10.1080/10749039.2012.665560
Kozulin, A. (1990). *Vygotsky's psychology: A biography of ideas.* Cambridge, MA: Harvard University Press.
Robbins, D., & Stetsenko, A. (2002). *Vygotsky's psychology: Voices from the past and present.* New York, NY: Noval Science Publishers.
Stetsenko, A., & Arievitch, I. M. (2010). Cultural-historical Activity Theory: Foundational worldview, major principles, and the relevance of Sociocultural context. In S. R. Kirschner & J. Martin (Eds.), *The sociocultural turn in psychology: The contextual emergence of mind and self* (pp. 231–252). New York, NY: Columbia University Press.
Veresov, N. (2014). Refocusing the lens on development: Towards genertic research methodology. In M. Fleer & A. Ridgway (Eds.), *Visual methodologies and digital tools for researching with young children: Transforming visuality* (pp. 129–149). Dordrecht, The Netherlands: Springer.
Vygotsky, L. S. (1987). Thinking and speech (N. Minick, Trans.). In R. W. Rieber & A. S. Carton (Eds.), *The collected works of L. S. Vygotsky: Vol. 1. Problems of general psychology* (pp. 39–285). New York, NY: Plenum Press.

Vygotsky, L. S. (1997a). *The collected works of L. S. Vygotsky: Vol. 4. The history of the development of higher mental functions* (M. Hall, Trans., R. W. Rieber, Ed.). New York, NY: Plenum Press.

Wertsch, J. V. (1995). The need for action in sociocultural research. In J. V. Wertsch, P. del Rio, & A. Alvarez (Eds.), *Sociocultural studies of mind* (pp. 56–74). Cambridge, MA: Cambridge University Press.

Marilyn Fleer
Monash University
Australia

SECTION I

EMPIRICAL RESEARCH ON USING ACTIVITY THEORY IN ANALYSING STUDENTS' AND TEACHERS' EXPERIENCES OF LEARNING AND TEACHING IN FACE-TO-FACE, BLENDED AND FULLY ONLINE LEARNING CONTEXTS

ALCUIN IVOR MWALONGO

2. USING ACTIVITY THEORY TO UNDERSTAND STUDENT TEACHER PERCEPTIONS OF EFFECTIVE WAYS FOR PROMOTING CRITICAL THINKING THROUGH ASYNCHRONOUS DISCUSSION FORUMS

INTRODUCTION

The use of asynchronous discussion forums has the potential for promoting students' critical thinking. Critical thinking is defined as the skills and dispositions "to think effectively about the matter in a sustained way" (Perkins, 2004, p. 359). Student teachers are likely to use asynchronous discussion forums as teaching-learning tools in their courses and during their future teaching career. As potential users of asynchronous discussion forums, examining their perceptions of the use of these tools becomes significant. Research on the use of asynchronous discussion forums for promoting critical thinking amongst students has mainly focused on gauging the evidence of critical thinking displayed on discussion forums (Corich, Kinshuk, & Jeffrey, 2011; Fahy, 2005; Jacob & Sam, 2010; Perkins & Murphy, 2006). Furthermore, some studies have suggested interventions for promoting critical thinking (Alexander, Commander, Greenberg, & Ward, 2010; Cranney, Wallace, Alexander, & Alfano, 2011; Shaul, 2009; Thompson, Martin, Richards, & Branson, 2003). However, little research has been done on student teachers' perceptions of effective ways for promoting critical thinking through the use of these forums. Examining students' perceptions of the use of asynchronous discussion forums is significant because it can help to know their intention for using these tools in their future teaching career. Based on their perceptions, intervention measures can be taken. To that end, this study examined student teacher perceptions of effective ways for promoting critical thinking through the use of asynchronous discussion forums. Activity Theory was used as a framework to guide the study.

ACTIVITY THEORY

Activity Theory was developed by Lev Vygotsky (1896–1934). His focus was on the mediation of the triad – the *subject*, *object* and *tools* (artefacts) in the interaction as indicated in Figure 2.1 (Engeström, 2001). Based on the conception of the triad,

D. S. P. Gedera & P. J. Williams (Eds.), Activity Theory in Education, 19–34.

Vygotsky identified methods that would help study and explain human activities (Yamagata-Lynch, 2010).

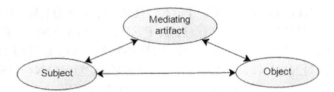

Figure 2.1. Mediation of the triad – the subject, object and mediating artifact. Adapted from Engeström (2001, p. 134)

Some elements of Activity Theory were introduced by Alexei Leont'ev (1904–1979). These elements are the concept of activity, object of activity and division of labour (Leont'ev, 1978). Leont'ev stressed that activities cannot exist without their objects. Division of labour was a result of individuals' specialisation in making and using tools (Kaptelinin & Nardi, 2012).

In the 1980s and 1990s, the activity system was further developed by Engeström. Engeström integrated elements of Vygotsky's and Leont'ev's frameworks. It was Engestrom who introduced the ideas of community, rules and outcomes (Kaptelinin & Nardi, 2012). Thus, based on Engeström's view, Activity Theory constitutes subjects, object, tools, community, rules, division of labour and outcomes as indicated in Figure 2.2.

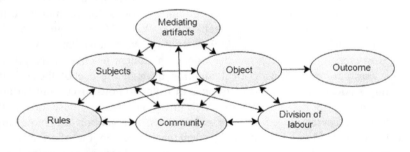

Figure 2.2. The Activity Theory. Adapted from Engeström (2003, p. 31)

In this study, the elements of Activity Theory (see Figure 2.3) were reflected in the following ways:

- *subjects* refer to student teachers using asynchronous discussion forums,
- *object* is the use of asynchronous discussion forums for promoting critical thinking,
- *tools* refer to asynchronous discussion forums and language used to express student teachers' thoughts,

- *community* refers to student teachers and lecturers,
- *rules* are regulations for using asynchronous discussion forums,
- *roles* are the responsibilities of student teachers and lecturers, and
- *outcome* refers to the promotion of critical thinking.

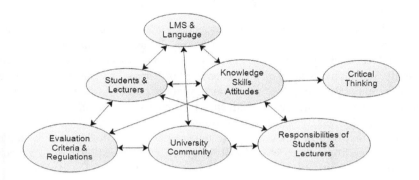

Figure 2.3. The Activity Theory in the current study. Adapted from Engeström (2003)

RATIONALE FOR USING ACTIVITY THEORY

Activity Theory was used as a theoretical framework for several reasons. First, the framework fits in this study because the learning process involved the use of asynchronous discussion forums as mediating tools for promoting critical thinking. Through the lens of Activity Theory, student teacher perceptions of the use of asynchronous discussion forums for promoting critical thinking and interaction through these tools could be analysed.

Second, through the lens of Activity Theory, a learning activity is understood within a specific social setting (Murphy & Rodriguez-Manzanares, 2008). The framework provides a helpful way to analyse and understand student teacher perceptions of the use of discussion forums for promoting critical thinking within the context of universities.

Third, Activity Theory is a suitable framework for online learning environments because it helps to understand the social structure of online environments that show a learner as an individual as well as a member of a larger community (Baran & Cagiltay, 2010). Thus, the framework helps to understand how each student used asynchronous discussion forums to promote critical thinking individually as well as how students as a learning community collaboratively used asynchronous discussion forums to achieve expected learning outcomes.

Finally, Activity Theory as a framework helps the researcher make sense of complex real-world data sets in a manageable and meaningful manner (Yamagata-Lynch, 2010). This study involved several variables such as perceptions of the student teachers of the use of asynchronous discussion forums, and interaction amongst themselves. Without the use of such a framework, it would have been difficult to manage and understand the processes involved in these tools individually or collaboratively.

EDUCATIONAL CONTEXT

This study examined student teacher perceptions of effective ways for promoting critical thinking through the use of asynchronous discussion forums in a pre-service teacher education programme in Tanzania. Three public universities were involved in the study. Tanzania is located on the eastern part of Africa. The education structure is as follows: three years of pre-primary, seven years of primary, four years of ordinary secondary education, two years of advanced secondary education, and three to five years of undergraduate education, depending on the programme of study. Research participants involved in this study were undergraduate students. After graduation, they would qualify to teach in either ordinary level, advanced level or in a teacher education institution.

RESEARCH QUESTION

The study was guided by the following research question: What are student teachers' perceptions of effective ways for promoting critical thinking through the use of asynchronous discussion forums?

METHODOLOGY

This section discusses sampling of participants, mixed methods approach, methods of data collection, and analysis.

Sampling

Sampling of research participants was done in two phases. The first phase involved the selection of universities and participants to be involved in the survey. The selected universities were to be public universities because all public universities follow a similar curriculum. They dealt with the preparation of teachers; and used Moodle as a teaching-learning tool. Participants from the three universities were to be involved in a compulsory course related to curriculum design and development. Participants were accessed through the invitation letters given to their respective universities. Fifty four students participated. Out of 54 students, 17 were in-service and 27 were pre-service. Ten students did not indicate their status of being in-service or pre-service. These participants were involved in completing the survey.

In the second phase, students, who were willing to participate in the interviews were selected from students involved in completing the survey. Part of the questionnaire item requested students willing to participate in follow-up study to provide their contact details for further communication. Eight students were interviewed.

Mixed Methods Approach

This study used a mixed methods approach which involves the collection, analysis, and interpretation of quantitative and qualitative data in a single study or in a series of studies that investigate the same underlying phenomenon (Leech & Onwuegbuzie, 2009). Both approaches were used for complementarity. In complementarity, different approaches are used to measure different aspects of the same phenomenon in order to elaborate, illustrate, enhance or clarify the results from another approach (Ary, Jacobs, & Sorens, 2010; Creswell & Creswell, 2005; Onwuegbuzie, Dickinson, Leech, & Zoran, 2009). Finally, a mixed methods approach was used to triangulate findings. Triangulation allows researchers to cross-check and get a more robust picture of the research problem (Williams, 2015). In triangulation, the quantitative and qualitative approaches are compared in terms of sources of data, methods, and respondents (Creswell, 2014; Onwuegbuzie et al., 2009; Onwuegbuzie, Slate, Lech, & Collins, 2007; Torrance, 2012).

Mixed methods approach designs used in the study. This study used two designs of a mixed methods approach: concurrent mixed methods design and explanatory sequential mixed methods design. The former is also known as convergent, parallel or triangulation design (Creswell, 2012). In this design, both quantitative and qualitative data are collected simultaneously, merged and used to understand the research question (Creswell, 2012). The use of both quantitative and qualitative data is to complement each other.

In explanatory sequential mixed methods design, quantitative data are collected first, then qualitative data. This design was used to ensure that the qualitative data helped to "refine, extend, or explain the general picture" obtained from quantitative data (Creswell, 2012, p. 542).

Methods of Data Collection

Data were collected through a survey and interviews.

Survey. The questionnaire items focused on student teacher perceptions of effective ways for promoting critical thinking through the use of asynchronous discussion forums. The questionnaires were in a Likert scale. Research participants had to rate the statements (strongly disagree, disagree, agree, and strongly agree) and give reasons to justify their rating (see Appendix A). In this way, the survey generated both quantitative and qualitative data. There was an open-ended question that was intended to elicit additional perceptions from the participants. The developed

23

survey was reviewed by two experts in assessment and evaluation. Based on their suggestions, one item was excluded because it did not capture the intended concept.

Prior to administrating the survey, ten students volunteered to participate. These students did not take courses related to curriculum development, and evaluation. The pilot was done in face-to-face mode. The pilot survey helped to examine questionnaire items in context and to get participants' views about the questionnaire items (Gideon, 2012). A discussion with students who were piloted indicated that the survey could be completed within 30 minutes and the questionnaire items were comprehensible.

After piloting the questionnaires, the survey was administered face-to-face in order to maximise return rates. Seventy six questionnaires were given, and 54 were returned.

Interviews. Semi-structured interviews were conducted with eight students. Semi-structured interviews were used because they are flexible as the researcher could probe research participants for further details (Wellington, 2015). The interviews focused on exploring student teacher perceptions of effective ways for promoting critical thinking through the use of asynchronous discussion forums. One of the interviews with four students was a focus group discussion, while the rest of the interviews were on a one-to-one basis because of their availability. The duration of the interviews was between 0:30:00 and 1:25:00.

Data Analysis

Data analysis involved survey and interview data. The details of the analysis are given in the following paragraphs.

Survey data. The questionnaire data were analysed using a Statistical Package for Social Sciences (SPSS version 22). Descriptive statistics were used. The results were displayed in the form of frequencies and percentages. Qualitative data generated from the reasons stated in the Likert scale and from open-ended questions were analysed using NVivo 10 to generate themes related to the research question. The two types of data were analysed separately, but results were presented side by side. The use of both quantitative and qualitative data in the survey helped to correlate the findings between the two types of data as well as complementing each other. That is, the statistical data (ratings) were compared with the reasons given for each rating so as to ascertain the reasons behind choosing a particular rating level.

Interview data. The transcribed qualitative data from the focus group discussion, and one-to-one interviews were analysed using NVivo 10. The texts were read word for word to gather themes related to the research question. Internal consistency reliability of the questionnaire was calculated using Cronbach's alpha. It was calculated using the following formula:

$$Cronbach's\ alpha = \frac{k}{(k-1)} \left(1 - \frac{\sum var(i)}{var(sum)} \right)$$

where k is the number of items, var(i) is the variance of an item, and var(sum) is the variance of the totals for each participant (Hinton, 2005). Results are displayed in Table 2.1. Cronbach alpha was 0.738. Tavakol and Dennick (2011) consider that acceptable values of alpha range from 0.70 to 0.95.

Table 2.1. Internal reliability of the questionnaire

Cronbach's alpha	Cronbach's alpha based on standardised items	No. of items
.738	.742	5

RESULTS

This section presents results from the survey and interviews. With reference to Activity Theory, the results have been presented from the view of *subjects* (student teachers) using *tools* (asynchronous discussion forums) to achieve a particular *object* (promotion of critical thinking).

Results from the Survey

A summary of student teacher perceptions of effective ways for promoting critical thinking through asynchronous discussion forums is presented in Figure 2.4.

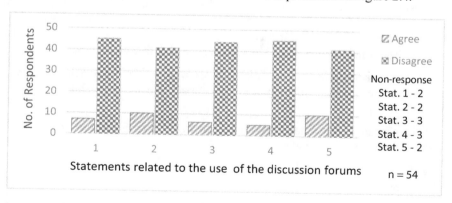

Figure 2.4. The degree of agreement and disagreement about statements related to the use of asynchronous discussion forums

25

Both quantitative and qualitative data have been presented side by side. A total of 153 reasons were generated. Only representative reasons have been used to illustrate ideas in question.

Most of the students (90.0%) believed that one of the effective ways for promoting critical thinking was to ensure that tasks in the discussion forums encouraged freedom of expression. Through freedom of expression, students had the opportunity to engage in problem-solving or decision-making as illustrated in the following extracts:

I am freely arranging my views privately. (Survey, Student 06)

Because in Moodle, students irrespective of their individual differences have equal chance of suggesting anything they think is logical. (Survey, Student 34)

It gives me a room for that and I can express my suggested solutions to the problems or issues under discussion. (Survey, Student 45)

Sometimes the issue is more complicated as it needs specialists to be involved, but I should suggest my own solution. (Survey, Student 19)

Some students perceived that when learning tasks were related to real-life situations, they were able to analyse issues being discussed. The following quotes illustrate the point:

Because most of the issues discussed related to our academic and social life, hence I have enough knowledge to give analysis of issues. (Survey, Student 34)

Most of the issues discussed are analysable, academic and social. (Survey, Student 37)

Most of the students (86.5%) perceived that critical thinking could be promoted when tasks related to the discussion forums encouraged interaction amongst students and with the lecturers. This interaction helped them analyse issues related to their courses. The following are typical responses reflecting this view:

Through various comments and observations from my fellow students and the lecturer's response, I can analyze the topic/issues we are discussing. (Survey, Student 45)

This is because of the interaction I have with my friends. So it becomes easy to judge them. (Survey, Student 17)

Various contributions from my colleagues help me to analyse issues. (Survey, Student 44)

Most of the students (80.4%) felt that critical thinking could be promoted when students were willing to learn from each other during the discussion forum sessions because colleagues brought divergent views. Accommodating different views from colleagues had the potential for promoting open-mindedness. The following are some of the extracts related to willingness to learn from each other:

Because everyone comes with his/her views I learn a lot from them. (Survey, Student 08)

Most with different people and of course they added many things in my experience. (Survey, Student 19)

When I read other people's views I get to know things that I had no knowledge of. (Survey, Student 34)

Yes, colleagues come up with a lot, some of them I have not yet thought about or was not expecting to learn on myself. (Survey, Student 45)

Though most students saw the need for learning from colleagues, more than half of the number of pre-service students (56.6%) felt that they could not accommodate other students' ideas, especially when such ideas contradicted their own beliefs. The reasons for not changing their views were that evidence given by colleagues was superficial, and that they were confident about what they believed.

If, I too, have evidence for what I support, I am a person my stand cannot be shaken by superficially supported evidence/proof. (Survey, Student 37)

I always trust what I know. I'm not a man driven by other people's view even if null. (Survey, Student 34)

It is confidence. (Survey, Student 41)

Most of the students (80.4%) believed that critical thinking could be promoted when colleagues' arguments presented in the discussion forums were supported with evidence and they considered multiple perspectives. Through the evidence given, students were able to evaluate the usefulness of the comments given by colleagues.

People will sometimes argue the idea with strong reasons. (Survey, Student 19)

No research no right to speak. (Survey, Student 16)

Evidences are a scientific way I have to consult. (Survey, Student 23)

They criticise me with no evidence. (Survey, Student 33)

You can get different views which can help to judge which is good or bad. (Survey, Student 25)

For promoting critical thinking, most of the students (88.0%) were of the view that the tasks related to the discussion forums need to help them draw conclusions about issues being discussed in their respective courses. In this case, conclusions could be drawn because through the tasks students had the opportunity to compare their views with those of their colleagues.

Due to the fact that I will be able to make comparisons with others views. (Survey, Student 04)

Because I can pass through different issues from different colleagues. (Survey, Student 11)

The following section outlines results related to student interviews. Some representative quotations have been used to support the arguments made.

Results from the Interviews

Themes generated from student interviews were related to freedom of expression, proper moderation and immediate feedback, and use of authentic and challenging tasks.

Freedom of expression. Most of the students believed that the discussion forums had the potential for promoting critical thinking when students were given the opportunity to express their ideas freely during discussions. It was in such cases that they could discover different views from different participants as illustrated in the following extracts:

In the discussion forum every student can express his views more freely. It is one of the best ways to express ideas because a person will be free to express his views. The discussion forum accommodates ideas from different students; therefore, it is something much better because you get different ideas from different people. (Interview, Student 03)

It allows students to actively engage themselves in learning. It gives students a wider opportunity to discuss their own ideas. (Interview, Student 08)

Immediate feedback and proper moderation. Since online discussion forums take place in the physical absence of the lecturers, most of the students had the view that feedback had to be given immediately. Immediate feedback could help students correct their mistakes.

Once you give a question, students should be able to display the answers. In the sense that they should know that in this question I have got it wrong and its answer ought to be this and that. (Interview, Student 02)

When I give a task to students I prefer giving the feedback immediately so that the student knows what s/he has got. (Interview, Student 03)

Furthermore, students felt that discussions need to be effectively moderated to be able to promote critical thinking. Moderation had the potential for making students more focused on the respective tasks.

But if the forum is moderated by the teacher, it will be good because the teacher will be able to guide students who put their own things and show their biases. (Interview, Student 07)

The lecturer will be monitoring on the students' progress. For example, so and so is logged on and is working on a particular task. In that way, the lecturer can see what students are doing and can also alert them in case the lecturer realises that corrections are needed. (Interview, Students 02)

Use of authentic and challenging tasks. Most of the students perceived that critical thinking could be promoted when the discussion forum tasks were authentic. Additionally, students believed that discussion forum tasks could promote critical thinking if challenging tasks were used. The following extracts support this view:

It should focus on political, economic, social as well as academic issues. It should focus on all the aspects in life. (Interview, Student 05)

It should have things that prompt learners to think and respond to something. (Interview, Student 07)

You may have a question that demands the use of your own experience. The experience can be job related, but at some point is a general experience. You need to sit down and think. For example, the way you think about the tasks, and come up with solutions. So you will have to think. Therefore, you think beyond the given task. (Interview, Student 08)

In summary, most of the students felt that critical thinking could be promoted through the use of asynchronous discussion forums, especially when freedom of expression was encouraged. Also the use of authentic tasks and proper moderation have the potential for promoting critical thinking.

DISCUSSION OF THE RESULTS

Discussion of the results reflects the framework of Activity Theory. In this framework, the perspectives of the subjects (students) are reflected in the use of tools (asynchronous discussion forums), their roles, rules, and the promotion of expected learning outcome (critical thinking).

Encouraging Freedom of Expression

Student teachers felt that freedom of expression is important for promoting critical thinking. Freedom of expression helps students share different views, learn from different participants, and evaluate colleagues' views and their own views. This view is evident in an interview with Student 03: "The discussion forum accommodates ideas from different students; ... you get different ideas from different people." In evaluating colleagues' points of view, most of the students suggested that arguments in the discussion forums need to be supported with evidence. Supporting views with evidence could help them draw logical conclusions, engage in decision-making processes, and evaluate the usefulness of colleagues' comments. In such cases, students are encouraged to be open-minded.

However, more than half of the number of pre-service students were less open-minded because they could not accommodate other students' ideas, especially when such ideas contradicted their own beliefs. The reasons for not changing their views were that evidence given by colleagues was superficial, and that they were confident about what they believed. This attitude could inhibit their learning. To help students learn from other students, teachers can use interactive tasks that encourage students to share ideas and see the points of view of other students.

The role of freedom of expression in promoting critical thinking is supported by previous research. Nentl and Zietlow (2008) argue that online learning as a community of inquiry needs to encourage individuals' freedom to explore ideas, question, and construct meaning. With reference to Activity Theory, these findings suggest that the manner in which tools are used by the subjects may influence the quality of expected outcomes. In this study, for example, the manner in which the discussion forums were conducted had the potential for promoting open-mindedness amongst students.

Proper Moderation of Discussion Forums

Students believed that proper moderation of discussion forums made them more focused on the tasks. Moderation is likely to save time that may be wasted on discussing irrelevant or unnecessary issues. Moderation also has the potential for encouraging interaction amongst students and with the teachers. Findings from this study have revealed that through moderation, the required levels of critical thinking can be raised. The results confirm previous studies that lecturers' feedback promotes students' critical thinking, and develops self-regulated and reflective learning (Arend, 2009; Borham-Puyal & Olmos-Migueláñez, 2011; Giacumo, Savenye, & Smith, 2013; Stein, Wanstreet, Slagle, Trinko, & Lutz, 2013; Wilkinson & Barlow, 2010).

Most of the students felt that moderation can be started by students as Student 05 pointed out during the interview: "... one student starts the discussion then another student contributes." When students are involved in initiating and facilitating discussions, they are likely to become more responsible learners, self-confident, and motivated to learn in online environments. Stein et al. (2013) support the view that student-led discussions can promote critical thinking and the sense of responsibility for learning.

However, student-moderated discussions are not intended to replace the role of the teacher. In the study by Xie and Ke (2011), it was found that student moderations were positively related to peers' low level of knowledge construction; while lecturer moderations were related to peers' high level of knowledge construction because even highly motivated students do not necessarily provide better quality moderation. This calls for lecturers to take new roles, different from those taken during face-to-face environments. To effectively moderate online discussions, online tutors and e-moderators need to adopt social, pedagogical, and intellectual roles (Vlachopoulos & Cowan, 2010), and give individual support to the student moderator (Quinton & Allen, 2014). The shift in students' and lecturers' roles is important, especially in a sociocultural context such as Tanzania, where traditionally teaching has mainly been teacher-centred. From the perspective of Activity Theory, these results suggest that asynchronous discussion forums are good mediating tools because, among other things, they are likely to change the dominant role of teachers that is so apparent in face-to-face environments. Furthermore, for the subjects to achieve expected outcomes, members of the community need to carry out their roles effectively. Since tools by themselves may not promote expected outcomes, conscious use of the mediating tools is important for promoting interactions amongst subjects.

Use of Authentic Tasks

Students believed that meaningful learning takes place when tasks are authentic. Students suggested that the tasks need to reflect real life and practical issues as illustrated by Student 05 from one of the interviews: "It [discussion] should focus on all the aspects in life." Since one of the main purposes of most education systems is to help students be able to solve real-life problems now and in the future, the use of authentic tasks in asynchronous discussion forums is likely to promote meaningful transfer of learning. Meaningful transfer of learning can help students see the connection between theories learnt in class and their applications in real-life situations. This view is also supported by Sansone, Fraughton, Zachary, Butner, and Heiner (2011). In their study, they found that students become active in online lessons, especially when the tasks explicitly show the connection of how the skills can be applied in real life. In the view of Activity Theory, for the subjects to see the application of tools in real-life situations and be able to solve real-life problems, authentic tasks need to be used during the teaching-learning process. The use of authentic tasks is likely to meaningfully engage the subjects in using the tools, in performing their roles, and in observing the rules in order to achieve expected learning outcomes.

CONCLUSION

Using a mixed methods approach, this study examined student teacher perceptions of effective ways for promoting critical thinking through the use of asynchronous discussion forums in a pre-service teacher education programme in Tanzania. Findings from this study suggest that discussion forums are likely to promote critical thinking through: encouraging freedom of expression, moderating discussion forums properly, and using authentic tasks. Activity Theory is seen as a useful framework to organise and analyse data related to student teacher perceptions of the use of asynchronous discussion forums, the purpose for using discussion forums, and the expected learning outcome. Since this study used a relatively small sample, further research could use a large sample. Also low levels of open-mindedness amongst pre-service teachers could be an area for further research.

REFERENCES

Alexander, M. E., Commander, N., Greenberg, D., & Ward, T. (2010). Using the four-questions technique to enhance critical thinking in online discussions. *Journal of Online Learning and Teaching, 6*(2), 409–415.

Arend, B. (2009). Encouraging critical thinking in online threaded discussions. *The Journal of Educators Online, 6*(1), 1–23.

Ary, D., Jacobs, L. C., & Sorens, C. K. (2010). *Introduction to research in education* (8th ed.). Belmont, TN: Cengage Learning.

Baran, B., & Cagiltay, K. (2010). The dynamics of online communities in the Activity Theory framework. *Educational Technology & Society, 13*(4), 155–166.

Borham-Puyal, M., & Olmos-Miguelánez, S. (2011). Improving the use of feedback in an online teaching-learning environment: An experience supported by Moodle. *US-China Foreign Language, 9*(6), 371–382.

Corich, S., Kinshuk, & Jeffrey, L. (2011). Automating the measurement of critical thinking for individuals participating in discussion forums. In D. Ifenthaler, P. Isaias, J. Spector, Kinshuk, & D. Sampson (Eds.), *Multiple perspectives on problem solving and learning in the digital age* (pp. 143–157). New York, NY: Springer.

Cranney, M., Wallace, L., Alexander, J., & Alfano, L. (2011). Instructor's discussion forum effort: Is it worth it? *Journal of Online Learning and Teaching, 7*(3), 337–348.

Creswell, J. W. (2012). *Educational research: Planning, conducting and evaluating quantitative and qualitative research* (4th ed.). New York, NY: Pearson.

Creswell, J. W. (2014). *Research design: Qualitative, quantitative, and mixed methods approaches* (4th ed.). London, England: Sage.

Creswell, J. W., & Creswell, J. D. (2005). Mixed methods research: Developments, debates, and dilemmas. In R. Swanson & E. H. III (Eds.), *Research in organizations: Foundations and methods of inquiry* (pp. 315–326). San Francisco, CA: Berrett-Koehler Publishers.

Engeström, Y. (2001). Expansive learning at work: Toward an activity theoretical reconceptualization. *Journal of Education and Work, 14*(1), 133–156. doi:10.1080/13639080020028747

Engeström, Y. (2003). Activity Theory and individual and social transformation. In Y. Engeström, R. Miettinen, & R.-L. Punamaki (Eds.), *Perspectives on Activity Theory* (pp. 19–38). Cambridge, MA: Cambridge University Press.

Fahy, P. (2005). Two methods for assessing critical thinking in computer-mediated communications (CMC) transcripts. *International Journal of Instructional Technology and Distance Learning, 2*(3), 13–28.

Giacumo, L., Savenye, W., & Smith, N. (2013). Facilitation prompts and rubrics on higher-order thinking skill performance found in undergraduate asynchronous discussion boards. *British Journal of Educational Technology, 44*(5), 774–794.

Gideon, L. (2012). The art of question phrasing. In L. Gideon (Ed.), *Handbook of survey methodology for the social sciences*. New York, NY: Springer.

Hinton, P. (2005). *Statistics explained* (2nd ed.). London, England: Taylor & Francis Group.

Jacob, S. M., & Sam, H. K. (2010). Perspectives on critical thinking through online discussion forums in engineering mathematics. In K. Elleithy, T. Sobh, M. Iskander, V. Kapila, M. A. Karim, & A. Mahmood (Eds.), *Technological developments in networking, education and automation* (pp. 121–126). Dordrecht, The Netherlands: Springer.

Kaptelinin, V., & Nardi, B. (2012). *Activity Theory in HCI: Fundamentals and reflection.* San Rafael, CA: Morgan & Claypool.

Leech, N. L., & Onwuegbuzie, A. J. (2009). A typology of mixed methods research designs. *Quality & Quantity, 43*(2), 265–275. doi:10.1007/s11135-007-9105-3

Leont'ev, A. N. (1978). *Activity, consciousness and personality.* Englewood Cliffs, NJ: Prentice-Hall.

Murphy, E., & Rodriguez-Manzanares, M. A. (2008). Using Activity Theory and its principle of contradictions to guide research in educational technology. *Australasian Journal of Educational Technology, 24*(4), 442–457.

Nentl, N., & Zietlow, R. (2008). Using Bloom's taxonomy to teach critical thinking skills to business students. *College & Undergraduate Libraries, 15*(1–2), 159–172.

Onwuegbuzie, A. J., Dickinson, W. B., Leech, N. L., & Zoran, A. G. (2009). A qualitative framework for collecting and analyzing data in focus group research. *International Journal of Qualitative Methods, 8*(3), 1–21.

Onwuegbuzie, A. J., Slate, J. R., Lech, N. L., & Collins, K. M. T. (2007). Conducting mixed analysis: A general typology. *Interdisciplinary Journal of Multiple Research Approaches, 1*(1), 4–17.

Perkins, C., & Murphy, E. (2006). Identifying and measuring individual engagement in critical thinking in online discussions: An exploratory case study. *Educational Technology & Society, 9*(1), 298–307.

Perkins, D. (2004). When is good thinking? In D. Y. Dai (Ed.), *Motivation, emotion, and cognition: Integrative perspectives on intellectual functioning and development* (pp. 351–384). Mahwah, NJ: Lawrence Erlbaum.

Quinton, S., & Allen, M. (2014). The social processes of web 2.0 collaboration: Towards a new model for virtual learning. In M. Gosper & D. Ifenthaler (Eds.), *Curriculum models for the 21st century: Using learning technologies in higher education* (pp. 35–54). New York, NY: Springer.

Sansone, C., Fraughton, T., Zachary, J., Butner, J., & Heiner, C. (2011). Self-regulation of motivation when learning online: The importance of who, why and how. *Educational Technology Research & Development, 59*(2), 199–212. doi:10.1007/s11423-011-9193-6

Shaul, M. (2009). Assessing online discussion forum participation. In L. Tomei (Ed.), *Information communication technologies for enhanced education and learning: Advanced applications and developments* (pp. 259–268). New York, NY: Information Science Reference.

Stein, D. S., Wanstreet, C. E., Slagle, P., Trinko, L. A., & Lutz, M. (2013). From 'hello' to higher-order thinking: The effect of coaching and feedback on online chats. *Internet & Higher Education, 16*, 78–84.

Tavakol, M., & Dennick, R. (2011). Making sense of Cronbach's alpha. *International Journal of Medical Education, 2*, 53–55.

Thompson, S., Martin, L., Richards, L., & Branson, D. (2003). Assessing critical thinking and problem solving using a web-based curriculum for students. *Internet and Higher Education, 6*(2), 185–191.

Torrance, H. (2012). Triangulation, respondent validation, and democratic participation in mixed methods research. *Journal of Mixed Methods Research, 6*(2), 111–123.

Vlachopoulos, P., & Cowan, J. (2010). Reconceptualising moderation in asychronous online discussions using grounded theory. *Distance Education, 31*(1), 23–36.

Wellington, J. (2015). *Educational research: Contemporary issues and practical approaches.* London, England: Bloomsbury Academic.

Wilkinson, S., & Barlow, A. (2010). Turning up critical thinking in discussion boards. *eLearning Papers, 21*, 1–12.

Williams, K. (2015). *Doing research to improve teaching and learning: A guide for college and university faculty.* London, England: Routledge.

Xie, K., & Ke, F. (2011). The role of students' motivation in peer-moderated asynchronous online discussions. *British Journal of Educational Technology, 42*(6), 916–930. doi:10.1111/j.1467-8535.2010.01140.x

Yamagata-Lynch, L. (2010). *Activity systems analysis methods: Understanding complex learning environments.* New York, NY: Springer.

Alcuin Ivor Mwalongo
Dar es Salaam University College of Education
Tanzania

APPENDIX A

A Sample of the Instrument Used to Collect Data

We are interested in finding out your opinions about Moodle as a tool for promoting your learning. We, thus, would like to know how you use Moodle.

Rate the following statements related to your use of Moodle by ticking (√) the most correct response (*Note*: Tick only one response for each given statement). Then, for each response you have chosen give reason(s) why you think so.

		Statements	Strongly disagree	Disagree	Agree	Strongly agree	Write your reason(s) in the space given below
Discussion Forums	1	Through the discussion forum I am able to analyse issues being discussed.					
	2	In the discussion forum, I can judge how good or bad my colleagues' comments are.					
	3	Using the discussion forum, I am able to generalise about issues being discussed and make logical conclusions.					
	4	Through the discussion forum I am able to suggest for solutions about the problems or issues being discussed.					
	5	Through the discussion forum I learn a lot from my colleagues.					

KATHRIN OTREL-CASS,
KAREN EGEDAL ANDREASEN AND LARS BANG

3. THE STANDARD CHILD

National Testing Made Complex through
the Lens of Cultural-Historical Activity Theory

INTRODUCTION

National testing is an institutionalised practice that has been the subject of much debate, including how it can be used by students, parents, and teachers as well as how outcomes affect decision making of principals, local authorities and policy makers. Testing of this kind has been reported to shape students' motivation for learning. For instance, based on a thorough literature review, Wynne Harlen and Ruth Dean Crick described in 2003 a number of factors that shape schools', teachers' and students' positive and negative responses to national testing. They point out that only a few studies had looked at the mediating effect testing has on educational communities. Dylan Wiliam reports in 2010 that the validity of standardised testing can be problematic in terms of the intended inferences. With a focus on the relationship between standardised testing and accountability he writes that:

> …standardized tests are rather inappropriate tools with which to hold districts, schools, and teachers accountable. Yet there is evidence that establishing an accountability regime that uses externally set tests, where the results of these tests have significant consequences for students, teachers, schools, and districts, can be a cost-effective way to increase student achievement, although the introduction of such regimes has the potential for a range of unintended outcomes, many of which will have a negative impact. (p. 120)

National testing typically involves designed assessment that sets particular testing conditions, uses specific questions and applies interpretation of testing data in a standardised manner. This allows for comparisons across schools (Morris, 2011). The reliability of such comparisons though can be questioned since, for instance, the context of testing might influence test results. While it is important to differentiate between standardised testing with high stakes, low or no-stakes (Morris, 2011), it is of interest to us how standardised assessment shapes how those involved or affected operate, and how they see themselves as educationally performing individuals. Test results (high or low stakes) may be used for different assessment purposes including summative or formative. Summative assessment typically refers to assessment of

D. S. P. Gedera & P. J. Williams (Eds.), Activity Theory in Education, 35–50.

academic skills and because the assessment outcomes are used to evaluate students' performances, this type of assessment comes with significant consequences for students (Morris, 2011). Formative assessment or assessment for learning supports the teaching and learning process because it does not focus so much on performance evaluation but rather the outcomes of formative assessment are used to modify teaching strategies, and highlight learning needs and students' learning strategies (Black & William, 1998).

Internationally there is continuing interest in the merits of standardised assessment practices and the kinds of tools used for examining student performances (OECD). It is important to note here that different assessment tools inform different interest groups. For instance, large scale international surveys such as PISA and TIMSS, primarily inform policy makers, while national testing can be used to provide insights and feedback both to policy makers and individual learners because learners receive, in contrast to for example PISA testing, the results of their assessment. This means that national testing can, potentially, be of formative value for both students and their teachers. The OECD report Synergies for Better Learning: An International Perspective on Evaluation and Assessment study (2013) highlights the benefits of standardised testing but stresses the crucial role classroom teachers play in orchestrating assessment. Making the most from any kind of assessment insights that can also be used for formative purposes has been called for by a number of researchers (see for example Pellegrino, 2010; Popham, 2006, 2011; Stiggins, Arter, Chappuis, & Chappuis, 2012; Volante & Fazio, 2007). Assessment plays a significant role in how learners see themselves, what they identify as important to learn about, or how to learn (Crooks, 1988). This means that assessment, whether standardised or not, at international level or devised by the class teacher, will have an impact on shaping students' perceptions and experiences of themselves while they are at school (Moreland, Cowie, & Otrel-Cass, 2013). This interest has also contributed to seeking a better understanding of an assessment divide between top down (standardised) and bottom up (constructed by teachers) assessment. It is therefore interesting to examine whether and in what way it matters to students' identity formation (subjectivity), who constructs, administers, and scores assessment and the interpretations that are communicated about their academic performances and progression.

Market oriented education systems place enormous weight on standardised testing and are responsible for "an environment in which both abstracted and common-sense models of intelligence and ability have been elaborated anew and individualised models of learners and learning have been rearticulated" (Gillborn & Youdell, 2000 as cited by Youdell, 2006, p. 1). Here we take a particular interest in the production of subjectivity when standardised testing is used. We see subjectivity or the "changing response to others" (Sullivan, 2012, p. 1) not as a passive result of an activity that one is exposed to. This is why we use the phrase 'production of subjectivity' because we want to highlight the active relationship between testing and the formation of self. When Paul Sullivan (referring to Bakhtin's ideas) highlights the process of shaping our own subjectivity, he alludes to the process of anticipation of how others may expect us to be. This position assumes we actively respond to and find justifications for an alignment with particular expectations or not. Research on subjectivity may raise questions about the circumstances of activities that create opportunities for engagement or a distance to the desired outcome and whether such encounters are experienced as something to oppose or embrace. Thus being interested in the potential tensions that standardised testing creates on subjectivity formation we find the theoretical lens of Activity Theory useful also because it allows us to adopt a reflexive position as researchers.

CULTURAL-HISTORICAL ACTIVITY THEORY AND EDUCATIONAL PERFORMANCE

We refer to ideas about the social and material aspects to learning processes developed by Alexei Nikolaevich Leontiev' (1981) and Lev Vygotsky (1978) to explore questions of subjectivity as addressed by Mikhail Mikhailovich Bakhtin (1981) who views subjectivity from a dialogic perspective, as the response to the subject of an action.

Vygotsky, Leontiev and others theorised learning to be a process that has to be explained by more than behaviourist ideas to propose a model that considers how (learning) activities are oriented towards an object and are mediated by artefacts. Aspects such as cultural tools, and division of labour that are grounded in historical developments underpinned this thinking that resulted in the development of a cultural-historical theory of activity.

Here we used an Activity Theory framework to interrogate the interactions between students and their teachers and the internal (psychological) or external (materials and artefacts but also language) cultural tools they use. We examined the complexities of standardised testing from observations and interviews conducted in grade 6 (12 year old students) Danish primary classrooms. Activity Theory helped us gain insights into the intricacies of standardised testing experiences, about what teachers and students did and why, and the influence of the community in which they were situated when they were tested nationally for the first time in Danish reading skills and mathematics. Activity Theory allowed us also to take note of the historical development in regards to standardised testing in Denmark in order to situate and shape our interpretations. For example, why and in what way it is important to consider that in Denmark the Ministry of Education decided to implement nationally standardised testing in public schools in 2005 with full implementation in 2010 (Ministry of Education, 2011). The main purpose of national testing was to use a standardised way of assessment that would have "a significant impact on the school career of pupils" by way of certification (Eurydice network, 2009).

Activity Theory provides researchers with "the tools for revealing the social and material resources that are salient in activity" (Roth & Lee, 2007, p. 197). Our intention was to use these theoretical tools to highlight what governments hoped to gain from such testing and whether this supports in fact students' development of academic skills, and produces reliable test results that can be used to compare and rank students, teachers and their schools. Standardised tests have to presuppose standard conditions of what can be expected from students and their teachers. Activity Theory provides a theoretical lens to show that school reality is a lot more complex than what can be expected from a 'standard' child because human development is shaped by a complexity of factors including rules and practices that shape and navigate experiences. Our argument is that using Activity Theory as an analytical tool allows us to take a critical perspective towards standardised testing in Danish primary schools. To interrogate desired, intended and unintended consequences we highlight how standardised tests shape perceptions of competency and incompetency of young people and their teachers.

In response to a then prevailing notion of behaviourist explanations to human activity Lev Semyonovich Vygotsky was inspired by revolutionary ideas to rethink such positions (for example Karl Marx's Thesis on Feuerbach, 1845). Vygotsky's ideas about learning concentrated on the notion that cultural tools and signs mediate learning activities and that learning is a matter of assisted performance. He conceptualised the 'Zone of Proximal Development' (ZPD) and wrote that it describes "the distance between the actual developmental level as determined by independent problem solving and the level of potential development as determined through problem solving under adult guidance, or in collaboration with more capable peers" (Vygotsky, 1978, p. 86).

Testing of the individual, however, represents educational performance done in isolation. This creates a number of challenges including whether tests can examine more than a student's/child's conceptual development but also identify other learning outcomes such as their growing procedural, societal and technical understanding in a given subject. Our analysis and data is primarily focused upon the context of testing in schools and how this affects subjectivity formation.

In 'Thinking and Speech' Vygotsky (1987, pp. 121–122) problematises the examination of conceptual development:

> Traditional methods for studying concepts fall into two basic groups. The first is typified by what is called the method of definition. This method involves the study of fully developed and fully formed concepts through the use of verbal definitions...

The method of definition is often used in national tests, especially in science, where a student is asked to explain the meaning of a given concept. Vygotsky continues:

> The second group of methods used in the study of concepts attempts to overcome the inadequacies of the purely verbal approach of the method of definition by focusing on the mental and processes that underlie the formation of concepts...

The inadequacy of this second group of methods is that they replace a complex synthetic process with an elementary one that constitutes only one part of the whole. The role of the word or sign in the process of concept formation is ignored. The result is that the process of abstraction is radically oversimplified... Thus, both of these traditional methods for studying concepts divorce the word from objective material. One begins by isolating the word from the objective material. The other begins by isolating the objective material from the word. (Vygotsky, 1987, pp. 121–122)

Denmark uses 'computer-adaptive testing' (CAT) which means that a test is geared to individual levels of ability through the use of adaptive software that modifies questions based on a student's response. Setting Danish standardised high stakes national tests is the sole responsibility of the Ministry and rests upon clearly defined expectations typically drawn from the national curriculum (Eurydice network, 2009). This means that even the more refined national tests seek to reward those who perform according to expected outcomes.

CULTURAL-HISTORICAL ACTIVITY THEORY AND THE EXPLORATION OF SUBJECTIVITY

This chapter aims to show how Cultural-Historical Activity Theory can be used as a qualitative analysis framework to explore the complexities of subjectivity formation through national standardised testing. As mentioned above, Activity Theory draws on Vygotsky's (1978) notion of mediated action and Alexei Nikolaevich Leontiev's (1978) ideas surrounding the structure of human activity. The theory assumes that activities are motivated by the need to transform an object into an outcome. An object can be material or an idea. Actions may lead to transformations and can be identified as being directional and undertaken by individual or groups of subject(s). Routine and/or automated actions are mediated by tools, and can be material objects or psychological tools, such as language. At this point it is also useful to draw on one of Vygotsky's ideas that thinking occurs first at an intermental plane (between people, activated through sociocultural interaction) and then individualised (within the individual) at the intramental plane.

Engeström (1987) expanded Leontiev's (1978) ideas to a triad – connecting subject, tools and object and expanded the system to also include community, the people who may share the same motive, rules presiding over the community and, division of labour that mediate collective actions that are being carried out by participants. What makes this theoretical lens so appealing is that it points at contradictions or tensions that are key to any transformational processes. Contradictions do not necessarily imply the existence of a problem or conflict but rather identify "historically accumulating structural tensions within and between activity systems" (Engeström, 2001, p. 137). What is important in Activity Theory is the focus on the artefact that represents collected history and the transformations that have come through "human ingenuity and creativity" (Roth & Lee, 2007, p. 199).

Returning to the connection between analysing for subjectivity formation and the problematisation of human activity, Ritva Engeström and James Wertsch incorporated Bakhtin's theory of addressivity, voice, multivoicedness, speech genre into Vygotsky's and Leontiev's conceptions of activity (Engeström, 1995; Wertsch, 1991). The authors expressed this confluence of ideas through the theorising of activity systems that affect each other through objects that give rise to the emergence of new activity systems in response.

Yrjö Engeström famously developed these ideas further to an activity triangle diagram that visualises and highlights rules/norms, division of labour and community relations to show also how multiple activity systems can share an object and expand learning activities (see for example Engeström, 1987 and Engeström & Sannino, 2010). The expanded version of Cultural-Historical Activity Theory concludes that learning communities contribute with diverse points of views, rules and interests (see also Figure 3.1). It is argued that learning (including potentials and dilemmas that may occur) can only be meaningfully interpreted against a historical examination. The tensions, problems or contradistinctions that may occur along an activity are the sources of change and continued development, thus giving rise to cycles of transformations and re-conceptualisations of objects and/or motives.

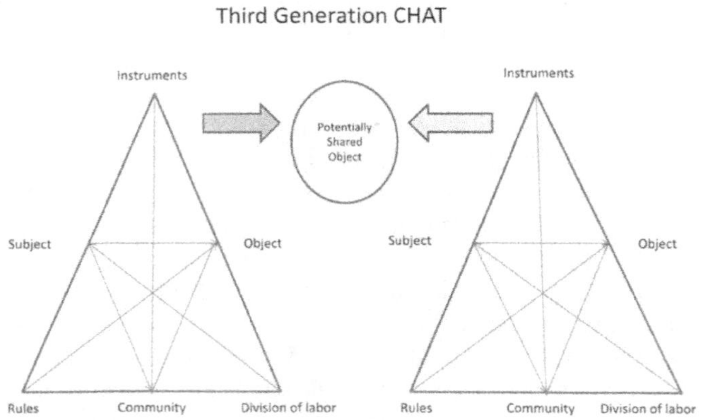

Figure 3.1. "Third Generation CHAT" by own creation – own work

Because Cultural-Historical Activity Theory allows for the identification of conflicts and the origin of multiple or sometimes contradictory voices but also cultural tools and rules that mediate these processes, it has been utilised by many researchers as an analytical lens to make sense of the complexity of learning processes.

INVESTIGATING ASSESSMENT ACTIVITIES
THROUGH CHAT IN THE DANISH FOLKESKOLE

In this chapter we used Cultural-Historical Activity Theory to analyse and conceptualise young people's subjectivity formation when they are engaged in the practices of national testing activities in Denmark. The data used for the analysis were collected over the period of two years from three Danish 'folkeskole' (primary school) classes. The 48 children who were observed were, at the beginning of the investigation, at the end of grade 5 (in spring 2010) and were followed until the end of grade 7 (spring 2012) when the students were between 12 and 13 years. The three different classes were selected to represent diversity of social backgrounds and academic levels. The intention of the research project was to get an in-depth understanding of the practices related to assessment activities and this included finding information about how students, teachers, and different kinds of experts who were involved in these processes experienced assessment. For this reason the study employed an ethnographic approach for the data collection (Hammersley, 2007; Walford, 2008a), using interviews, document analysis, observations, and data from the tests that were conducted by the teachers and by the Ministry of Education during the study period.

The three classes were situated at municipal schools in three different Danish cities. The intention was to select schools from neighbourhoods that could be characterised by differences as to their socio-economic composition. The intention was not to make a comparison between the schools, but to point out and be sensitive towards social, economic and historical differences when discussing the different pedagogical practices, and to explore the research questions in relation to the three different study contexts (Walford, 2008b). Thus the selection of the three schools followed these criterions: The residential areas of the schools should differ to support diversity among the students as to their socio-economic backgrounds, the selected school classes should represent diversity as to academic skills as described by the teachers, ethnicity and social backgrounds and of course also gender.

Interviews with students in groups and individually, were conducted three times during the study period. Interviews with teachers were organised twice. The principals of the schools were interviewed once, as well as interviews with selected experts at the schools (in reading for instance). The interviews were focusing on students' reflections on and descriptions of their experiences related to assessment and corresponding themes from school life, teachers descriptions and reflections on their pedagogy and test practices, and similar questions as reflected on by schools' principals and experts at the schools. Observations were conducted regularly during the two year period (approximately 100 hours in total) capturing everyday situations in the classroom and different school activities that were done by all three schools including a project week, assessment activities, including national standardised assessments, and the mandatory student-teacher conversation following these assessments.

Using selected data, we will highlight the active role that students take in the formation of their subjectivity when they have to operate in the world of standardised testing artefacts. All human activity can be connected to particular motives or reasons, and can be seen as series of conscious actions and mental operations that are shaped by particular conditions (Leontiev, 1978). We will elaborate on the elements that shape subjectivity formation based on the tripartite notion of Cultural-Historical Activity Theory. We will present the trickledown effect that rules, norms and conditions have that are connected to standardised testing and how this shapes in the end the formation of children's subjectivity.

RULES AND CONDITIONS: TESTING IN DANISH PRIMARY SCHOOL AS FRAMED BY LEGISLATION

In 2005 the Danish government implemented standardised national testing (Ministry of Education, 2014a). The related legislation describes and frames the use of these tests and similar kinds of assessments (Andreasen & Rasmussen, 2014). The law also links testing to the national curriculum as described by the ministry in "Fælles mål" [Learning goals] (Ministry of Education, 2014b). The executive order specifies teachers' obligation to use the results from different kinds of tests and assessments, among these also the results from the standardised national tests, to underpin a student's individual learning plan (Ministry of Education, 2009). Once a year teachers have to describe students' academic achievements and progress that form the basis for a mandated teacher-student conversation, and also for a recommended teacher-parent talk (Ibid.). Further it is stated that:

§ 2. The student plan will contain information about the agreed upon follow-up on the results of the on-going evaluation, including follow-up on the tests, as stipulated in the Folkeskole Act § 13 subsection 3, in selected subjects and in specific grades and about possible agreements about the parents' and the student's involvement in the student's achievement of the stated learning objectives. (Ministry of Education, 2009)

Test results are also used in the assessments of the quality of schools, and reported in a so-called "quality report" which was introduced in 2007 (Ministry of Education, 2007). This report needs to be made by the school once a year and published and made public on the homepage of the school that is accessible for anyone to read. This report is also used by the municipal council to form "a basis for assessing the academic level at the municipal public schools and make decisions accordingly ..." It says that this report should include:

...relevant information about results for each of the municipality's public schools and for the general school system, including information about:

1. Grading in the public school's final exams
2. Results of the tests mentioned in § 13, subsection 3 of the Act, cf. § 55 b, and

3. Any results of other types of evaluations that are used broadly in the municipal school system, for example to assess the students' proficiency and skills in areas (threshold objectives) that are not comprised by the tests mentioned in item 2 (Ministry of Education, 2007).

The legislation frames the practices for national standardised testing. It describes how the test should be used, in which contexts, by whom and for which purposes. Referring to Leontiev (1978) we might say, that the legislation describes the process by which an object – students' academic performances – are turned into an outcome. This process can be expected to influence and shape the pedagogical practices that are linked to the national curriculum, and the implementation of the idea of the "standard student" or "standard child", a norm, against which all students are compared. Rules, the constitutive elements of the voices of power never stand free of the socially defining patterns on how we deal with each other. The schools' quality reports, the teaching plan and the individual student-learning plan represent artefacts, which mediate these processes.

CONDITIONS FOR EDUCATIONAL PRACTICES: THE SCHOOL'S QUALITY REPORT

The quality report a school has to produce in Denmark shapes the educational activities, including how learning goals are set, and what is communicated to parents, students and the community. One principal of twelve years who was interviewed reflected on the new testing regime and felt that it dominates the daily routines at school more and more. He pointed to the problem associated with comparing results from national testing between schools and the ranking. Schools that are located in areas with families of low socio-economic background, where children produce lower test scores are challenged on how to interpret and use these.

I have followed the development ... and it is all about: results, result, results. ... The ranking means that schools are tried and tested (målt og vejet). Fundamentally I am not against it. But the problem is, as I see it, it is more interesting to focus on the improvements, rather than to focus on the comparison of schools, which are not comparable. It is like comparing apples and pears and bananas... And this is what we [the schools] are assessed on... (Principal, School C)

The outcomes from the national standardised tests are mediating what is prepared for a school's quality report and shape the students' learning plans. The Principal here commented also that these tools influence the school's understanding and reflections on students' attainment goals. He said that it shapes what can be considered more or less important subject knowledge, and what is the desired and legitimate way of presenting this knowledge, for instance by performing well in a test. These considerations influence further assessment strategies and decisions on pedagogical strategies and selections of more desired areas in the curriculum, as well as a teacher´s further professional development according to this. One of the principals explained how the school had taken steps to educate teachers to achieve higher test scores. He also considered that the students' learning plan is a very important tool that influences students' academic achievement in direct relation to the test scores students receive.

> We are training extra teacher aids in English and science, we already have one for reading. This means that we will have such teacher aides for all the subjects that are being tested in the national standardised tests and will align this with the students' learning plans and improve the way they are used… Several things can be improved, the way test results are reported to the parents for instance … (Principal, School B)

NORMS OF TEACHING PRACTICE: PEDAGOGY STEERED BY NATIONAL TESTING

Observations in the three classrooms showed that the pedagogy was adapted to support national standardised testing, both in respect to academic content and also in the ways this was tested, like in the observation below from a lesson in Danish. The first part of the lesson was focusing on reading books the students had chosen while in the second part of the lesson the teacher focused on assessing content by using the kinds of questions used in the national test. The specific focus was on two kinds of questions, one about proverbs and sayings and another addressing skills concerning the identification and combination of words. The observation was conducted in a Danish language lesson approximately one month after the national test had been introduced at school and illustrates the power and effect such tools have on the pedagogy in classrooms.

> The topic of the day is sayings and phrases (which is also a focus in the national test). The teacher is handing out worksheets with problems related to this. Different sayings and phrases are split in two parts and mixed up, and the students have to find, read, identify and combine the correct parts. The conversation in the classroom between the teacher and some of the students makes it clear that this is a difficult task for some of the students. … In some of the phrases a word is missing which the students should find to complete the sentence. Several students seem not to be able to do this, especially some of the bilingual children find it difficult. … The next task on the worksheet requires the students to produce as many words as possible using one syllable (for instance the syllable "head") and then combine it with another syllable. This task presents similar problems to those given in the national test. (Observation, School A)

An observation in another class in the following spring revealed similar practices as above in response to testing. In the example described below the students were being prepared for taking the national test within a few weeks. The class was engaged in solving test problems using "teaching to the test" pedagogy.

In the first part of these lessons the class starts going through problems that were discussed in previous lessons. They are similar to the kind of problems presented in the national test in which students have to split one long word correctly up into three single words. They are talking about each single problem and the students present their suggestions on how to split the words. Afterwards they get some new problems, also similar to those of the national test, for instance reading recipes and answering related questions. The class are working concentrated and quietly. In the last part of the lesson they are going through their answers, the students read their answers loud for the class, and they are discussing what could be the correct answer. (Observation, School C)

SHAPING MOTIVATION: STUDENTS' LEARNING PLANS AND THE MANDATORY STUDENT-TEACHER CONVERSATION

Danish national tests are digitally conducted and scored by computers. Teachers receive test results a couple of hours after the students have finished sitting the tests. An automatically generated mail sends a report with test results for each student in a class. Results are presented in reference to standardised categories. Five point categories are used: well above average (1), above average (2), average (3), below average (4), and well below average (5). As stated by the legislation teachers have an obligation to use the test results and report them in the student's learning plan, along with results from other kinds of assessments. The student learning plans represent artefacts that are used as key tools used in the mandatory student-teacher conversations, in which the teacher and the student discuss the student's academic progress and attainment level, and make plans for future improvements. The observation is from one such student teacher meeting and shows how the test results were central in the student's learning plan and shaped the feedback given to the student. Ahead of the national test school classes can choose to try out the test and the system in a pre-test, from which the scores do not really count. But in these student-teacher conversations they play an important role. The following observed conversations took place in a small room next to the normal classroom and just the teacher and one student at the time were present.

The teacher presents the test results to each student by starting with the results from the pre-test, and afterwards presenting the results from the actual test. Most of the children performed better in the last test (the actual test) than they did in the pre-test. Some even performed much better in the second test situation, and were very happy to hear that. The teacher presents the test score in each of the three categories and describes how each category is defined. She also makes suggestions how the students can raise their test scores, for instance by reading more. (Observation, School B)

SUBJECTIVITY FORMATION OF THE STANDARD CHILD

Practices related to preparing students for, and reviewing students' achievements after national testing, and working with the results from the standardised scoring from the national test shaped both principals' and teachers' discourses about the pedagogy as can be seen from the examples above. Mediated by these practices the test scores, and the standardised ways of assessing and reporting students' academic performances also play a role in teachers' understandings of the subject, the child, and students' understandings of themselves in reference to the standards.

In the following example two boys describe how they assess themselves and their performances compared to the average of students in the whole country, since this is a national test in Denmark.

Boy 1:   I prefer not having scores below the average for the whole country.

Boy 2:   It is better to be average or above average.

Interviewer: Why is that [you prefer not having scores below average]?

Boy 1:   It means, that you are not as smart as the others. If your scores are below average, then you are not as smart (*klog*), as those above average. And you do not want to be less smart than the others. (Boys 1 and 2, School B)

A girl reflected in similar ways, describing how her classmates might compare test scores and performances and the potential problems of this practice if your performance is not as good as that of your mates.

Girl: If I'm going to say I am clearly above average and my friend has been clearly below the average, is it ok not to tell, or do I talk about it? I do not know if I would want to talk about it.

Interviewer: Why?

Girl: Because then you feel quite bad compared to the other person if you did that. I do not know if it has something to do with how to behave in a group. If it has something to do with it, then it has to do with that you do not want to be the only one who has been clearly below average. So you will probably try to do your best to show that you will manage at moving up to the 7th grade. (Girl, School B)

The girl in the example above did not just worry and reflect upon her own performance but was concerned how her performance may be perceived or received by the group of students she associates with. This, she describes, will play a role in how you perceive yourself, and affect the perception others may have about you. The reflections from the two boys show how the two thought about their performance and how this referred to specific academic levels and defined categories. The social group to which the students belong seems to play an important role in these processes. It also appeared that the students found the defined categories important (more important perhaps than the comments and evaluations the teacher might give them about their performances). They clearly connected the standardised categories with their ideas of being smart or not.

TESTING, PRACTICES AND SUBJECTIVITY – IN CONCLUSION

We are applying in our analysis socially constructed perspectives that take into account the position of the speaker and consider the perspectives of cultural-historical situations (Engeström, 1995, p. 211). Ritva Engeström's ideas that voice is a form of action was based on her interpretation of Mikhail Mikhailovich Bakhtin's notion that literature is an inseparable component of culture, where a subject (person) uses their active voice to reproduce a form of social language. This follows also the argument on Activity Theory by Michael Roth and Yew-Jin Lee "…that human beings are not merely at the mercy of extant institutional contexts but that they are endowed with the power to act (agency), which allows for critique and revision" (Roth & Lee, 2007, p. 210). However, what becomes apparent in our example is that this reflexivity on the power of standardised testing plays a significant role in how activities and subjectivities are shaped.

We found that the quality report of the school, the student's learning plan, the student's individual learning plan, the national curriculum (Fælles Mål) (Ministry of Education, 2014b) and the national test are physical artefacts, documents that are semi-stable and are used in different ways by different communities. In this case they shape the standardised descriptors of individual work efforts. Empowered through legislation and shaped by educational practices in the classroom they influence the outcome on how young people see themselves in this environment. These documents are integrated in distinct practices, such as the student's learning plan, which directly feeds back the systematised assumptions on an individual's performance in a given subject. The high impact the standardised outcome has on a student's subjectivity formation reflects that there are preferred ways of categorising student's knowledge, skills and potentials, through the ways of presenting and communicating test scores and performances. The legislation also defines the practices as to when and where teacher student meetings take place, who is expected to participate, and what should be the object of the conversation and reports, and who is the subject.

Generally, it was found that testing practices paired with the standardised feedback played an important role in influencing students' ideas about their academic skills and potentials but showed also their sense of responsibilities towards what is expected of them as a functioning and well performing group member. This feeling for communal responsibility and individual action taking based on ranked student test scores influenced the principals' reflections on the quality of their schools, and shaped the pedagogical strategies to improve test scores. The teachers were referring to the test results and rankings and adapted their teaching to better suit the content of the test. The categories referred to in the responses to the students (both the oral and the written response) play a role in shaping the students' reflections on and understanding of their own and others' academic potentials.

The recent educational testing history in the Danish education culture developed a set of tools with particular purposes for using them. Standardised testing, a cultural tool, has created particular ways and means of thinking that reflect the needs of the different groups that are involved. As humans are inherently social the students' reflections about the meaning of standardised assessment outcomes encompass also their earlier discussions they will have had with parents, teachers or students in the social cultural interactions they share.

The standards used in the design of the national test seemed to be an integrated way of thinking about students' academic potentials. The research showed that the categories of the assessments influenced discourses related to students' academic progress strongly. Both principals and teachers are referring to this standard in their reflections on pedagogy and curriculum. The students are referring to it in their reflections on their own and classmates' academic potentials. As subjects they understand themselves related to this standard.

Using the theoretical lens of Activity Theory to analyse how standardised tests shape the active roles of human individuals when they are constructing their subjectivity, we highlight the central role of mediating artefacts. For the standardised test this includes both physical artefacts (the test, the student learning plan, the school report, the teaching plans) and abstract artefacts (grades and their meaning for the social groups, speech) and how they mediate relationships with the world. These artefacts form the basis for various actions that are socially, culturally and historically bounded, including the formation of identity within a certain subject. These activities are motivated or reasoned and achieved through a series of conscious actions with specific goals (alignment with legislation, shaping of pedagogical practices, doing your best as a 7th grade student). Multiple inner mental operations support achieving those goals, such as the girl referring to the role of group behaviour. In a world of standardised testing artefacts and related activities, students' subjectivities are produced and return to act back on this world.

The collective practice of standardised testing in Danish schools leads to the creation of the standard child. Therefore, such policy becomes self-fulfilling because of the feedback loop in improving the response to any outcomes. The result of this is a high success rate in standardised testing where the standards cascade through different levels and transformations. In anticipation of the different expectations, including those of their peers, young people's subjectivity construction is shaped through this interconnectivity between history, power and the artefact—the standardised test.

REFERENCES

Andreasen, K. E., & Rasmussen, A. (2014). I was just an average girl : Student identities in the context of testing. In *Performative educational experiences of learners across the world: An international collection of ethnographic research* (pp. 131–152). Essex, England: Ethnography and Education.

Bakhtin, M. M. (1981). *The dialogic imagination: Four essays* (M. Holquist, Ed., C. Emerson & M. Holquist, Trans.). Austin, TX: University of Texas Press.

Black, P., & Wiliam, D. (1998). Inside the black box: Raising standards through classroom assessment. *Phi Delta Kappan, 80*(2), 139–148.

Cowie, B., Moreland, J., & Otrel-Cass, K. (2013). *Expanding notions of assessment for learning: Inside science and technology primary classrooms.* Rotterdam, The Netherlands: Sense Publishers. doi:10.1007/978-94-6209-061-3

Engeström, R. (1995). Voice as communicative action. *Mind, Culture and Activity, 2*(3), 192–215.

Engeström, Y. (2001). Expansive learning at work: Toward an activity theoretical reconceptualization. *Journal of Education and Work, 14*(1), 133–156.

Engeström, Y., & Sannino. (2010). Studies of expansive learning: Foundations, findings and future challenges. *Educational research review, 5*(1), 1–24. doi:10.1016/j.edurev.2009.12.002

Eurydice network. (2009). *National testing of pupils in Europe: Objectives, organisation and use of results.* Brussels, Belgium: Education, Audiovisual and Culture Executive Agency (EACEA P9 Eurydice).

Hammersley, M., & Atkinson, P. (2007). *Ethnography: Principles in practice* (3rd ed.). London, England: Taylor & Francis.

Harlen, W., & Crick, R. D. (2003). Testing and motivation for learning. *Assessment in Education: Principles, Policy & Practice, 10*(2), 169–207. Retrieved from http://doi.org/10.1080/0969594032000121270

Leontiev, A. N. (1978). *Activity, consciousness, and personality.* Englewood Cliffs, NJ: Prentice Hall.

Leontiev, A. N. (1981). *Problems of the development of mind.* Moscow, Russia: Progress.

Marx, K. (1845/1967). Theses on Feuerbach. In E. Kamenka (Ed.), *The portable Marx.* New York, NY: Penguin Books.

Ministry of Education. (2007). *Bekendtgørelse om anvendelse af kvalitetsrapporter og handlingsplaner i kommunalbestyrelsernes arbejde med evaluering og kvalitetsudvikling af folkeskolen* (BEK nr 162 af 22/02/2007). København, Danmark: Undervisningsministeriet.

Ministry of Education. (2009). *Bekendtgørelse om elevplaner, elev- og uddannelsesplaner samt uddannelsesplaner i folkeskolen* (BEK nr 750 af 13/07/2009) [Executive order about the students plan]. København, Danmark: Undervisningsministeriet.

Ministry of Education. (2011). *Brug testresultaterne – Inspiration til pædagogisk brug af resultater fra de nationale test* [Use the test results – Inspiration for pedagogical use of results from the national tests]. København, Danmark: Skolestyrelsen. Undervisningsministeriet.

Ministry of Education. (2014a). *Bekendtgørelse af lov om folkeskolen* [Executive order about the Folkeskole]. København, Danmark: Undervisningsministeriet.

Ministry of Education. (2014b). *Bekendtgørelse om formål, kompetencemål og færdigheds- og vidensmål for folkeskolens fag og emner (Fælles Mål).* København, Danmark: Undervisningsministeriet.

Morris, A. (2011). *Student standardised testing: Current practices in OECD countries and a literature review* (Working Paper). Paris, France: OECD. Retrieved from http://localhost:8080/jspui/handle/123456789/2511

OECD. (2013). *Synergies for better learning.* Paris, France: OECD.

Own Creation – Own Work. (n.d.). Licensed under Public Domain via Wikimedia Commons. Retrieved from https://commons.wikimedia.org/wiki/File:Third_Generation_CHAT.jpg#/media/File:Third_Generation_CHAT.jpg

Pellegrino, J. (2010). *The design of an assessment system for the race to the top: A learning sciences perspective on issues of growth and measurement.* Paper presented at the Exploratory Seminar: Measurement challenges within the race to the top agenda, December 2009, Princeton, NJ. Retrieved from http://www.k12center.org/publications.html

Popham, J. (2011). Assessment literacy overlooked: A teacher educator's confession. *The Teacher Educator, 46*(4), 265–273. doi:10.1080/08878730.2011.605048

Popham, W. (2006). Needed: A dose of assessment literacy. *Educational Leadership, 63*(6), 84–85.

Roth, W.-M., & Lee, Y.-J. (2007). "Vygotsky's neglected legacy": Cultural-historical activity theory. *Review of Educational Research, 77*(2), 186–232.

Stiggins, R., Arter, J., Chappuis, S., & Chappuis, J. (2012). *Classroom assessment for student learning: Doing it right – using it well.* Portland, OR: Assessment Training Institute, Inc.

Sullivan, P. (2012). *Qualitative data analysis using a dialogical approach.* Los Angeles, CA: Sage.

Volante, L., & Fazio, X. (2007). Exploring teacher candidates' assessment literacy: Implications for teacher education reform and professional development. *Canadian Journal of Education, 30*(3), 749–770.

Vygotsky, L. S. (1978). *Mind and society.* Cambridge, MA: Harvard University Press.

Vygotsky, L. S. (1987). *The collected works of L. S. Vygotsky: Volume 1: Problems of general psychology, including the volume thinking and speech* (M. Norris, Trans., Vol. 1). New York, NY: Plenum Press.

Walford, G. (2008a). The nature of educational ethnography. In G. Walford (Ed.), *How to do educational ethnography.* London, England: The Tufnell Press.

Walford, G. (2008b). Selecting sites, and gaining ethical and practical access. In G. Walford (Ed.), *How to do educational ethnography.* London, England: The Tufnell Press.

Wertsch, J. V. (1991). *Voices of the mind: A socio-cultural approach to mediated action.* New York, NY: Harvard University Press.

Wiliam, D. (2010). Standardized testing and school accountability. *Educational Psychologist, 45*(2), 107–122. Retrieved from http://doi.org/10.1080/00461521003703060

Youdell, D. (2006). *Impossible bodies, impossible selves: Exclusions and student subjectivities/by Deborah Youdell* (Elektronisk udgave). Dordrecht, The Netherlands: Springer.

Kathrin Otrel-Cass
Aalborg University
Denmark

Karen Egedal Andreasen
Aalborg University
Denmark

Lars Bang
Aalborg University
Denmark

SECTION II

INSIGHTS IN IDENTIFYING HISTORICAL AND SYSTEMIC TENSIONS IN EDUCATIONAL CONTEXTS USING ACTIVITY THEORY

DILANI S. P. GEDERA

4. THE APPLICATION OF ACTIVITY THEORY IN IDENTIFYING CONTRADICTIONS IN A UNIVERSITY BLENDED LEARNING COURSE

INTRODUCTION

Engeström identifies three generations of Activity Theory (Engeström, 2001). Vygotsky's mediated action triangle is the first generation of Activity Theory. The following figure represents Vygotsky's basic mediated action.

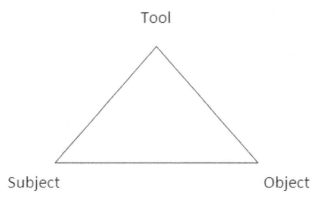

Figure 4.1. Vygotsky's basic mediated action (Vygotsky, 1978)

Through Figure 4.1, Vygotsky illustrates that the *Subject* is the participant(s) of the activity, the *Tool* can be the artefacts or participants' prior knowledge that influences the experience of mediated actions/activity and the *Object* of the triangle represents the goal of the activity. Vygotsky's (1978) notion of mediated action thus explains the semiotic process of the development of human consciousness, that is, individuals make meaning of the world through interactions with artefacts and other individuals in a particular environment. The participants play an active role as they engage in the meaning making processes while they interact with artefacts, tools and people to create and modify activities.

However, Vygotsky's tripartite model focuses on the notion of mediation; it is located at the level of individual actions and does not explain the collective nature of

D. S. P. Gedera & P. J. Williams (Eds.), Activity Theory in Education, 53–69.

activity. This led Leont'ev (1981) to explore the collective nature of human activity which is described in the second generation of Activity Theory.

Leont'ev's (1981) concept of the collective nature of human activity and Engeström's activity systems model are considered the basic elements of the second generation of Activity Theory. Vygotsky's attempt to fully develop the concept of activity was not successful during his short lifespan, and the development of the concept of activity was taken over by Leont'ev. As a significant contribution, Leont'ev identified the three hierarchical levels of activity: operations, actions and activity (Barab, Evans, & Baek, 2004). He emphasised the importance of the *object* of an activity which is related to goals and motives of the participants. In addition, he showed distinct differences between object-oriented activity and the goal-directed actions (Yamagata-Lynch, 2010). Goal-directed actions which are temporary in nature can be a step that the participants are taking while participating in a durable object-oriented activity. In addition, goal-directed actions are more individually focused, whereas object-oriented activities are considered more collective in nature. Developing Vygotsky's (1978) theory of mediated action, Leont'ev (1981) produced a model of activity that consists of the three levels (Figure 4.2). Greenhow and Belbas (2007) illustrate that Leont'ev's model "articulated the developmental transformation of social activity to individually internalised cognitive structures. At the foundational level of human activity is the object or "motive" which he theorised as the underlying driving force of human activity" (p. 366). This transformation is considered developmental.

As Leont'ev (1981) explains, operations are at the basic level of an activity. With a series of operations, actions take place at the next level. Taking part in an activity means carrying out a series of conscious actions which are associated with individual skills and knowledge. These actions can be individual or collective. At the highest level is the activity which is associated with goals and motives. Figure 4.2 shows the distinction between the hierarchical levels of an activity and the dynamics between these relationships with bi-directional arrows.

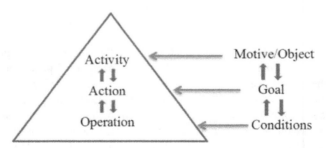

Figure 4.2. Hierarchical levels of an activity (Leont'ev, 1981)

Leont'ev (1981) illustrates the distinctions between these hierarchical levels of an activity by giving an example of hunting:

A beater, for example, taking part in a primaeval collective hunt, was stimulated by a need for food or, perhaps, a need for clothing, which the skin of the dead animal would meet for him. At what, however, was his activity directly aimed? It may have been directed, for example, at frightening a herd of animals and sending them toward other hunters, hiding in ambush. That, properly speaking, is what should be the result of the activity of this man. And the activity of this individual member of the hunt ends with that. The rest is completed by the other members. This result, i.e., the frightening of the game, etc. understandably does not in itself, and may not, lead to satisfaction of the beater's need for food, or the skin of the animal. What the processes of his activity were directed to did not, consequently, coincide with what stimulated them, i.e., did not coincide with the motive of his activity; the two were divided from one another in this instance. Processes, the object and motive of which do not coincide with one another, we shall call "actions". We can say, for example, that the beater's activity is the hunt, and the frightening of the game his action. (1981, p. 210)

This excerpt depicts how Leont'ev (1981) differentiates activity, action and operation. At the level of activity which is associated with a motive, it explains *why* something is done. At the second level which is driven by conscious actions, it shows *what* is done and at the third level, which consists of operations, it explains *how* it is done.

Activities are generally differentiated from one another according to their objects. These objects cannot be converted into outcomes immediately, but through several phases. The subject and the object of an activity are in a mutual relationship in which the subject is transforming the object and the constituents of the object transform the subject. This phenomenon in the activity system is called internalisation (Kuutti, 1996). Jonassen and Murphy (1999) assert that "with practice and internalisation, activities collapse into actions and eventually into operations, as they become more automatic, requiring less conscious effort" (p. 63).

Engeström's (1987) expanded Activity Theory offers other analytic tools that are appropriate for modelling activity systems. Figure 4.3 below shows the basic structure of Activity Theory on which this research is based.

An activity is comprised of elements which together form activity systems, and these systems are meaningful units through which to understand human activity (Kuutti, 1996, p. 25). Activity systems exist within socio-cultural settings like a classroom, school context or a society. Thus, learning processes cannot properly be studied solely at the individual level, but one should consider the socio-cultural setting which provides a more holistic approach (Lim, 2002). As shown in Figure 4.3, an activity comprises a variety of mediators such as tools, rules and community and division of labour. These elements in an activity system act as mediators and the relationships between these elements are constantly mediated. For instance, a tool (computer) mediates between the subject (participant) and object (writing an

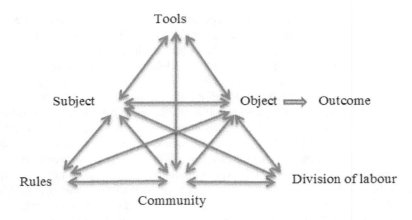

Figure 4.3. The basic structure of an activity system (adapted from Engeström, 1987)

essay), and rules (communication etiquette) mediate between subject (participant) and community (peers).

Activities are not rigid or fixed, but under continuous change and development (Kuutti, 1996). The development of the activities is rather discontinuous as the activities are not straightforward. The reason for discontinuation is that every action has its own history and as the activities develop, it is important to understand that history in order to grasp the current situation. In addition, activities are not isolated units. Other activities and the changes in their environments bring effects to activity systems. These external effects give rise to imbalances in the activity system and also among the elements of the activity. In this context, the imbalances are called contradictions.

According to Activity Theory, contradictions expose themselves as obstacles, interruptions, conflicts and gaps; however, contradictions are believed to be helpful in the development of activity systems. Contradictions can occur within an activity system, between the elements of an activity system or between activity systems. For instance, when a new technology is introduced to a group of students, if they lack knowledge of how to use the tool, this might create tension. This may lead some students to question the current situation or get frustrated when they are unable to use the new tool. Contradictions can even result in an expansion of an activity. This is known as an "expansive transformation" (Engeström, 2001, p. 137). As Engeström (2001) explains, this transformation takes place when "the object and motive of the activity are reconceptualised to embrace a radically wider horizon of possibilities than in the previous mode of the activity" (p. 137).

The third generation of Activity Theory proposed by Engeström describes the expansion of one activity system to two or more interacting activity systems. As Kuuti (1996) explains, "activities are not isolated units but are more like nodes in crossing hierarchies and networks, they are influenced by other activities and other changes in their environment" (p. 34). Figure 4.4 shows the third generation Activity Theory model developed by Engeström.

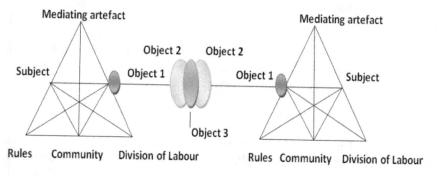

Figure 4.4. The third generation Activity Theory model (Engeström, 2001, p. 136)

Third generation of Activity Theory expands the unit of analysis from one activity system to two minimal activity systems as the unit of analysis (Engeström, 2001). For example, Engeström (2001) explored the relationships and contradictions among a health centre, a children's hospital and a patient's family in Helsinki. Through the resolutions of tensions such as healthcare agreement model, maps and document guides, the working practices could be transformed to improve the patient care services. The tensions and contradictions that exist within and between activity systems are thus considered sources of change and development in activity systems.

Since the aim of my research is to explore the contradictions that affect students' engagement with e-learning activities and the fact that I do not intend to compare activity systems, for the purpose of this chapter, Engeström's (1987) basic Activity Theory framework is used as a research tool.

CONTRADICTIONS

Contradictions are considered a key principle of Activity Theory and defined as "a misfit within elements, between them, between different activities, or between different developmental phases of a single activity" (Kuuti, 1996, p. 34). Contradictions are also referred to as structural tensions that have been accumulated over time. These tensions exist within and between activity systems. The activity systems which are generally open to the outside tend to embrace new elements, which may collide with the old elements. For instance, if a new technology is introduced to an activity system, it might collide with the existing practices such as the distribution of responsibilities (division of labour) or the time limit within which the activity should be carried out (rules).

Engeström (1987) proposes four levels of contradictions (1) primary, (2) secondary, (3) tertiary and (4) quaternary. The primary contradictions occur within the elements of activity systems (e.g. within the community). Secondary contradictions arise between the elements of an activity system (e.g., between the community and participants), tertiary contradictions arise when activity participants face situations where they have to use an advanced method to achieve an objective (e.g. when they are introduced to a new technology), and quaternary contradictions occur between the central activity system and outside activity systems. These contradictions may create conflicts, interruptions and clashes; however, through the resolution of conflicts, they can also be sources of change or development.

RESEARCH CONTEXT AND QUESTION

This chapter is based on a university blended learning course. This Post Graduate Diploma in Teaching course was offered in semester A of the 2012 academic year. The structure of the course included lectures, class presentations and an online discussion. The class hours were from 4pm to 7pm each Tuesday. The components of the course included an online discussion worth 10%, two face-to-face oral presentations worth 10%, and three written assignments. The written assignments were: Summary, Impact and Questions (SIQ) (30%); Summaries and position paper (20%); and Final report on a self-chosen topic (30%). For my purposes, I focused on the online discussion component of this course that was supported by Moodle. There was a required text book for this course and a recommended subject-related dictionary. The supplementary readings were provided on a CD-ROM to students at the beginning of the course. There were nine students in the course comprising both local and international students who were or wanted to be teachers. Out of these nine students, five students participated in my research.

The lecturer teaching this course was an experienced academician who had worked in different countries for over 40 years mostly in teaching, teacher education and administration. The lecturer also had a teaching assistant who is a PhD student in the university. The teaching assistant conducted three of the lectures and helped with the assessment tasks of the course.

This chapter is structured to answer the research question:

What were the contradictions that affected students' engagement in a university blended learning course?

DEFINITION OF LEARNER ENGAGEMENT

My study defines online learner engagement as students' active participation in e-learning activities (i.e., discussion threads, virtual classroom) in achieving learning goals where students:

- feel a sense of belonging to a learning community
- use collaborative ways to co-construct knowledge

- interact with the content and technology
- maintain social and academic interactions with the peers and the lecturer (Gedera, 2014).

RESEARCH METHODS

The main data collection methods used in this study included individual interviews with the participants, observations of learning activities, document analysis and a student profile questionnaire. The students, the lecturer and the teaching assistant were interviewed twice during the semester.

PRAGMATIC INTEGRATION OF ACTIVITY THEORY FRAMEWORK

Activity Theory provides a framework for understanding and analysing human activity. However, integrating the Activity Theory framework in an educational context requires some alterations to the terminology. According to Engeström's (1987) Activity Theory framework, the basic elements of activity systems comprise –*instruments, subject, object, rules, community, division of labour* and *outcome*. Engeström's use of the Activity Theory framework is limited to work-related contexts, and thus the terminology does not easily translate to an educational context. This specialised abstract terminology of Activity Theory can be confusing at times. For example, in Activity Theory, the term *object* is used instead of objective to refer to the purpose of an activity. Semantically this use can be considered correct; however, practically, in referring to the purpose of an activity in a classroom, this creates confusion, as the term *object* can mean a real object (i.e., a computer or a book). The term *object* generally is used as a noun, part of a noun phrase or as a pronoun that refers to a person or thing that is affected by the action of a verb in a sentence. In Activity Theory, the term *object* means a purpose or an objective of an activity. This is further complicated with different terminology used to refer to the elements of activity systems in the literature. Therefore, to suit the needs of my research as well as to avoid confusion, the following terms specified in Table 4.1 are adopted. The table below shows the terminology related to Activity Theory, in the literature, and how I adapt it in my study.

My specific terminology adaptation related to the elements of Activity Theory is associated with the following meanings:

- *Participant* – refers to the principle participant(s) of the activity—the students. Participant(s) accomplishes an objective through the use of tools.
- *Tools* – can be physical (such as a computer, a pen), mental (a plan), psychological, symbolic or abstract (a language, an experience) or virtual (functions of a website). Tools mediate the objective of an activity and assist in transforming an objective into an outcome. This element shows the principle of mediation in an activity.

Table 4.1. Activity Theory framework terminology

Original terminology used in Activity Theory framework by Engeström's (1987)	Terminology used in the literature	Terminology used in this study
Subject	subject, agent, actor, respondent	participant
Instruments	tools, artefacts, mediating tools	tools
Object	object, motive, stimulus	objective
Rules	rules	rules
Community	community, players	community
Division of labour	roles, division of labour	roles
Outcome	outcome	outcome

- *Objective* – is the purpose of an activity which can be a motive. The objective is transformed into an outcome and the objective distinguishes actions and sub-activities in an activity system.
- *Rules* – are the norms, practices, expectations that control or influence actions and interactions in the activity system. The *rules* can be implicit or explicit depending on specific communities.
- *Community* – represents the co-participants of an activity other than the principle *participant(s)* who share the same *objective* of an activity. In the case of my study, *community* includes peer students, lecturer and a teaching assistant. This element shows the collective nature of an activity.
- *Roles* – represent the distribution of roles, tasks and responsibilities among principle *participant(s)* and co-participants (*community*) of an activity. This element also denotes status and power divisions.
- *Outcome* – refers to a desired result of an activity. Objectives are transformed into an outcome through tool mediation.

For my purposes, I developed an activity system model for an asynchronous discussion forum (see Figure 4.5) which was carried out in the case study using Engeström's Activity Theory framework to demonstrate ways that learning activities can be analysed using the frame of Activity Theory.

In this model, *participants* are the students, *tools* include learning resources, computers and other learning practices. The *participants* accomplished an *objective* through the use of *tools*. A central factor to consider here is the way that students engage with *tools* to achieve their *objectives* that are transformed into *outcomes*. The *tools* mediate this process.

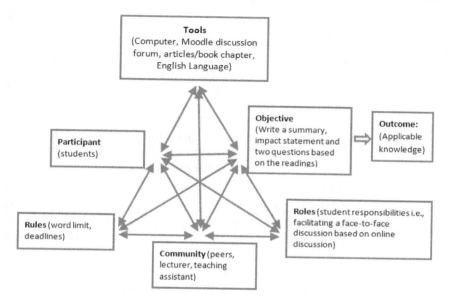

Figure 4.5. Moodle discussion activity system

FINDINGS

The contradictions identified in this case study were mainly related to the aspects of (1) Student-lecturer different opinions on feedback (2) Imbalance of student participation (student roles) (3) Divergent objectives, and these contradictions led to misunderstandings and frustrations among students.

In this case study the lecturer and the teaching assistant did not participate in the online discussions, but copied all the students' work from Moodle and pasted it in a word document in order to provide feedback. The feedback was given in the form of a short paragraph and was sent via email by the lecturer. In terms of feedback, the students' pointed out that they needed more specific comments; however, the lecturer and the teaching assistant assumed that the feedback and comments they provided were helpful. In addition, the students' participation (student roles) in activities in this case study did not seem to be balanced. In the following section these contradictory issues are discussed.

Student-Lecturer Different Opinions on Feedback

David (the lecturer) described how the students' SIQs were graded. First, Lise (the teaching assistant) looked at students' SIQs and comments to other students and then she graded them, adding a paragraph of feedback. Then David added his comments and emailed the feedback to students. David believed that he provided detailed feedback. As he explained:

> Lise would look at the SIQs and draft feedback which she would send to me and then I would add to that on the SIQs. And then I also looked at their responses to the questions and gave some detailed feedback. For instance, with the SIQs not much you can say, you did the right lengths, you covered the main points. Lise did that and sometimes I added to that. And she gave a grade and I generally I accepted the grade although I tended to up it rather than lower it in most cases. Then I would dictate my comments on their responses patching into Lise's SIQ comments and then I would email it to the students individually and copy it to Lise. (lecturer interview 2)

Lise who was a PhD student, commented positively on her experience of providing feedback to students in this course, partially because it was her research area. She said that she "learnt a lot in giving feedback" and she also commented:

> My style of providing feedback has changed a lot compared to the past partly because of my studies and also both the theoretical and the practical applications. So, my views of providing feedback, has changed tremendously. And I will not provide feedback that I used to give in the past. (teaching assistant interview 2)

However, the students felt that the feedback they received on SIQs seemed to not be specific and detailed enough. Lorraine mentioned:

> He gives feedback on our SIQs. His feedback is quite distinct, quite short. I find the previous lecturer (when she was doing another paper) is little better because when we get our feedback, we get our SIQ in the printed format handed to us and little bit highlighted that's good and little comments on the side. Whereas in this course our lecturer says you need to consolidate more or you did cover the main points, but it would be nice to have little bit more. The previous lecturer's style was more specific in that sense. (student interview 1)

Ken had similar expectations and he mentioned that he preferred "more explicit feedback. I'd like to know how I can get an A+. It'll be really helpful" (student interview 2). Melissa also felt that she needed some specific feedback that could guide her to improve her grade.

In general, in terms of feedback, students and the lecturer had opposing views in this study.

Imbalance of Student Participation

The imbalance of student participation was mainly related to participant roles in this case. The lead in-class discussions took place during face-to-face class hours weekly and these in-class discussions were supposed to be based on online discussions. Each student presented at least twice during the semester and only the second presentation was assessed by Lise and David. By looking at students' presentations David commented:

> Those lead-in presentations varied. Some of them were little bit too trivial, a little bit too schoolish whereas the recent one was really excellent. It was a series of activities which led one to the other. (lecturer interview 2)

In the in-class discussions, students were to work with a partner to plan and present their ideas. One particular student had an issue with working with her partner in lead in-class discussions. Lorraine explained that the male student she had to work with did not contribute much and she had to do it all by herself, but in the end he expected to get the same grade as Lorraine. She also stated that "I didn't want to work with him and no one was putting up their hands, so David said "how about him and Lorraine", I just said "ok", but I wasn't happy. It wasn't very good" (student interview 2). She described what took place:

> I had to work with him on a lead-in discussion and he was pretty bad because he had done no preparation for it. I did the whole thing and then I was a bit stressed and tired at that time because I had other things on. We didn't even get together properly to practise how we are going to do it. In the end, I said to him "you say that and you say that and I'm doing the rest" because I thought I do all this work and if he stands out there and goes "ah now we are going to ..." I thought that's not good. It was a bit embarrassing because at the end David said to him "Why didn't you talk much"? He (group member) is very impolite and he never even said "Lorraine thank you, you did all the work", only what he said was "oh I hope we get the same mark" and I was like "oh wow". (Lorraine, student interview 2)

When Lise was asked about the imbalance of student participation in activities, she said that some students were domineering, taking over the whole discussion and leaving the other student behind. She said that even she was not sure how much they had contributed, but she assumed that they had done their part and graded their work. Lise said:

> The lead-in discussions maybe they have problems because there is one dominating the whole discussion. Taking over the whole discussion and leaving the poor person behind as if the other person is not doing their work at all. And you are not sure whether this person has contributed, but you try to think positively and think that person has. (teaching assistant interview 2)

The issue of imbalance of participation was also apparent in the classes I observed. For example, Nicky was presenting with Melissa in the first round of presentations and Nicky's presentation was brief compared with Melissa's presentation (3 April, Observation). In the second round of presentations, Nicky presented with Ken and most of the discussion parts were done by Ken whereas Nicky talked very little (15 May, Observation).

In general, during face-to-face in-class discussions, students' participation did not seem to be balanced. Some of the students felt that they did not have an opportunity to clarify things and most of the time only one or two people talked in the class. Lorraine said that "certain people like me and Ken interrupt quite a lot and ask questions" (student interview 2). In David's point of view, "people who asked questions tended to be the native speakers. That I expected because it is difficult to formulate a question when you are trying to process it" (lecturer interview 2). However, Melissa who is also a native speaker felt that she did not have an opportunity to ask questions:

> When David is teaching, there should be opportunities for people to do some feedback within this class…face-to-face interactions because there is a guy called Ken and he is always putting up his hand and asking questions and clarifications, and there is no time and David doesn't set up that. There is no time for us to ask questions and feedback from other people and join the conversation because I have a lot of questions too. (student interview 2)

It is apparent from Melissa's comment that students needed well-designed opportunities to interact and communicate in this course. Although this course had both online and face-to-face spaces, the mechanisms for this did not appear to be structured.

Divergent Objectives

David mentioned that on the whole, he was "satisfied with the balance of the course" (lecturer interview 2). However, some students raised a concern regarding the objective of the main in-class activity which was supposed to be based on the online discussions on SIQs each week. According to David, "the purpose of that (online discussions) is to get them to interact online because the first part of their next class is a discussion of those issues" (lecturer interview 1). The course outline specified the details of the in-class discussion as:

> Each week, on a rotating basis, one or two students will lead an in-class discussion of ideas discussed in the articles (or book chapters). This is not a presentation or summary of the reading, as you may assume that everyone in the class has already read it. In order to start the discussion, you can develop your own questions about the reading, or you can read through the SIQ assignment questions posted by your classmates and select the ones that you find particularly interesting or salient (10 minutes maximum). You will then lead the class in an exploration of issues discussed in the readings. (course outline)

Ken pointed out that although the lead in-class discussion was supposed to be based on online discussions on SIQs, students practised rather a different method where they developed activities but without many discussions.

People seem to develop and develop until it becomes whole lot of activities that have become less and less useful. I think it has become like people feel obliged to do a certain amount of lead in a certain amount of activities and ask "have you finished" and "have you finished" and "let's move on" and less discussions. (Ken, student interview 2)

According to Ken, the activities students put together for lead in-class discussions were from one slide of David's previous lecture and Ken considered it rather an ineffective method of leading a discussion.

So far the lead-in is quite didn't...yeah it didn't really...I was hoping that there'll be comments on what we've done, but it was totally you know...I mean one lesson and totally different expressions and they all came from one slide of classroom projection. There was one particular slide taken from 30 or whatever and that was the chunk of the lead-in. I was like "I don't even know what these terms are or there's no use to me". I want to get excited and something that interests us, be more useful and get stuck to a smaller area of discussion, discuss more deeply rather than...you know. (Ken, student interview 2)

He suggested that there should be a link between SIQs and lead in-class discussions. As he said, "Probably it's good to get that linkage of SIQs and lead-in discussions and the discussions we have are being further in-class at the beginning and then we continue it". In linking these two activities, he said, "The person who does SIQ and the lead-in has to take all of the questions asked and look at whatever everyone is interested in and maybe misunderstandings and go from there...draw over it" (student interview 2). Ken emphasised that when that linkage is not there, students naturally feel that they should not worry about such activities that do not take them anywhere.

It's interesting and it's amazing to see that as a learner, if the teacher doesn't link something up, pretty soon you think "wow, I'm not going to even bother with those things because it's not going anywhere" and what I need to do is to focus on the assessment which is different. (Ken, student interview 2)

Overall, students' and lecturer's opposing views on feedback, imbalanced student participation and divergent objectives of learning activities reflected some contradictions that occurred in this case study.

DISCUSSION

Contradictions constitute a key principle in Activity Theory and they appear as conflicts, ruptures, breakdowns and tensions in activity systems. As illustrated by the lightning-shaped arrows in Figure 4.6, in my study, contradictions emerged within and between (primary and secondary) the elements of the activity systems as well as between the main activity system and its neighbour activity system (quaternary).

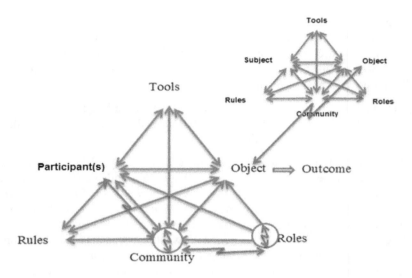

Figure 4.6. Contradictions within and between activity systems

The contradictions identified in this case were within and between the elements: *participants, roles* and *community* of the activity systems.

The analysis revealed that the opinions of the *participants* (students) and the *community* (lecturer and teaching assistant) on the SIQs feedback were contradictory. Contradictions occurred between the elements: *participants* and the *community* (secondary contradiction) as well as within *roles* (primary contradiction) of activity systems. The lecturer, David and the teaching assistant, Lise believed that they provided a lengthy paragraph of feedback that was useful for the students. However, the students' views demonstrated that they were quite disappointed that they did not receive specific feedback that could guide them to improve their assignments and grades. Students' comparison to the previous course in which they received explicit feedback, which they found satisfying, informed the students' expectations in this course.

The imbalance of student participation that emerged as a primary contradiction in activities was related to the element *roles* in the in-class discussion activity system in this case. In the case of Lorraine, although it was paired work, she had to prepare the presentation all by herself and in the end, her working partner expected to get the same mark. In the literature this is known as the 'free riding' problem associated with group work where some students are reluctant to contribute to tasks. Lorraine was unhappy with this situation, as she was under stress juggling the presentation with her other commitments. In this case, there was no specific way to assess students' individual contributions, but the lecturer assumed that they all contributed equally in activities. One way to solve this problem is to carefully consider group as well as individual efforts put into the task and award marks (Davies, 2009).

Similarly, the student *roles* in the in-class discussions were not balanced. The presentation conducted by Nicky (non-native speaker) and Melissa (native speaker) at the beginning of the semester and the presentation by Nicky (non-native speaker) and Ken (native speaker) at the end of the semester were apparent examples of imbalanced participation in activities in this case. Consistent with the findings of Freiermuth's (2001) study, when native speakers were paired with non-native speakers, because of their different language competencies, the native speakers tended to dominate the discussion. The literature suggests that when native speakers and non-native speakers are mixed in learning activities, opportunities for non-native speakers are limited (Freiermuth, 2001). Warschauer (1996) accentuates that, in particular, Asian students do not feel comfortable participating in oral discussions due to their previous experiences. This could be because in many Asian countries, it is uncommon to have oral discussions as part of learning activities. The non-native speakers in the case of my research were also mostly from Asian countries.

However, some of the native speakers in the class were also quite frustrated and disappointed, as they felt that they did not have enough opportunities in the class to ask questions and clarify issues related to the lesson. This could be interpreted as lecturer's poor pedagogy, as there were not enough opportunities for questions in the class; however, this issue could possibly be addressed by the provision of an online space for asking questions and interacting with each other without limiting themselves within the four walls of the classroom.

Engeström's (1987) fourth level contradictions (quaternary) refer to the contradictions that occur between the central activity system and neighbour activity systems. Activity systems are never isolated as the constituents of one activity system are somehow always related to other activity systems. For example, in my research the unit of analysis was the activity system (the main activity system). However, when studying contradictions, if a neighbour activity system is interconnected with the main activity system and relevant to the study, it is important to study all the connected activity systems. This was evident where contradictions occurred between the virtual and physical classroom activity systems.

In the activity system of the online SIQ activity, the neighbour activity system was the in-class face-to-face discussion activity. These two activity systems were related because of the linked objectives of two activities. David (lecturer) affirmed that the objective of the online SIQ activity was to "get them to interact online because the first part of their next class is a discussion of those issues". The lead in-class activity was becoming less constructive when the students realised that it was not linked up with the online discussions. Although it was stressed in the course outline that the class discussions were to be based on the SIQ online questions or students' own questions on readings, it was interesting to note that almost all the in-class discussions were a series of activities based on David's (lecturer) previous lecture, which was supported by students' views.

The contradictions arose between these two systems when these activities were not planned and carried out in a way that linked the objectives of two activity systems. As a result, the students were frustrated and it affected their participation in activities. Students' suggestions included that those who do the lead in-class discussion should first consider online questions (posted by the students) and based on students' ideas, questions and concepts, they should then develop the face-to-face discussion activity.

CONCLUSION

Contradictions can be characterised as conflicts, ruptures, disturbances and breakdowns (Engeström, 2001). Contradictions can be "the motive force of change and development" (Engeström & Miettinen, 1999, p. 9) if they are acknowledged or resolved. In the context of my research the contradictions that occurred were related to community, participant roles and physical and virtual classes.

In conclusion, the contradictory views on feedback revealed the students' expectations in this course and their disappointment in not receiving explicit feedback on their performance. The analysis also revealed that students needed more opportunities for interactions and discussion in this course. The missing linkage between the virtual (online) and physical (face-to-face) activity systems also affected the way students participated in the activities.

In relation to student roles, pairing up students who have different levels of competencies (i.e., language in this case) resulted in imbalanced student participation in activities and as a result a student was frustrated when she had to do the bulk of the work, but both students received the same grade. These frustrations were identified as contradictions that precluded students' full participation in activities. Therefore, lecturers should be mindful not to pair up students who are at different competency levels related to specific tasks. In implementing e-learning activities in blended learning contexts, it is crucial to make sure that the linkage between the objectives of the virtual and physical classes are well established.

REFERENCES

Barab, S. A., Evans, M. A., & Baek, E. O. (2004). Activity Theory as a lens for characterizing the participatory unit. In D. H. Jonassen (Ed.), *Handbook of research on educational communities and technology* (pp. 199–214). Mahwah, NJ: Lawrence Erlbaum Associates.

Davies, W. M. (2009). Groupwork as a form of assessment: Common problems and recommended solutions. *High Educ, 58*, 563–584.

Engeström, Y. (1987). *Learning by expanding: An activity-theoretical approach to developmental research*. Helsinki, Finland: Orienta-Konsultit.

Engeström, Y. (2001). Expansive learning at work: Toward an activity-theoretical conceptualization. *Journal of Education and Work, 14*(1), 133–156.

Engeström, Y., & Miettinen, R. (1999). Introduction. In Y. Engeström, R. Miettinen, & R. L. Punamäki (Eds.), *Perspectives on activity theory* (pp. 1–18). Cambridge, England: Cambridge University Press.

Freiermuth, M. R. (2001). Native speakers or non-native speakers: Who has the floor? Online and face-to-face interaction in culturally mixed small groups. *Computer Assisted Language Learning, 14*(2), 169–199.

Gedera, D. S. P. (2014). *Mediational engagement in e-learning: An Activity Theory analysis* (Unpublished doctoral thesis).The University of Waikato, Hamilton, New Zealand.

Greenhow, C., & Belbas, B. (2007). Using activity-oriented design methods to study collaborative knowledge-building in e-learning courses within higher education. *Computer-Supported Collaboraive Learning, 2*(4), 363–391.

Jonassen, D. H., & Murphy, L. R. (1999). Activity Theory as a framework for designing constructivist learning environments. *Educational Technology, 47*(1), 1042–1629.

Kuutti, K. (1996). Activity Theory as a potential framework for human computer interaction research. In B. Nardi (Ed.), *Context and consciousness: Activity Theory and human computer interaction* (pp. 17–44). Cambridge, MA: MIT Press.

Leont'ev, A. N. (1981). *Problems of the development of mind.* Moscow, Russia: Progress.

Lim, C. P. (2002). A theoretical frame for the study of ICT in schools: A proposal. *British Journal of Educational Technology, 33*(4), 411–421.

Vygotsky, L. S. (1978). *Mind in society.* Cambridge, England: Harvard University Press.

Warschauer, M. (1996). Comparing face-to-face and electronic discussion in the second language classroom. *Calico Journal, 13*, 7–26.

Yamagata-Lynch, L. C. (2010). *Activity systems analysis methods: Understanding complex learning environments.* New York, NY: Springer.

Dilani S. P. Gedera
Otago Polytechnic
New Zealand

MELISSA HARNESS AND LISA C. YAMAGATA-LYNCH

5. SYSTEMIC TENSIONS IN AMERICAN TEACHER UNIONS

An Activity Systems Analysis of Teacher Unions and Their Role in Society

INTRODUCTION

Cultural Historical Activity Theory (CHAT) offers a broad approach to analysing complex contexts. CHAT has been employed in analysis of activities specifically within learning contexts for many years (Yamagata-Lynch, 2010). We find that the CHAT approach to the analysis of learning and learning environments is attractive because of its ability to recognise the intertwining of human thought and action (Engeström, 1987; Galperin, 1995; Leontiev, 1981). Essentially CHAT allows both educational researchers and participants to engage in the examination of institutional affordances for action; in other words, the ability to see action when members of the system are constrained by that very system (Dijk et al., 2011). The precise understanding needed to research and begin to unravel the complexities and changes within society, governmental systems, policies, and organisational entities are also well suited for use within an activity systems analysis methodology (Foot, 2014).

In this chapter we will report on how we relied on CHAT and activity systems analysis while examining the complexities involved in teacher unions in the United States. To us, labour unions in general are a very interesting and provoking subject matter to study, especially when the ideas surrounding collective bargaining have such a strong pull in a nation (United States) that values extreme individualism. The idea of coming together as a community of individuals to garner power for a group over those who seek to use their hegemony to overrun workers in society, to us, is a fascinating avenue for study. Our predilection for desiring to study unions, specifically teacher unions, has been reignited with the demonstrations and subsequent destruction of teacher unions all over the country, most notably in the state of Wisconsin where collective bargaining by public sector workers has been largely outlawed; the demonising effects in the city of Chicago where teachers, unions, and its members have been vilified as only interested in protecting and furthering their needs and desires and not those of their students; and most recently in the state of California where tenure and seniority rights have been removed.

What follows will be guided by our research question: What are the systemic tensions associated with teacher unions within the United States, and what entities have been perpetuating these tensions? We will rely on various popular news media

D. S. P. Gedera & P. J. Williams (Eds.), Activity Theory in Education, 71–85.

sources such as the Washington Post (Porter & Trottman, 2014), the New York Times (Brill, 2010), and POLITICO (Simon, 2014) as our data sources. We first engaged in a qualitative document analysis primarily relying on the constant comparative method (Charmaz, 2014; Corbin & Strauss, 2015; Glaser & Strauss, 1967; Saldaña, 2013) then while writing the narrative results of our qualitative analysis we engaged in activity systems analysis. We believe that by using CHAT we will demonstrate and expose the gap between what is being stated about teacher unions, and the ramifications of their dismantling, as well as, why it should really matter to teachers, parents, politicians, and society in general.

We will conclude the chapter with a discussion about how activity systems analysis can help tease out the systemic tensions related to teacher unions to understand what really is occurring rather than what is sensationalised in popular media. We will discuss how CHAT allows us to understand how and why outsiders, as well as the insiders of education are demonising unions. Our analysis brings about the ability to see and understand that there is much more to tensions in teacher unions than meets the eye, and we will demonstrate with this chapter why analysis of these means needs to be done more, especially concerning the government and political entities. CHAT, in the end will give us the research tools to focus this study and examine the inner workings to a deeper level than we could understand before.

UNDERSTANDING COMPLEX SYSTEMS

Changes in educational policy and practice are demanding that researchers examine issues surrounding education, teacher unions included, from a new perspective, one that allows us to understand the complexities that education systems are facing as a social system in a globalised world. Activity Theory (AT) and especially Cultural Historical Activity Theory (CHAT) provides a methodological approach that takes a developmental view of the human mind in context (Cole, 1996; Wertsch, 1985). CHAT is particularly well suited to study schools and policies surrounding education. CHAT as a framework allows for changes to occur in the activity being observed and for consideration of how those changes are affecting the activity itself, participants, and society. This is an advantage when analysing politics and education because CHAT allows researchers to consider how changes in policy and popular educational practices have far reaching individual and societal impacts. CHAT provides a rich description of the "participants, their activities, and the activity setting" which allows for a very detailed understanding of the issues and tensions that are part of a situation which the researcher is studying (Yamagata-Lynch, 2010). We are not the first researchers to rely on CHAT to study socio-political systems and implications on human daily activity. Other scholarly work relying on CHAT to study socio-political systems includes (a) Foot (2001) who traced activities related to non-violent conflict management after the Soviet Union was dismantled; (b) Lee and Roth (2008) who studied a state sponsored salmon enhancement program in British Columbia and its implications to food production, saving salmon as a species, and providing employment to workers; and (c) Igira and Aanestad (2009) who examined implications brought upon by contradictions found in healthcare practices in Zanzibar that was uncovered while designing a new healthcare information system. Our work fits within this area of research relying on CHAT analysis methods to uncover socio-political tensions in our case specifically related to public policy, or politics of teacher unions.

TEACHER UNIONS PROJECT PARTICULARITIES

Understanding the Need to Study Teacher Unions

The CHAT research that will be introduced here has led us to better understand the discontent with teacher unions within the U.S. that rests heavy on the minds of many individuals within American society. Within this discontent for many lies an unsurmountable feeling of loss and a genuine disheartening over what simply can be coined 'the loss of America's competitive edge' (Peterson, 1999). Several different players within and outside the realm of education explain this loss in many ways. However it is explained, there seems to be an unpretentious and sometimes misguided desire to make education better by all involved (Lieberman, 2004).

This desire to see education as it is perceived as once being at a pinnacle for all to admire in the world, comes at a price. The price for this nostalgic view of education, and its accompanying unprecedented return, has begun in the last decade to forsake long standing teachers' unions. Although the attack against labour unions has been ongoing since the 1970s, beginning in the early part of the twenty-first century we can begin to see the hard push in the political parties, and in other both governmental and non-governmental entities throughout the U.S. against teacher unions. For instance, in 2010 Newsweek ran a story titled The Key to Saving American Education, in which they call for the end of tenure rights for classroom teachers (Thomas & Wingert, 2010). The attacks on teacher unions have continued in popular media outlets as well with movies such as Waiting on Superman (2013), where students are portrayed as needing to be saved from poor, failing schools. These understandings have continued on to the present day, and thus teacher unions, the entities that once stood as formidable professional support and a negotiator for teachers throughout the U.S., have now been caught off guard with negative imagery and extremist propaganda that has been created by critics of the teacher unions and cynics of labour unions including, the mass media, government officials, those in law, and most surprisingly, teachers themselves (Bidwell, 2015).

Anger both for and against teacher unions within the U.S. has been building over the last several years. Many groups that are calling themselves 'reformers' have come from many avenues, governmental systems, private industry, and from parents. These 'reformers' have created a narrative that lets them claim moral high ground in public debates, and paints teacher unions as having their own interests in mind, and that in fact, teacher unions do not have students' best interest at heart at all (Burke, 2010). They claim that ineffective teachers, supported by corrupt and unprogressive unions are unduly and particularly harming minorities and students in poverty, already some of the most disenfranchised students. Likewise, the reformers are claiming that if teacher unions really cared about students and helping to improve education, they would rescind on long standing pressured issues like tenure and seniority rights (Bascia & Osmond, 2012; Simon, 2014).

Accordingly, teacher unions are outraged at the attacks they say are unwarranted and uncalled for. They claim that they have both the students' and teachers' best intentions at heart, and their interests are backed by a century or more of research and experience in the field of education (National Education Association, 2014). However, reformer groups have put so much money into their efforts at creating a negative picture of teacher unions, as well as, backing high profile individuals all the way up to the U.S. President, that the reformers rhetoric has largely prevailed, and teacher unions are losing ground even with seasoned unionised teachers (Bidwell, 2015). By no means did all teachers throughout the history of the unions support everything they did; however, there has always been a feeling of comradery between professionals in the education field, and in many ways there is a clear lack of feeling of any disheartenment by the prospective that teacher unions may not be around in the near future in many places within the U.S. There has been a 'brand identity' that has been created by the reformers that demonstrates that they are the ones who are most interested in improving education; and that 'branding' is winning out.

The new 'branding' of education that has occurred is being mimicked and regurgitated throughout society as the way we are going to solve the issues in education in the U.S. Politicians from all over the country have jumped on the band wagon that education has to be 'fixed,' teachers must be held accountable, inefficiency must be phased out, students need improved test scores, and teachers' unions must be disbanded. Even long term supporters of teacher unions, namely the Democratic Party, have seemed to turn their back on them and the issues that they are trying to fight for. In many instances where law suits have been filed by 'reformers,' long time unions supporting Democrats have in turn become part of the party that fights against the teacher unions, thus adding an unforeseeable element to the criticisms the unions face.

Throughout all the rhetoric that surrounds the politicians and the government becoming so heavily involved in the debates about teacher unions, runs a vein of neoliberalism that cannot be ignored (Simon, 2012; Torres, 2010). As politicians try to campaign for the disbandment of labour unions within the education field, they support the notions surrounding charter schools, and other types of corporatism into public education (Burke, 2010). They feel that these entities infused into our current systems will vastly improve overall academic success for all students. However, teacher unions and others both in and outside the field of education find that the flux of neoliberal principles in the field of education is a hindrance to social justice and equity. Further, the repercussions of having private industry infiltrate public spaces are vastly under researched, especially in education.

Finally, the teacher unions take the stance that they are scapegoats for the perceived problems in the U.S. educational systems. It can be viewed that this may be a critical moment in time, where the unions' positionality and influence will become so hotly debated, and in some ways their very existence come into question, that it seems imperative that more significant research and time be used to determine the effects of unions upon education. As politicians and government try to 'fix' laws that have been long established concerning teachers, the unions are going to fight back against a media storm of negative imagery and bad societal perception as we have seen in the CHAT research that will follow.

Data Sets

In this project, we engaged in CHAT analysis of teacher unions based on three articles that come from reputable news organisations. We first began by simply typing in a scholarly search engine, *Teachers Unions*. After reading briefly through several articles that appeared and not finding the articles to be overtly pertaining to what might be going on in the U.S. concerning the degradation of teacher unions, we refined the search to include *Issues* surrounding teacher unions. The following three articles are the results of the second, more refined search. We chose to look at these three articles because we believed them to have a good source of information about our subject matter and they came from reputable news sources. In addition we limited our choice to three articles in order to focus intently on the content of the material.

The first article we chose to use in the analysis comes from the *Wall Street Journal*, and is entitled *Teachers Unions Under Fire* (Porter & Trottman, 2014). Further, the second article that we chose comes from *The New York* Times. The title of the article from the Times is named, *The Teachers' Unions' Last Stand*. We chose the *Wall Street Journal* and *The New York* Times articles as sources for analysis because the *Journal* and *Times* are read all over the U.S. and both are considered to be reliable and reputable sources to garner information. Both also write about many current social issues that are politically and legally pervasive in the media.

The third article that we chose to use comes from *POLITICO*. *POLITICO* is an American political journalism organisation that was founded in 2007, that distributes its news content via newspaper, radio, television, and internet (Anonymous, 2014). Although *POLITICO* has not been around as long as the *Wall Street Journal* and *The New York* Times, its reputation for reporting accurate, reliable political, legal, and social content material has been acquired through the various awards that it can now claim. The article that we found titled *The Fall of Teacher Unions* is an article that demonstrates the ability of the journalists working within POLITICO (Simon, 2014).

The data that we found within these three articles garnered a wealth of information about what has been happening within the U.S. concerning teacher unions. These data sources serve as an excellent example for this CHAT analysis about the current state of teacher unions in the US. In the following section we will lay the foundation for the types of questions that we chose to examine when researching this topic.

Research Questions

When thinking about teacher unions and the attacks that have taken place on them in U.S. society in recent years, we directed our research question toward understanding what might be some of the causes and issues surrounding teacher unions:

> What are the systemic tensions associated with teacher unions within the United States, and what entities have been perpetuating these tensions?

We found while reflecting on the literature and examining the data that the following questions emerged and should also be addressed, as they pertain to the above questions in inquiry:

- What tensions are occurring between the different entities concerning teacher unions (parents, teachers, administrators, politicians, the law, and the union representatives)?
- What roles do government and politicians play concerning teacher unions?
- What might be possible outcomes if teacher unions are effectively absolved throughout the U.S.?

Through this study our goal was to examine what role the activities of teacher unions play within the larger context of society, thereby bridging the gap between teachers, parents, individual politicians, and society at large. Thus, these questions help to delve deeper into the understanding of the culture and history of teacher unions, and to be able to examine more closely why it seems they are under attack.

Qualitative Activity Systems Analysis

Qualitative activity systems analysis is a process that helps researchers to gain a detailed understanding of the subject that they are studying (Yamagata-Lynch, 2010). The steps to the process of providing a qualitative activity systems analysis may vary depending on the researcher and their needs based on the topics being addressed. In this study we relied on Saldaña's (2013) methods introduced in *The Coding Manual for Qualitative Research*, as well as, Glaser and Strauss's (1967) book *The Discovery of Grounded Theory: Strategies for Qualitative Research* and Corbin and Strauss's (2015) work in *Basics of Qualitative Research: Techniques and Procedures for Developing Grounded Theory*. As Yamagata-Lynch (2010) introduces constant comparative method, as a way for investigators to engage in "an intense, systematic process of examining and re-examining the data while comparing one source with another to find similarities and differences," (p. 73) we too used this method as a way to begin the initial analysis of activities. As in the constant comparative model discussed in Charmaz (2014) and Corbin and Strauss (2015) Saldaña (2013), it begins with open coding (looking for words or phrases that stand out), followed by re-reading of the material and finding any other units of data that might be helpful to the researcher, this is done until saturation of the data occurs (no other information can be coded or 'pulled' from the data). The next steps are to re-read the data, and where the codes are placed, begin to look for patterns within the codes; these patterns are then assigned a word or a short phrase that might denote how the particular code is related. Through this process, filters are then attached to the patterns that are then categorised and placed into themes, "a process that permits data to be segregated, grouped, regrouped and relinked in order to consolidate meaning and explanation" (Saldana, 2013, p. 8). After this process is completed, sometimes many times over, the codes and their subsequent categories are then generated into a workable theory. This rectification process allows data to become more trustworthy as a source of valid representation of a phenomenon.

Being trustworthy during coding is of upmost importance, as this can be one of the major criticisms when researchers look at using CHAT as a viable methodology within research. Careful processes for reiteration and member checking help to satisfy some of the critique that may be brought about concerning the methodology. According to Yamagata-Lynch (2010), the following questions are helpful to address during coding when performing an activity theoretical qualitative research:

> What are the key activities related to this study that are in the data set? What is the activity setting in which these activities are situated? Who are the subjects of these activities? What is the shared object of these activities? Do different subjects participating in the same activity view the activity and the object differently? If yes, why? What tools, rules, community, and division of labour are involved in these activities? What systemic contradictions are bringing tensions into these activities? What are the outcomes of these activities? What historical relationship does one activity have with another? How does one activity interact with another? (p. 75)

Having these questions in the back of the mind, in conjunction with the research questions that are being pursued, helps during the coding process as can be witnessed in the steps that were taken in this study, which are found in Figure 5.1.

By step 5 we gained an understanding of a workable theory that addressed our research questions; essentially, the theory allowed us to see connections among various components of the data collected, which help us explain the activities that are occurring throughout the U.S. concerning teacher unions (Creswell, 2013).The categorisation and themes further helped to filter through some of the questions that we had pertaining to the issues that we wanted to examine in this CHAT analysis.

Findings

As previously stated in the beginning of the chapter, and as we came to find during our research, teacher unions have had many issues that are explicitly public

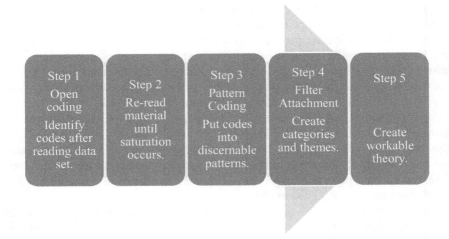

Figure 5.1. Steps involved in qualitative activity systems analysis

concerns throughout their histories that have continued and even worsened into the 21st century; such as, tenure, and seniority rights, of which both were negatively discussed throughout the articles that we examined. Examples of new laws in both California and Wisconsin were given that illustrated both the governments' and societies' desire to 'fix' the issues concerning tenure and seniority rights.

Further, it became evident that teacher unions have other issues both internally and externally within both the major teacher unions (NEA and AFT). According to the data, most teacher unions have seen a small drop in the number of enrolees into the unions, approximately 7% across the board (Brill, 2010). Their revenues have dropped, but more significantly over the last decade, which has hurt their ability to mobilise externally, as well as, provide campaign funding for individuals that have the best intentions for education. Teacher unions seem to be squashed in some states as to what they can do to represent teachers and their needs; in many places discussed in the data, collective bargaining and striking are strictly prohibited by law.

Furthermore, teacher unions have had to become more flexible in their dealing with school systems and state legislatures. This has led to other internal strife that has been reflected in the splintering of groups within the organisations themselves. One such group that was exemplified within the data was BATS (Bad-Ass Teachers Society) (Members of BATS, 2015). These internally splintered groups have been voicing their discontent with issues of testing to accountability, and welfare to public spending. The data shows their anger and discontent over being disenfranchised by society concerning issues of education. This is reflected in the manner in which many of the group's members personally attack those that they feel are not supporting their claims in a more aggressive manner, including the unions they are a part of themselves.

It seems that although some of the criticisms that were levelled against teacher unions within the data, is rightly deserved, opponents of teacher unions have simply had the loudest voices. Teacher unions responses both from the NEA and AFT have been slow, and have come from an often times un-united front.

This data shows a telling picture of the tensions that surround teacher unions. In Figure 5.2 we have compiled the thick description narrative of the data into an activity systems visual representation. This visual representation gave us the ability to discern and pick apart the intricacies of the research work, specifically the tensions uncovered.

Looking at the activity system that emerged from our analysis in this project, we can see that the overall object for teacher unions is to give support to teachers in their professional needs within the educational realm. To achieve this object, the teacher unions have various tools, including lawsuits, political campaigning, active factions within their unions, and ingenuity of individual minds. On the other hand, teacher unions also have to deal with tools that are not as helpful to them, such as, falling membership rates and declining funding, which in the long run could hurt some of the more positive aspects of the unions. Also, as was evident in the research, the various factions within the unions can also have a negative impact on their overall goal and outcome, especially if the factions go against the best interest of all other union members. Therefore, although many of the tools that are available to the teacher unions to achieve their goals are positive and helpful, some are also detrimental to the long term outcome for teacher unions and members.

Further, the community for this activity system includes a good majority of society, including teachers, teacher unions (NEA/AFT), government and politicians, parents and advocacy groups, and lawyers and judges. Not all of these individuals seemed to be willing participants, especially those who were opposed to teacher unions from the beginning, such as parents and parental advocacy groups. Even some of the government officials and politicians seemed not to want to be involved with things that surrounded the teacher unions (both good and bad), but that seemed to be pulled in one way or another by various entities. We believe that this non-participatory desire by many involved caused various roles that are evidenced within the activity system. Hence, the roles that were created for teacher unions in particular are varied and many. They, along with all other members of the community involved here had to have at least a rudimentary understanding of the judicial system and the laws surrounding education, as well as, an appreciation of social justice and educational issues for students, parents, and especially teachers, all the while taking into account the unaligned principles surrounding the ideas of neoliberalism.

Hence, the tensions in this project are many (see Appendix, Table 5.2 for full list). In numerous respects it seems that the teacher unions are up against very rigid ideas surrounding what everyone perceives as beneficial to the field of education. Teacher unions seem to be in tension with everyone from parents, politicians, government officials, political factions, teachers not associated with unions, and even those

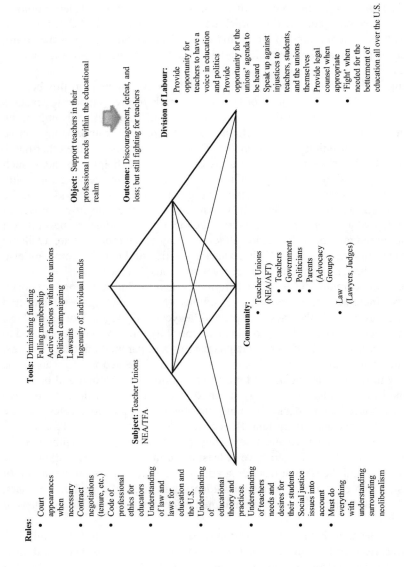

Figure 5.2. Teacher unions' activity system

Tools: Diminishing funding
Falling membership
Active factions within the unions
Political campaigning
Lawsuits
Ingenuity of individual minds

Object: Support teachers in their professional needs within the educational realm

Outcome: Discouragement, defeat, and loss; but still fighting for teachers

Subject: Teacher Unions NEA/TFA

Rules:
- Court appearances when necessary
- Contract negotiations (tenure, etc.)
- Code of professional ethics for educators
- Understanding of law and laws for education and the U.S.
- Understanding of educational theory and practices.
- Understanding of teachers needs and desires for their students
- Social justice issues into account
- Must do everything with understanding surrounding neoliberalism

Community:
- Teacher Unions (NEA/AFT)
  - Teachers
  - Government
  - Politicians
  - Parents (Advocacy Groups)
- Law (Lawyers, Judges)

Division of Labour:
- Provide opportunity for teachers to have a voice in education and politics
- Provide opportunity for the unions' agenda to be heard
- Speak up against injustices to teachers, students, and the unions themselves
- Provide legal counsel when appropriate
- 'Fight' when needed for the betterment of education all over the U.S.

within their own ranks, neoliberalism, and the very ideas held within the most basic democratic principles. These tensions within and outside the teacher unions contribute to a hostile environment for all involved.

The outcome from this activity seems to be one of discouragement, defeat, and loss for teacher unions and those who stand with them. Although teacher unions seem to be a 'scourge' of the education system in the U.S. for many; for others, like teachers and administrators, dependent on their knowledge about various entities, including legal and political; teacher unions keep fighting for teachers and better educational systems throughout the U.S.

Further Discussion

We were surprised initially at the findings that we came upon concerning the data about teacher unions. We went into this project with some pretty big questions, and some vague ideas about what might be happening regarding the unions and the larger society, and what we might be able to discover by using a CHAT analysis as a methodology within our research. We had an awareness about what teacher unions do, who was involved with them and why, and how contentious they have become over the last decade within the U.S. However, we had no idea how much the government itself, the politicians, the parents, and even in many instances, the teachers themselves were rallying against the unions to create a perfect storm of controversy and anti-union bullying. Tensions abounded out of this project; many more than we could have ever anticipated.

According to this analysis, teacher unions really do want to help education improve; and in general, they have the best interests at heart for teachers, students, and society. However, they are increasingly becoming frustrated at the lack of support and recognition that they are receiving from even long term supporters. Using a metaphor to explain the plight of unions, they are seemingly playing a game that has all new rules for them, and that has many more unsympathetic players than ever before. And unlike in previous generations of teacher unions, the divisions of labour for them have become numerous and go far outside the scope of simply understanding teachers and educational issues, but continue on into politics, law, and government.

This frustration and loss can be felt when viewing the various tensions that were discovered while doing this research. The tension between the unions and government are somewhat understandable, as government and organisations that deal with social justice and questioning power relationships within society can be problematic with any entity, even those outside the realm of education. Again, in many ways society, parents, and teachers can understandingly be in conflict with one another in one way or another, although the amount of tension that was witnessed in the data between everyone was somewhat surprising. But what was most surprising was that many of these tensions that are involved in this activity system have very little connection with the actual teacher unions themselves, but are in fact issues that have become persistent problems outside of education that seemingly have spilled over into the field. For instance, the tension concerning the hard stance against labour unions in the twenty first century would seem to be a tension that would have been dispelled over a century ago when labour unions had to fight for existence within the U.S., a fight they eventually won. It is the compounding of these tensions taken together that is seemingly making the teacher unions the scapegoat for a perceivably 'failing' U.S. education system. But are the teacher unions in fact even an issue at all? This is a question for another analysis.

Further, the data brought to light for us the need to be aware that no one, including many researchers who closely examine the mass media's attempts at shaping public perception, particularly those that are politically fuelled, seems to understand the impact that it has on the institutions and people within our society. At the surface level, the information presented seems harmless and just a presentation of facts: informative and important. We became very surprised to see in the data collection for this particular project a wealth of simple propaganda. The sources we chose are considered to be reliable, seemingly non-partisan sources for gathering information about a host of broad topics; but what we examined when looking at the data very closely, coding it, and eventually analysing it using the CHAT methodology, is how very political, and at times very one-sided the information appears to be.

Implications for Future Research

The activity systems analysis helped answer the research questions by helping to organise the material into a visual representation of what is happening concerning teacher unions within the U.S. It helps to begin examining and understanding how and why the unions have become demonised. This analysis of teacher unions using CHAT helps researchers to grasp that there is much more to this problem than meets the eye, and most important to observe, is the fact that we are leaving this project with many more questions and much more analysis that needs to be done, especially concerning the government, public policy, and political entities, as well as, the mass media.

The goal of this project for us was to gain an understanding of some of the issues surrounding teacher unions, particularly the tensions, all the while methodically using a research methodology that is not prototypical of those found in public policy and the like. Further, we also find it noteworthy that by using this method, it seems that even very novice researchers can employ the techniques, getting viable and helpful information from the issues they are undertaking.

CHAT also seems to be able to provide a way, even for those who would not consider themselves classically trained researchers, such as those in the media, politicians, government officials, and those that study these entities, to have the ability to more thoroughly examine presented material, and begin to critically analyse it in ways that make it easier to understand, both representationally and visually. The visual component to this research makes it worthwhile in and of itself; it allows for easy access and breakdown of messy and complicated information.

As far as qualitative research is concerned, the lack of visual representation within the data can be problematic for many who want to understand it; CHAT adds that component and much more. We would call for individuals to start beginning to see how this methodology might begin to help people understand complex activity systems throughout our society, not just those within the realm of education.

CONCLUSION

CHAT and activity systems analysis have not been used within the domain of issues surrounding public policy, or politics in which teacher unions often find themselves situated. Although these issues within public policy domains deal directly with matters surrounding human activity, activity systems analysis is not a common methodology for those doing research in the public policy, political, or mass media arenas. One of the charges that CHAT researchers must contend with is how to raise the profile of associated methods in various principles outside of the field of education, which it is heavily used within. In this way, by introducing activity systems analysis, as we have done above, as a viable and worthwhile avenue to research policy, political issues, and the mass media, we hope to open an opportunity for others to explore CHAT's profound usefulness.

Furthermore, activity systems analysis allows the researcher to capture a picture of what is happening around us, and to better understand the complexities within that picture, than what other methodologies are able to do. It also allows the researcher to describe the tensions and conflicts that may be occurring surrounding the issues that are being researched; however, one of CHAT's main objectives is to bring these issues to light, so that they may be further analysed, and changes can be made based on the findings. This is a very important implication that CHAT contributes, and again, something that needs to be addressed in the fields of public policy, politics and the mass media.

Overall, by employing the use of activity systems through CHAT in this particular research endeavour concerning teacher unions, we believe that we have been able to better understand how the conceptual tools of the methodology can help the dialogue and multiple perspectives that CHAT brings to light in our analysis. These perspectives need to be examined, challenged, and developed further. With every new research endeavour using CHAT, the chance to add to the base of knowledge and enhance the tools of the trade, is one step closer to better understanding the world around us.

REFERENCES

Anonymous. (2014). *About us.* Retrieved from http://www.politico.com/magazine/aboutus/#VGKHMIGvDw

Bascia, N., & Osmond, P. (2012). *Teacher unions and educational reform: A research review.* Washington, DC: National Education Association. Retrieved from http://feaweb.org/_data/files/ED_Reform/Teacher_Unions_and_Educational_Reform.pdf

Bidwell, A. (2015, January 26). Teachers take union dues to supreme court. *U.S. News*. Retrieved from http://www.usnews.com/news/articles/2015/01/26/teachers-petition-supreme-court-to-overturn-forced-collective-bargaining-dues

Brill, S. (2010). The teachers' unions' last stand. *The New York Times*. Retrieved from http://www.nytimes.com/2010/05/23/magazine/23Race-t.html?pagewanted=all&_r=0

Burke, L. (2010). *Creating a crisis: Unions stifle education reform*. Washington, DC: The Heritage Foundation.

Creswell, J. W. (2013). *Qualitative inquiry and research design choosing among the approaches*. New York, NY: Sage.

Dijk, S. V., Berends, H., Jelinek, M., Georges, A., Romme, L., & Weggeman, M. (2011). Micro-institutional affordances and strategies of radical innovation. *Organizational Studies, 32*(11), 1485–1513.

Foot, K. A. (2014). Cultural-historical activity theory: Exploring a theory to inform practice and research. *Journal of Human Behavior in the Social Environment, 24*(3), 329–347.

Members of BATS. (2015). *Bad-ass teacher society*. Retrieved from http://www.badassteacher.org/

National Education Association. (2014). Teacher unions: What we do and how students benefit. *NEA Today*. Retrieved from http://neatoday.org/must-reads/teachers-unions-what-we-do-and-how-students-benefit/

Office of Lieberman, Senator Joseph I. (2004). *Offshore outsourcing and America's competitive edge: Losing out in the high technology r&d and services sectors*. Washington, DC: United States Senate.

Peterson, B. (1999). Survival and justice: Rethinking teacher union strategy. In B. Peterson & M. Charney (Eds.), *Transforming teacher unions fighting for better schools and social justice*. Milwaukee, WI: Rethinking Schools, Ltd.

Porter, C., & Trottman, M. (2014). Teachers unions under fire: Educators plan to fight back after California ruling gutting tenure emboldens critics. *The Wall Street Journal*. Retrieved from http://online.wsj.com/articles/teachers-unions-under-fire-1409874404

Saldana, J. M. (2013). *The coding manual for qualitative research* (2 ed.). New York, NY: Sage Publishing.

Simon, S. (2012). Teacher unions fight to keep clout with democrats. *Reuters*. Retrieved from http://www.reuters.com/article/2012/05/25/us-usa-campaign-obama-teachers-idUSBRE84O12Y20120525

Simon, S. (2014a). The fall of teachers unions. *Politico*. Retrieved from http://www.politico.com/story/2014/06/teachers-union-california-court-decision-107816.html

Simon, S. (2014b). California teachers unions lose big in court. *Politico*. Retrieved from http://www.politico.com/story/2014/06/california-teachers-tenure-vergara-ruling-unions-107656.html

Thomas, E., & Wingert, P. (2010). The key to saving american education. *Newsweek*.

Torres, C. A. (2010). *Education and neoliberal globalization*. New York, NY: Routledge.

Yamagata-Lynch, L. C. (2010). *Activity systems analysis methods: Understanding complex learning environments*. New York, NY: Springer.

Melissa Harness
University of Tennessee
USA

Lisa C. Yamagata-Lynch
University of Tennessee
USA

APPENDIX

Table 5.1. Data collections procedure summary

Methodology	Sources	Procedure
Document Analysis	Washington Post Article The New York Times POLITICO Article	Read materials for all three articles and decided if they contained enough information for the questions that we wanted to address within the research. We looked for meaningful and relevant pages of text or other data that would make them a good representation of other materials that we had seen the last several years concerning teacher unions. Meaning upon first reading the material, we could identify some key elements and initial themes that we had noticed in our research surrounding teacher unions.

Table 5.2. Tensions of activity system

Tensions:

- What teachers want vs. What teachers need
- What teachers unions desire vs. What teachers desire
- What teachers unions desire vs. What government and politicians desire
- What teachers unions are involved in vs. What parents believe is best for students
- What teachers unions want vs. What helps students the most
- What the government desires vs. What education needs
- What society perceives is the best for education vs. What all other entities believe is best
- Political factions and their stance on education issues vs. Teachers unions
- Political factions and their stance on labour unions vs. Teachers unions
- A democratic society vs. neoliberalism
- Education vs. neoliberalism
- Social justice issues vs. government
- Social justice issues vs. neoliberalism

LEE YONG TAY AND CHER PING LIM

6. AN ACTIVITY THEORETICAL APPROACH TOWARDS DISTRIBUTED LEADERSHIP FOR ONE-TO-ONE COMPUTING IN A SINGAPORE ELEMENTARY SCHOOL

INTRODUCTION

Adopting the sociocultural Activity Theoretical perspective, this ethnographic case study examined how distributed leadership supported one-to-one computing implementation in an elementary school under the FutureSchools@Singapore programme. The FutureSchools@Singapore programme aimed to develop prototypes for the seamless and pervasive use of Information and Communication Technology (ICT) to enhance teaching and learning in schools.

Observations and field notes of significant events in relation to the implementation of one-to-one computing were triangulated by reviewing planning documents, reports and publications. Sociocultural Activity Theory was used to examine how the distributed leadership of the school's teaching community (i.e., the principal, ICT coordinator, curriculum coordinators and teachers) worked towards addressing the disturbances (disturbances are manifested as a result of the presence of systemic contradictions) of adopting one-to-one computing in the school. The more significant actions and repair actions of the school's teaching community to address the disturbances in implementing the one-to-one programme were highlighted, discussed and analysed. The discussion of these actions was then used to formulate a more generalised one-to-one computing activity system where more meaningful analysis and interpretation could be made. This in-depth analysis of the contradictions and tensions illuminated the less visible but very important social mediators: the relations between the subject, tool and object were mediated by these social factors (i.e., rules, community and division of labour). There were physical infrastructure and technical issues in the integration of ICT into schools, but the sociocultural factors (e.g., mindset and the level of acceptance of parents to procure computers for their children, teachers' beliefs and practices in using ICT in their lessons and working with external agencies to fund the purchase of computing equipment for financially challenged students) were equally, if not, more important in the implementation process.

This ethnographic case study, with a focus on distributed leadership, also serves as an instance of the implementation of a one-to-one programme in an elementary

D. S. P. Gedera & P. J. Williams (Eds.), Activity Theory in Education, 87–104.

school for sharing, emulation and further refinements by others. In other words, this chapter presents a useful empirical case study resource for those who are in the field of educational technology for the purpose of ICT integration and one-to-one computing in schools.

BACKGROUND

As one of the schools under the FutureSchools@Singapore programme, the school's learning framework was consciously designed for leveraging ICT to enhance teaching and learning process. The ICT implementation included a hybrid model of notebook computer use (2:1 or 1:1; i.e., two students to one computer or one student to one computer ratio) in a wireless environment, with interactive whiteboards in every classroom, and other relevant tools which supported the attainment of the expected learning outcomes in the various school-designed programmes. The notebook computer was chosen because it allowed for greater mobility.

The school took a progressive approach by providing the necessary computing devices (i.e., notebook computers) to the students in their initial years in the school. The Beacon one-to-one (B121) computing learning environment programme provided each student in Primary 1 to 3 with one school-owned computer, and subsequently requested students of Primary 4 and above to procure their own notebook computers. The conceptualisation of this two-tiered, one-to-one model was developed with the notion of sustainability in mind. Students would need to procure their own digital learning device for extension of their learning beyond the school. Financially challenged students could apply for a special computer ownership scheme where more than 85% of the cost of a full-featured notebook computer and Internet broadband subscription (3 years) were subsidised by the Infocomm Development Authority, Singapore. This programme and scheme also acted as a social leveller for these students. Since then, the school had become a 'model' and case for adoption and sharing of one-to-one computing among schools (Infocomm Development Authority – Singapore, 2014).

SOCIOCULTURAL HISTORICAL ACTIVITY THEORY

In this ethnographic case study, Activity Theory, proposed by Engeström (1996 & 2000), was used to organise and analyse the actions, repair actions and identify the disturbances in the activity systems (at the action level) of the school principal, ICT coordinator, curriculum coordinators and teachers. The difference between the operation, action and activity levels was illustrated in Figure 6.1. An activity would involve a chain of actions and actions can be understood as driven by a more specific goal; the realisation of the actions is done through operations (*see* Liu, 2011). An activity system "comprises the individual practitioner, the colleagues and

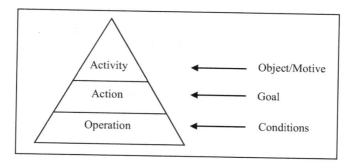

Figure 6.1. The hierarchical structure of activity (Leont'ev, 1978)

co-workers of the workplace community, the conceptual and practical tools, and the shared objects as a unified dynamic whole" (Engeström, 1992, p. 12).

For better clarity and ease of presentation and analysis of the actions of the aforementioned stakeholders, we first considered them as an individual activity system at the action level, and then considered them as a whole for a better understanding of how the programme was conceived and implemented.

In Activity Theory, deviations from the standard scripts are called disturbances, which typically indicate developmentally significant systemic contradictions and change potentials with the activity (Engeström, 2000). Through this process, more systemic contradictions can be identified. "The identification of contradictions in an activity system helps practitioners and administrators to focus their efforts on the root causes of problems. Such collaborative analysis and modelling is a crucial precondition for the creation of a shared vision for the expansive solution of the contradictions" (Engeström, 2000, p. 966). Barab, Barnett, Yamagata-Lynch, Squire, and Keating (2002) also used Activity Theory to examine actions (or sequences of actions) in their study of a technology-rich introductory astronomy course, and framed these in terms of the mediating components that constitute an activity system. They argued that using Engeström's (1987) triangle to explain instances of activity at the action level was useful, meaningful, and theoretically consistent with Activity Theory. This was also confirmed by Engeström in his personal email (Barab, Barnett, Yamagata-Lynch, Squire, & Keating, 2002, p. 84). The analysis of these actions was then used to formulate a more generalised one-to-one computing activity system. They stressed that "the challenge is not to eliminate the systemic tensions or contradictions but to balance the interplay so that it enriches system dynamics and facilitates motivation and learning" (p. 102).

In Activity Theory, the distinction between short-lived, goal-directed action and durable, object-oriented activity is of central importance. A historically evolving collective activity system, seen in its network relations to other activity systems, is taken as the prime unit of analysis. Goal-directed actions, as well as automatic operations, are relatively independent but subordinate units of analysis, eventually understandable only when interpreted against the background of entire activity systems. Activity systems realise and reproduce themselves by generating actions and operations. (Engeström, 2000, p. 964)

LITERATURE REVIEW

Research in the area of ICT usage in schools has been focusing on the identification of the possible factors and the removal of barriers to facilitate ICT use among teachers and students in the teaching and learning process. A number of factors have been found: (1) technological infrastructures; (2) teachers' beliefs and practices; (3) curriculum; (4) school leadership; (5) professional development; and (6) subject area differences (Ertmer, 1999; Hew & Brush, 2007; Howard & Maton, 2011, 2013; Howard, Chan, & Caputi, 2014; Lim & Oakley, 2013; Tay, Lim, & Lim, 2013).

However, the main focus of this chapter is not discussing or analysing of these factors. Instead, this chapter presents the key actions taken by the various subjects – the school's teaching community (i.e., principal, ICT coordinator, curriculum coordinators, and teachers) in the implementation of the one-to-one computing activity system. This chapter serves as an empirical case study highlighting the critical and essential actions and tasks to be taken by the teaching community (the division of labour among the teaching community) for the implementation of one-to-one computing.

Distributed Leadership

The responsibility of leadership functions can be distributed in various ways, and studies have revealed that this responsibility can be undertaken by multiple leaders – not just principals – who work in a collaborative fashion at times and in parallel at others (Heller & Firestone, 1995).

Arguably, the salient feature of distributed leadership is its unique leadership practice which is viewed as the product of the interactions of school leaders, followers, and their situation (Spillane, 2005). Spillane, Halverson and Diamond (2004), building on Activity Theory and distributed cognition theories, proposed that leadership practice is constituted in the interaction of school leaders, followers and the situation. Leadership practice should not be seen as solely a function of an individual's ability, skill, charisma, and/or cognition. Rather, they argued that it can be best understood as a practice distributed over leaders, followers and their situation. As such a situation is more than a backdrop for leaders' practices. Spillane et al. (2004) considered the sociocultural context as a constitute element of leadership practice, an integral defining element of that activity. The consideration of tools, rules and the community would enable a better understanding of the situation or sociocultural context.

Ho, Chen and Ng (2015) also used Activity Theory as an interpretive lens to examine distributed leadership in a Singapore school. Activity Theory embraced the concept of division of labour which is aligned to the concept of distributed leadership with individuals or groups with different roles and motives. Applying the lens of the third-generation Activity Theory, they revealed two interrelated activity systems performed by the senior and middle management with regard to the integration of ICT. Their research study highlighted the role played by social norms in mediating the leadership activity. Activity Theory enabled research on distributed leadership to identify and examine interrelated activity systems of the school leaders, followers and the situation. This allowed for a more in-depth analysis and understanding of the roles played by the various individuals and groups within the school's activity system.

Distributed leadership from an Activity Theoretical perspective is adopted in the analysis of the activity systems of the various individuals and groups, with the aim of seamless and pervasive use of ICT by the students in the school. The actions of the various individuals and groups (i.e., the Principal, coordinators and teachers) are described in detail for a more in-depth understanding of the tasks carried out by them.

RESEARCH DESIGN AND METHODS

An ethnographic case study approach (Stake, 1994, 1995) was used in this research to examine the actions of the school's teaching community (i.e., the Principal, ICT coordinator, curriculum coordinators and the teachers). This case study took place from 2008 to 2015, involving the Principal, ICT coordinator, 6 subject coordinators and teachers in the school. The one-to-one computing programme constituted the case, and it was ethnographic in nature as the first author was in the teaching faculty of the school since the inception of the school in 2008. This chapter was reported from the point of view of the subjects of the study. Their actions, disturbances and repair actions were discussed and analysed to formulate a more generalised activity system for the school's one-to-one computing programme.

Observations and field notes of significant events in relation to the implementation of one-to-one computing by the authors were triangulated with internal (e.g., scheme of work, lesson plans, planning documents and evaluation reports) and published documents (e.g., book chapters and articles published in journals regarding the school's efforts in ICT integration). The various data mentioned above were reviewed, triangulated, analysed and the key actions of the teaching community were presented using the Engeström's (1987) triangle. Although there were many actions that were taken by the teaching community, only the key and significant ones were presented and analysed. The Activity Theoretical framework also highlighted the importance of sociocultural and historical contexts that needed to be considered, for instance, how ICT had been integrated and used in the school context and the value of ICT in teaching and learning as perceived by teachers, parents and the society at-large.

The triangles depicting the actions (i.e., Figures 6.2 to 6.5) were drawn in grey and the disturbances were represented with two-headed, dashed lightning-shaped arrows. The triangle depicting the activity (Figure 6.6) was drawn in using solid black lines and the contradictions were represented with two-headed, solid line, lightning-shaped arrows.

FINDINGS

Actions of the Principal

The Principal led by setting the direction (i.e., mission) for the school – to nurture and inspire learners to work to the best of their potential through innovative approaches in an engaging environment, leveraging on technologies and research. In the area of distributed leadership, the Principal was arguably the 'leader of leaders' – the Principal was one of the subjects who propagated the integration of ICT into the curriculum, and had continuously been a strong proponent of ICT usage in education.

The disturbances from the Principal's perspective were depicted in Figure 6.2, with the help of two-headed, dashed lightning-shaped arrows. The main disturbances came from the teachers and the parents – between the object-community and object-division of labour. The Principal needed to work with teachers and school staff to change their perspective regarding the use of ICT in the classrooms and also to redesign and redistribute work among them. In addition, the parents also needed to be convinced of the potentials of one-to-one computing and their willingness to procure a notebook computer for their children. In order to ease the tension between the community (i.e., teachers) and the object, the Principal had not only encouraged and authorised the provision of necessary resources (e.g., ICT infrastructure) but also conducted several local and overseas study trips to learn more about the integration of ICT through one-to-one computing. This was epitomised by the focus on teachers' professional development, especially in the area of ICT integration. Teachers were encouraged to attend courses, workshops, seminars and conferences to enhance their knowledge and skills. In addition, the school had been organising cluster-level professional development seminars annually from 2009 to 2015 for teachers from several schools located within close geographical proximity to share insights and experiences on how ICT could be used to enhance teaching and learning. Teachers needed the knowledge and skills to bring out the potentials of ICT in their classrooms. The practices of the teachers would define how ICT would be used in the classrooms, and in that sense teachers are pivotal in the use of computers. A good teacher is probably worth more than a computer with a lousy teacher (Oppenheimer, 1997). However, teachers' practices needed to be enhanced via a variety of professional development activities.

Technical glitches also posed a real challenge. The Principal worked closely with the ICT coordinator to help address and reduce technical failures. She would sit in during the various staff meetings to understand and assist the teachers in the challenges they faced during the use of ICT in their classrooms. The Principal worked with the ICT coordinator and technicians to address these technical challenges through better division of labour and workflow.

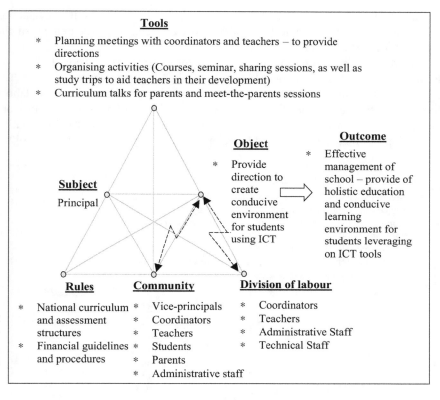

Figure 6.2. Actions of the principal

Another important stakeholder in the community was the parent. Parents arguably were the ones who had great influence over whether the one-to-one computing effort could be implemented. Parents not only needed to support the idea of the use of ICT for their children's learning but also needed to procure a personal learning device (i.e., a notebook computer) after Primary 4, and also support their children in using it at home. Parents were informed and updated via the various communication channels – letters, school website, meet-the-parents sessions, curriculum talks, and prize presentation ceremonies. Constant communication with parents was critical for the success of the programme. Parents needed to be informed and prepared in advance for the programme and the procurement of the computers.

Actions of the ICT Coordinator

From the perspective of distributed leadership, the ICT coordinator played the primary role in advocating the use of ICT for teaching and learning vis-à-vis the one-to-one computing initiative. The ICT coordinator was mainly responsible for the introduction of innovative pedagogical approaches for the use of ICT, evaluation of the effectiveness of the ICT infusion, and overseeing the procurement of the technological infrastructure.

The disturbances from the ICT coordinator's perspective were depicted in Figure 6.3 (indicated by the double-headed, dashed lightning-shaped arrows). The tensions came from the object-rules, object-community and object-division of labour links, quite similar to that of the Principal. The ICT coordinator needed to work and negotiate with the community (including external vendors, the Information Technology Branch and Infocomm Development Authority for the setting up of the

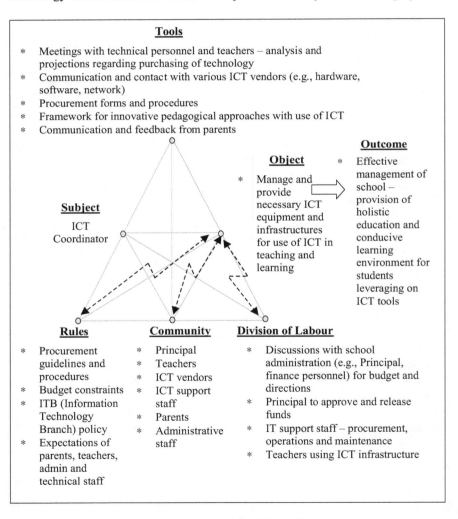

Figure 6.3. Actions of the ICT coordinator

infrastructure; the teachers in using ICT in their classrooms for both pedagogical and technological aspects; the school clerical staff to prepare for purchase of the equipment; and the school technicians in the infrastructural and maintenance work) for the implementation of the one-to-one computing programme. This would inevitably translate into redesign and redistribution of work among the community members just mentioned above.

These tensions arose mainly because of the 'rules' and sociocultural expectations as set by the community. Conventionally, in a local context, computing devices for teaching and learning purposes were supplied by the school, especially in the elementary and secondary school levels. However, the school had only provided computers for students up to Primary 3 level. This had inevitabily created tension between the parents and the school's one-to-one computing effort as it had been the culturally and historically accepted norm (or rule) that computing devices were to be provided by schools.

The ICT coordinator, with the direction and support from the Principal, conducted annual focus group discussion sessions with parents for each Primary 4 cohort to explain the concept of one-to-one computing and the school's computer ownership programme for all students up to Primary 4. Feedback and suggestions from each cohort of students and parents were collected and analysed to constantly refine the programme. The cost and weight of the computing device were two main factors that were important to the parents. The ICT coordinator and his technical team had been on the lookout for notebook computers that were reasonably priced and light-weight to recommend to the students and parents. The school also encouraged students to bring their own digital devices if they already owned one. In addition, the ICT coordinator also worked with the local information communication authority to provide notebook computers and Internet connection at a heavily subsidised rate for financially constrained families.

The ICT coordinator also needed to work – in terms of division of labour – with the technicians and clerical and administrative personnel on the maintenance and procurement of ICT infrastructure. For instance, the ICT coordinator needed to mobilise the technicians to handle the increase in maintenance work due to the students' owned computers, as well as the clerical administrative staff in the application of subsidised computers and mobile broadband for students who were under the financial assistance scheme. Apart from the procurement of computing devices and infrastructure, the ICT coordinator also engaged in training the teachers on using the ICT hardware devices and software applications. In addition, with the help from the technicians, the ICT coordinator also looked into the maintenance, stock taking and technological refreshing of the ICT infrastructure and equipment. ICT technicians were hence constantly engaged in supporting teachers in resolving technical issues in their classrooms. Common technological problems included issues with: wireless Internet connection, computing devices, LCD projectors, and software applications. The introduction of ICT into the teaching and learning equation had indeed added another layer of work and preparation. For one-to-one computing to work, it required the technicians to provide the necessary support and troubleshooting when the need arose.

In essence, the ICT coordinator needed to work and manage the expectations of the teachers, parents, technical and administrative staff for the one-to-one computing programme.

Actions of the Curriculum Coordinators

The curriculum coordinators played an important leadership role in the school's efforts in one-to-one computing. They were the teachers who designed and developed the curriculum for the students with the use of ICT explicitly spelled out in the curriculum plans and schemes of work on how ICT would be used in the classroom. The curriculum coordinators for the various subjects (e.g., English, Mathematics, Science, Mother Tongue languages and Social Studies) worked with their fellow teacher colleagues to create detailed lesson plans.

The disturbances from the curriculum coordinators' perspective were depicted in Figure 6.4 (see the two-headed, dashed lightning-shaped arrows). The tensions came from the object-rules, object-community and object-division of labour relationships. Quite similar to the disturbances faced by the ICT coordinator, the curriculum coordinator needed to deal with the 'expectations' and rules that were set by the community. By-and-large parents and some teachers were still uncertain about the effectiveness of ICT and learning, although they understood and agreed with the importance of acquiring ICT skills and knowledge. To date, the link between ICT usage and students' performance had yet to be established. The curriculum coordinators, with the help of the teachers, adopted practical and innovative pedagogies, such as digital storytelling for the teaching and learning of languages and within the rules and boundaries as set by the national curriculum. More work and thinking were required by the teachers to develop and plan ICT-infused lessons and hence there existed the tension between the object and division of labour.

The curriculum coordinators had initiated various programmes to incorporate ICT into the classrooms. For instance, digital storytelling was used in the teaching of languages, an approach shared and adopted by all teachers of the school. Digital storytelling was an efficient and simple approach that allowed students to create their digital 'compositions', with the enhancement of various digital elements such as images, as well as digital narrations. In Mathematics lessons, students created pictorial graphs with spreadsheet software applications to analyse trends and patterns. In Science, teachers propagated the use of relevant videos and online resources to be shared with the students.

Actions of Teachers

In distributed leadership, the teachers played the important role of executing the plans. They were ones who conducted the lessons, with the direction set by the

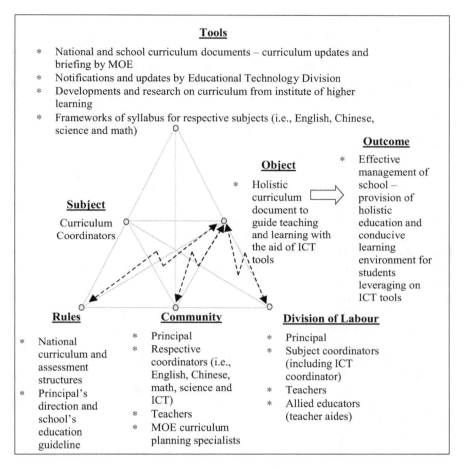

Figure 6.4. Actions of the curriculum coordinator

school, technology infrastructure setup by the ICT department and curriculum guidelines set by the various departments. While titled 'actions of teacher', this section would cover the actions of different subject teachers, namely the English, mathematics, science and mother tongue languages.

The main object of the teachers was to effectively integrate ICT and enhance students' learning. However, professional development effort was deemed necessary to develop skilful and competent teachers who can effectively leverage ICT to facilitate and enhance the process of teaching and learning. Teachers needed to be well-versed in their content, and pedagogical, as well as, technological skills and knowledge (*see* Mishra & Koehler, 2006; 2009 for more details for Technological Pedagogical Content Knowledge – TPACK) in order to more effectively use ICT in their classrooms. Several avenues were available for teachers to update and refine their skills and knowledge – through courses, seminars, conferences (local and overseas) and on-the-job training.

Teachers in this school also engaged in action research projects and shared their learning points and insights through seminars, conferences and publications; linking their practices with theories. This was further made possible with the local ministry's effort to support teachers' upgrading skills – to encourage non-graduate teachers to obtain their degrees and graduate teachers to acquire their masters. The local education ministry gave heavy subsidies and professional development leave schemes to facilitate and encourage capacity building of the teachers.

Teachers of various subjects explored different ways to use ICT during their lessons. For instance, English and mother tongue languages (i.e., Chinese, Malay and Tamil) teachers used simple presentation software applications to engage their students in the creation of their digital stories. Students wrote texts, used digital images, animations and voice over to learn their languages and also acquire ICT skills. Mathematics teachers used online game-like applets and software applications to facilitate students' learning of arithmetic skills (e.g., addition, subtraction, multiplication and division). The game-like online applications provided a more engaging online learning environment for students to practice the conventionally less interesting but essential mathematical skills. Teachers also designed step-by-step mathematics problem sum solutions with the animation function of the presentation software to allow for students' self-paced learning. Some mathematics teachers used screen capture and video software applications to teach problem solving procedures and mathematical concepts. Science teachers searched for useful online videos, experiment-based applets and online concept mapping software applications to facilitate students' learning and mastery of science concepts.

The disturbances of the teachers were depicted in Figure 6.5 (see the two-headed, dashed lightning-shaped arrows).

The main tension came from the subject-tools disturbance, in which teachers needed to have the relevant technological, pedagogical and content knowledge in order to integrate the use of ICT into teaching and learning. Teachers also needed to regularly update and upgrade their skills and knowledge through seminars, courses and conferences. Tensions might arise when teachers with a lack of skills or belief used ICT in their lessons. Professional development efforts by the teachers might also further compound the tension with the introduction and use of ICT as more time, effort and resources would be demanded from the teachers.

DISCUSSIONS OF THE CONTRADICTIONS BEHIND THE DISTURBANCES

The findings of this chapter were presented in terms of the actions of the four main stakeholders – the Principal, ICT coordinator, subject coordinators and teachers in the one-to-one computing programme. The disturbances and some of the subsequent repair actions were analysed to provide insights and learning for a wider and more

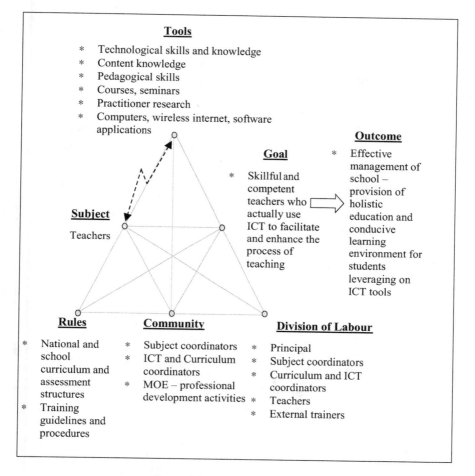

Figure 6.5. Actions of the teachers

stable system of collective activity, that is, the one-to-one computing programme, as shown in Figure 6.6.

The disturbances described above were not just accidental and arbitrary; they seemed to be systemic (Engeström, 1992; 1996; 2000). The disturbances mentioned in the above discussion were caused by the more systemic contradictions within the one-to-one computing programme activity system. The contradictions were depicted with the aid of two-headed, solid line, lightning-shaped arrows.

In essence, the school teaching community, which was made up of the Principal, ICT coordinator, subject coordinators and teachers, were important stakeholders of the one-to-one computing activity system. Starting with the Principal, she led by setting the direction for the school and the pervasive use of ICT in teaching and learning.

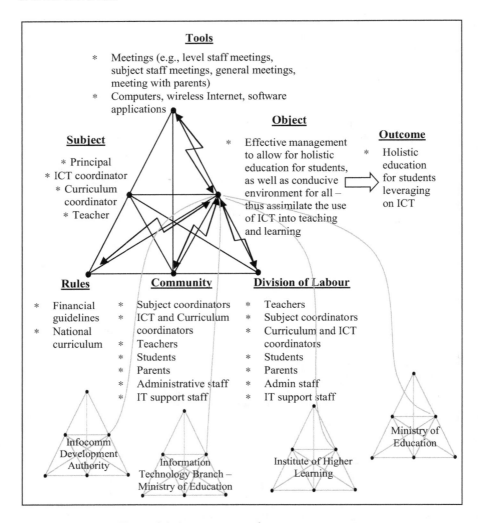

Figure 6.6. Activity system of one-to-one computing

To the Principal, both the parents and teachers were critical stakeholders – parents needed to support the procurement and use of computers for their children's learning and teachers needed to be willing to use ICT in their classrooms. The contradictions were mainly between the object-community (i.e., parents and teachers) and also the division of labour, requiring a change in the workflow or additional work with the introduction of the one-to-one computing programme. Frequent and constant communication between the school and community was necessary to mediate these contradictions.

Apart from setting up the technological infrastructure and wireless network, the ICT coordinator recommended computing devices to parents and students on an annual basis. Briefing and discussion sessions were conducted to provide information for the parents and to answer their queries. In addition, the ICT coordinator also invited experts from the Institutes of Higher Learning (IHLs) and other external agencies for the professional development of teachers, worked with the Infocomm Development Authority to provide subsidised computers for financially disadvantaged students, and consulted and negotiated with the Information Technology Branch for computer and network related issues. The contradictions were again between the object-rules, object-community and object-division of labour. The ICT coordinator needed to work with the parents, the teachers and also external agencies to mediate these contradictions; to work with parents, teachers, technicians and administrative staff to change historically laid down 'rules' as set by the community and better division of labour. For pervasive use of ICT in the classrooms to be implemented, the ICT coordinator needed to pay special attention when working and negotiating with the teachers, technicians, administrative (clerical) staff, and parents.

Curriculum coordinators led by mobilising teachers to plan for the integration of ICT into the teaching and learning process. The contradictions were between the object-rules, object-community and object-division of labour. Together with the curriculum coordinators; teachers needed to put in the extra effort in their own professional development, draw out lesson plans, source digital resources, and conduct lessons with the use of ICT, within the guidelines of the national curriculum. For pervasive use of ICT in the classrooms to be implemented seamlessly, the curriculum coordinators had to pay special care and attention when working and negotiating with the teachers.

For teachers, the main contradiction was between the tool and the object. Teachers needed to know how to use the computer hardware, software applications, and also the appropriate pedagogical skills and knowledge to integrate ICT into their lessons. The tools in this instance would refer to the computing devices and also the pedagogical skills that would allow the teachers to leverage on ICT for teaching and learning. Such an endeavour required the teachers to keep up-to-date with their technological and pedagogical knowledge.

In addition, it was necessary to consider external agencies (or external activity systems, for instance, the Infocomm Development Authority, Information Technology Branch, Institutes of Higher Learning and the Ministry of Education) to further support the one-to-one computing programme or activity system, as shown in Figure 6.6.

IMPLICATIONS

The use of the Activity Theory and the analysis of the disturbances and contradictions present a fresh and meaningful perspective of a case study on one-to-one computing in an elementary school in Singapore.

This case study outlines and highlights the actions carried out by the school's teaching community – which is made up of the Principal, ICT coordinator, subject coordinators and teachers – for the implementation of the one-to-one programme. Communication with parents and teachers seems vital; both parents and teachers alike need to understand the rationale and planning work done by the school for such an endeavour. Apart from the setting up and procurement of the necessary ICT infrastructure, teachers need to be involved in the development of curriculum and lesson plans to integrate ICT into their lessons. Teachers also need to be trained technologically and pedagogically. The Principal, the coordinators, and teachers need to take the lead in their various positions to initiate actions – with the Principal setting the direction and communicating the school's vision with its stakeholders (e.g., parents and teachers); ICT and subject coordinators setting up the technological infrastructure, coordinating professional development efforts for the teachers, and working with teachers to design ICT-based lessons; and with teachers, learning how to use ICT in their lessons.

In addition, it is also essential for the ICT and curriculum coordinators to work with external agencies, such as institutes of higher learning for innovative ideas and teachers' professional development, the Infocomm Development Authority for subsidised computers and broadband network for students who are financially disadvantaged, and the Information Technology Branch for technical advice, assistance and wireless Internet setup. These external agencies and institutions also initiated several schemes (e.g., provisions of wireless Internet access to all schools, subsidised computers for financially disadvantaged students, and professional development modules for ICT in teaching). These schemes and initiatives have further assisted and facilitated the implementation of one-to-one computing in the school.

CONCLUSION

The concept of distributed leadership, where the various teaching staff in the school take the lead in their respective area of responsibility to engage in tasks that work towards the implementation of a one-to-one computing programme, seems to be an effective approach towards ICT integration in schools.

In addition, the analytical lens of the Activity Theory in viewing the actions of the members of the teaching community has illuminated useful insights of the critical actions to be taken by the respective members of this community.

This chapter proposes a distributed leadership from an Activity Theoretical perspective of looking at the critical actions taken by the school's teaching community. The school's teaching community needs to work together to redesign workflow, redistribute workload, and acquire pedagogical and technical knowledge to effectively run the one-to-one computing programme. Capacity building of the teachers, technicians and establishment of buy-ins from the stakeholders and community are also essential actions to be taken. In addition, the historical, sociocultural and contextual are elements that need to be considered – how ICT has been historically used and its perceived importance by teachers, parents and the society at-large need to be looked into.

We hope that this chapter could be a useful empirical case study resource for those who are in the field of educational technology for ICT integration and one-to-one computing.

ACKNOWLEDGEMENT

The authors would like to thank Mr Ethan Tan Hym and Miss Yang Danlin for the assistance rendered in the writing of this chapter.

REFERENCES

Barab, S. A., Barnett, M., Yamagata-Lynch, L., Squire, K., & Keating, T. (2002). Using Activity Theory to understand the systemic tensions characterizing a technology-rich introductory astronomy course. *Mind, Culture, and Activity, 9*(2), 76–107.

Daniels, H. (2001). *Vygotsky and pedagogy*. London, England: RoutledgeFalmer.

Engeström, Y. (1987). *Learning by expanding: An activity theoretical approach to developmental research*. Helsinki, Finland: Orienta Konsultit.

Engeström, Y. (1992). *Interactive expertise: Studies in distributed working intelligence* (Research Bulletin No. 83). Helsinki, Finland: Helsinki University Dept. of Education. (ERIC Document Reproduction Service No. ED349 956)

Engeström, Y. (1996). The tension of judging: Handling cases of driving under the influence of alcohol in Finland and California. In Y. Engeström & D. Middleton (Eds.), *Cognition and communication at work* (pp. 199–233). New York, NY: Cambridge University Press.

Engeström, Y. (1999). *Changing practice through research: Changing research through practice*. Keynote Speech presented at the 7th Annual International Conference on Post Compulsory Education and Training, Griffith University, Australia.

Engeström, Y. (2000). Activity Theory as framework for analysing and redesigning work. *Ergonomics, 43*(7), 960–974.

Engeström, Y. (2001). Expansive learning at work: Toward an activity theoretical reconceptualization. *Journal of Education and Work, 14*(1), 133–156.

Ertmer, P. A. (1999). Addressing first- and second-order barriers to change: Strategies for technology integration. *Educational Technology Research and Development, 47*(4), 47–61. Retrieved from doi.org/10.1007/BF02299597

Heller, M. F., & Firestone, W. A. (1995). Who's in charge here? Sources of leadership for change in eight schools. *Elementary School Journal, 96*(1), 65–86.

Hew, K. F., & Brush, T. (2007). Integrating technology into K-12 teaching and learning: Current knowledge gaps and recommendations for future research. *Educational Technology Research and Development, 55*(3), 223–252. Retrieved from doi.org/10.1007/s11423-006-9022-5

Ho, J. M., Chen, V. D. T., Ng, D. F. S. (2015). Distributed leadership through the lens of Activity Theory. *Educational Management Administration & Leadership, 43*(3). Advance online publication.

Howard, S., & Maton, K. (2011). Theorising knowledge practices: A missing piece of the educational technology puzzle. *Research in Learning Technology, 19*(3), 191–206. Retrieved from doi.org/10.1080/21567069.2011.624170

Howard, S. K., & Maton, K. (2013). *Technology & knowledge: An exploration of teachers' conceptions of subject-area knowledge practices and technology integration*. Paper presented at the 2013 Annual Meeting of the American Educational Research Association, San Francisco, CA. Retrieved from the AERA Online Paper Repository.

Howard, S. K., Chan, A., & Caputi, P. (2014). More than beliefs: Subject areas and teachers' integration of laptops in secondary teaching. *British Journal of Educational Technology, 46*(2), 360–369. Retrieved from doi.org/10.1111/bjet.12139

Infocomm Development Authority – Singapore. (2014). *Good practice from 1-to-1 computing implementations in Singapore schools*. Retrieved April 26, 2015, from http://www.ida.gov.sg/~/media/Files/Programmes%20and%20Partnership/Initiatives/2014/ExperimentationSchools/GoodPracticesGuide.pdf

Koehler, M. J., & Mishra, P. (2009). What is technological pedagogical content knowledge? *Contemporary Issues in Technology and Teacher Education, 9*(1), 60–70. Retrieved from http://www.citejournal.org/vol9/iss1/general/article1.cfm

Leont'ev, A. N. (1978). *Activity, consciousness and personality*. Englewood Cliffs, NJ: Prentice Hall.

Lim, C. P., & Oakley, G. (2013). Information and communication technologies (ICT) in primary education: Opportunities and supporting conditions. In L. Y. Tay & C. P. Lim (Eds.), *Creating Holistic Technology-Enhanced Learning Experiences: Tales from a future school in Singapore* (pp. 1–18). Rotterdam, The Netherlands: Sense Publishers. doi.org/10.1007/978-94-6209-086-6_1

Liu, Z. (2011, May 28). Activity Theory: Levels of activity [Web log post]. Retrieved from http://www.zcliu.org/archives/activity-theory-levels-of-activity

Mishra, P., & Koehler, M. J. (2006). Technological pedagogical content knowledge: A framework for teacher knowledge. *Teachers College Record, 108*(6), 1017–1054.

Oppenheimer, T. (1997). The computer delusion. *The Atlantic Online : Digital Edition*. Retrieved April 14, 2015, from http://www.theatlantic.com/magazine/archive/1997/07/the-computer-delusion/376899/

Spillane, J. P. (2005). Distributed leadership. *The Educational Forum, 69*(2), 143–148.

Spillane, J. P., Halverson, R., & Diamond, J. B. (2004). Towards a theory of leadership practice: A distributed perspective. *Journal of Curriculum Studies, 36*(1), 3–34. Retrieved from doi.org/10.1080/0022027032000106726

Stake, R. E. (1994). Case studies. In N. K. Denzin & Y. S. LinColn (Eds.), *Handbook of qualitative research* (pp. 236–247). Thousand Oaks, CA: Sage Publications Inc.

Stake, R. E. (1995). *The art of case study research*. Thousand Oaks, CA: Sage Publications, Inc.

Tay, L. Y., Lim, S. K., & Lim, C. P. (2013). Factors affecting the ICT integration and implementation of One-to-One computing learning environment in a primary school – A sociocultural perspective. In L. Y. Tay & C. P. Lim (Eds.), *Creating holistic technology-enhanced learning experiences: Tales from a future school in Singapore* (pp. 19–37). Rotterdam, The Netherlands: Sense Publishers. Retrieved from doi.org/10.1007/978-94-6209-086-6_2

Lee Yong Tay
Beacon Primary School
Singapore

Cher Ping Lim
The Hong Kong Institute of Education
Hong Kong SAR

SECTION III

UNDERSTANDING CONCEPTUAL AND CONTEXTUAL ASPECTS OF EDUCATIONAL CONTEXTS THROUGH ACTIVITY THEORY

JINRUI LI

7. THE INTERACTIONS BETWEEN EMOTION, COGNITION, AND ACTION IN THE ACTIVITY OF ASSESSING UNDERGRADUATES' WRITTEN WORK

INTRODUCTION

Tutors are important members of the teaching staff in universities. Nevertheless, in the area of teacher cognition studies, the beliefs and practices university tutors draw upon when assessing students' written work have rarely been explored. Issues and theoretical perspectives relating to the assessment of undergraduates' written work are more researched in the domains of applied linguistics and composition studies. Formative feedback on scripts written by non-native English speaking students has been a research focus in applied linguistics, while composition studies have explored comments on scripts written by native English-speaking students in various disciplines. The focus of discussion in both groups of studies has been on how to improve the effectiveness of feedback so that it can inform students' learning. Strategies for effective feedback, such as integrative feedback (Broad, 2003; Sitko, 1993), portfolios (Weigle, 2007), and assessment dialogues (Carless, 2006) have been proposed over time. However, these strategies have not been widely applied to the assessment of students' written work across a range of faculties. The summative role of assessment feedback predominates, with the formative aspect often being limited to formal issues of writing (Carless, 2006; Mutch, 2003; Stern & Solomon, 2006). Thus tutor feedback to students tends to lack advice on how they can improve their written work (Osmond & Merry, 2011).

A number of contextual issues have been found to constrain the ability of tutors to provide feedback, for example, a lack of time, the modular patterns of programs, and organisational policies (Bailey & Garner, 2010; Lilly, Richter, & Rivera-Macias, 2010). In addition, Deluca and Klinger (2010) found that there is also a lack of training that can equip new staff with sufficient assessment knowledge, and Carless (2006) and Crisp (2008) have shown that emotional factors also affect assessment practices. These issues all indicate that there is a need for in-depth study into the impact of context on tutors' beliefs and practices when providing assessment feedback.

According to Vygotsky (1978), context is the key to understanding cognitive progress. Burns (1996) and Lee (2009) have found that contextual factors affect teachers' beliefs and practices. However, the concept of context varies in teacher

D. S. P. Gedera & P. J. Williams (Eds.), Activity Theory in Education, 107–119.

cognition studies. The context either involves only factors within or around classrooms (e.g., Borg, 2006; Woods, 1996) or it refers broadly to any social, cultural, or political aspects relevant to the activity being studied (Cross, 2010). As very few teacher cognition studies have included think-aloud and stimulated recall data in a real educational context, there is, moreover, a lack of understanding of how contextual factors interact with the individual teacher's cognition (Salomon, 1997).

In addition to context, emotion is an important aspect of cognition. For Vygotsky (1986), emotion has a dialectical relationship with cognition. Engeström (2009) points out that emotional issues should be addressed in Activity Theory. Roth (2009) also argues that studies on human activities need to include both the emotional and structural aspects of cognition.

This case study aims to meet a gap in the research by exploring the interaction between contextual factors and cognitive processes of tutors when engaged in the activity of assessing undergraduates' written work. It will also address the role that emotion plays in that activity. The theoretical framework of the study is based on Engeström's (1987) expanded model of Activity Theory. This chapter briefly introduces the research design and findings, then discusses the application of Activity Theory to the study, before concluding with comments on the use of Activity Theory in this study.

RESEARCH DESIGN AND FINDINGS

This case study presents an interpretive naturalistic inquiry into tutors' beliefs and practice in the context of providing written feedback on student assignments. It takes a qualitative approach to data collection and a grounded theory approach to data analysis.

The intention of the study is first to explore what subject tutors believe about giving written feedback on students' written assignments in that particular context, and what their actual practices are when giving assessment feedback. Secondly, it explores the extent to which the tutors' actual practices converge with or diverge from their beliefs, both individually and as a group across departments/disciplines. Thirdly, it aims to reveal the sociocultural factors that influence tutors' beliefs and practices. Finally, the fundamental question to answer is how the findings to the above research questions add to academic understanding of what constitutes tutors' beliefs and the possible tension that arises in putting these beliefs into practice.

To answer these research questions, the study takes a multimethod approach to data collection. The context of the data collection was an Arts and Social Sciences faculty of a New Zealand university. It is the practice of 9 of the 10 departments in the faculty to provide assessment feedback on students' written work. The faculty's students were both native and non-native English speakers who had varying levels of background knowledge on writing. Assessment was carried out by the teaching staff whose professional titles ranged from professor to senior tutor. Sessional and part-time tutors were also employed to run tutorials and mark assignments for courses with large numbers of enrolled students. These part-time tutors were recruited from amongst the faculty's third-year undergraduate, master's, and doctoral students.

The data were first transcribed and open coded using NVivo8 and then manually analysed using thematic analysis for deeper understanding. The study found that tutors had convergent and divergent beliefs about and practices of assessment which were related to the sources of their beliefs. Moreover, a third element—emotion—was found to play an important role in the activity of assessment in two ways. First, the tutors had emotional reactions to the contextual factors in the activity system; as a result, they regulated their emotions in order to achieve the goal of assessment. Secondly, tutors were aware of students' emotional reactions to the assessment and feedback; therefore, they tried to regulate students' emotional reactions through positive feedback.

The following section will explain in detail how the data collection, data analysis, and discussions were guided by Activity Theory.

THE APPLICATION OF ACTIVITY THEORY

This case study adheres to an interpretive paradigm in that it explores tutors' beliefs and practices in their natural context of work. An interpretive case study needs to address two issues. The first issue is that the interpretive paradigm, relatively speaking, neglects the power of structural influences on the shaping of participants' practices (Cohen, Manion, & Morrison, 2000); the second issue concerns how to define the boundary of a case (Creswell, 2007). Both issues can be well addressed by Activity Theory. First, Activity Theory provides a clear framework of the activity system that explains the contextually formed and transformed practices. Secondly, Activity Theory defines the activity system as the unit of analysis. It not only provides the clear boundary of a case, but also specifies seven key components (subject, object, instruments, rules, division of labour, community, and outcome/goal) in an activity system. These help researchers to analyse the complexity of the case.

Moreover, Activity Theory's strength lies in its ability to provide a systematic approach to data collection, data analysis, and interpretation of the findings. These aspects are detailed in the following sections.

Application of Activity Theory to Data Collection

Activity Theory based research requires ethnographic methods of data collection such as participant observation, interviews, and discussions in real-life contexts (Scribner, 1985; Vygotsky, 1978). To get rich data from real-life settings, this case study took a multimethod approach to data collection using survey (with both closed and open-ended questions), semi-structured interview, think-aloud, stimulated recall, and focus group discussion.

The survey was used to collect information from the community at a faculty level. It covered the tutors' biographical data and their attitudes towards providing

109

assessment feedback. The survey was also used to recruit participants for the qualitative stages of data collection.

On the basis of the survey results, 16 tutors were selected for interview in their work settings. The interviews were guided by semi-structured questions designed to uncover tutors' beliefs on providing assessment feedback. The interviewed participants were also invited to participate in the next stage of data collection: i.e., think-aloud, and stimulated recall.

Nine of the 16 tutors participated in the think-aloud and stimulated recall sessions. The think-aloud approach in this study is based on Vygotsky's (1962, 1978) theories that language is a tool that mediates thinking and that thinking happens first on the social and then on the individual plane. Unlike Ericsson and Simon's (1984) think-aloud model which was used in laboratory settings, the think-aloud activities in this study took place in the real-life setting of assessment. The think-aloud task was the routine work that the tutors carried out in their own offices, and it had actual social effects. The participants in this study were expected to think aloud what came into their minds while marking students' written assignments and providing assessment feedback.

Finally, focus group data were collected from seven of the tutors who had participated in the previous data collections. Two focus group discussions were carried out in a faculty common room. The tutors were given a summary of the previous findings and were left to themselves to discuss any points that interested them. The aim of this discussion was to reveal any common concerns among the tutors as they interacted naturally.

This multimethod approach to data collection enabled the gathering of rich data about tutors' beliefs and practices both individually and collectively in their working context. Here Activity Theory guided me in the selection of appropriate methods of data collection, as the seven basic components of the activity system highlighted the key aspects of data that needed to be collected.

Application of Activity Theory to Data Analysis

Established by Glaser and Strauss (1967), grounded theory is a common approach to qualitative data analysis. The main feature of this approach is that theory is generated inductively from data through concurrent data collection and analysis, and constant comparisons between data.

Grounded theory has the advantage of inductively generating a theory from raw data. However, as Silverman (2006) warns, while grounded theory may result in groups of categories, it may also, if used unintelligently, fail to find themes. One major issue in the process of data analysis is, therefore, how to find themes without becoming lost in a vast amount of open coded data. Unfortunately, grounded theory did not provide a practical answer to this issue, and so, in seeking a practical approach to data analysis, Braun and Clarke (2006) proposed thematic analysis. Based on grounded theory, the main steps of thematic analysis include: initial coding, searching for themes, reviewing, and naming themes. Although I followed these steps in this case study, I nevertheless still faced the problem of how to search effectively for themes within the large number of open codes. Applying Engeström's (1987) expanded model of Activity Theory provided an efficient solution to this problem; the model also assisted with my data analysis in the following three ways.

First, I used the key elements of the activity system to group the initial codes after the process of open coding. In conjunction with the two main domain beliefs and practices of the activity, these key elements formed the core categories of my data. Interestingly, examination of codes that had been excluded from the initial code map, revealed that a significant number of the initial codes (e.g., trust, anxiety, empathy, and confidence) pointed to a new core category—emotion. Consequently, this new category added a significant dimension to my study of the tutors' beliefs and practices in the activity system.

Secondly, Activity Theory guided me in the search for themes. Theme searching requires insights into the interconnections between the main categories. The triangles of Engeström's (1987) expanded model of Activity Theory reveal the interconnections between the key elements in the activity system. According to Engeström (1987, 1999), one of the major features of the links between the elements is contradictions. By looking for connections and contradictions between the key categories, I found that one of the major themes was the contradiction between the tutors' intended goal of helping students through feedback and the summative role of feedback. This theme provided an answer to my research question which asked to what extent the tutors' actual practices converge with or diverge from their beliefs.

Finally, the unique strength of Activity Theory is that it is a philosophical and theoretical framework of human activity rather than a concluding theory in a specific area of study. It outlines the mechanisms of human activity and provides a practical means of analysing the complexity of an activity. Activity Theory guided my search for themes because it allowed me to analyse the interconnections between each element but did not hinder me from finding a new emergent theme, i.e., the interactions between emotion, cognition, and action. The discovery of this theme contributed to answering my last research question: What constitutes tutors' beliefs, and the possible tension that arises in putting these beliefs into practice.

Understanding Cognitive Development in the Activity System

Engeström's expanded model of Activity Theory, as the theoretical framework of this study, provided a holistic view of the contextual issues that constituted and constrained tutors' beliefs and practices. Engeström's (1987) concepts of the context of an activity and contradictions within the activity system were found especially helpful in interpreting the findings in my study.

Context and contradictions as sources of cognitive development. In my study of tutors' beliefs and practices when providing assessment feedback, contextual factors interacted with tutors' beliefs and affected their practices. According to Engeström (1987), the context is the activity system that is constructed from seven elements: subject, community, division of labour, object, goal, tool, and rule. Figure 7.1 illustrates the activity system in my study (as cited in Li, 2012):

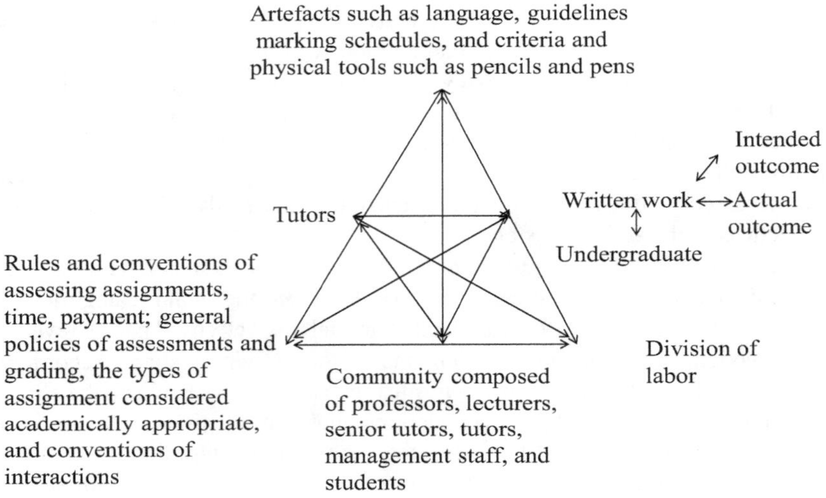

Figure 7.1. The expanded model of Activity Theory (Adapted from Engeström, 1987, p. 78)

In terms of its application to my study, the object was the assignment written by undergraduates who majored in social sciences. The actualised goal was to get the assignments assessed, while the intended goal was to assist students' cognitive development in their study. The instruments or tools were artefacts such as language, marking schedules, criteria, and guidelines, as well as physical tools such as pencils and pens. The subject was the individual tutors who were employed to assess undergraduate students' written work. These tutors belonged to a local community of practice which was hierarchically composed of professors, lecturers, senior tutors, management staff, and the students. The rules included institutional policies of assessment, the explicit rules for marking a specific assignment, and the requirements for feedback. As regards the division of labour, the lecturers and senior tutors distributed marking schedules, sample answers, and provided other oral requirements or guidelines to tutors individually or collectively in meetings. In addition, the tutors were temporarily employed on a part-time basis only.

This context constituted the direct source of the tutors' cognitive development. Contradictions were found both within and between the contextual factors (Engeström, 1987). For example, at the primary level, there was the contradiction between the goals of providing assessment feedback: Tutors believed they should use feedback to help students make improvement; however, they also knew that the actual goal of their feedback was to justify the grade awarded. In effect, the assessment feedback provided by the tutors was expected to be both summative and formative, yet the tutors were given only marking schedules or criteria as their tools. They were provided with neither the tools nor sufficient training to enable them to give feedback on the students' writing per se. Thus, the tutors provided written feedback in line with the types of feedback they received on their own work and on the basis of the instruction/criteria given by their supervisors. In this context, the tutors found themselves in a double bind situation (Engeström, 1987, 2001): They were expected to achieve both the summative and formative goal of the activity of assessment, yet were not supported with sufficient resources.

At the secondary level, contradictions were found between individual tutors' practices and those in the community of practice, especially regarding the actions that were taken when they assessed essays. Tutors usually took action in three circumstances: When there were too many grammatical errors; when they had to weight grades, especially when they had to fail an assignment; and when they were composing written feedback.

Both grammatical errors and written feedback required the tutors to take linguistic actions. The more actions the tutors took, the longer time the tutors spent on an assignment. The actions the tutors took to address grammatical issues in an assignment varied. For example, one tutor corrected all the grammatical errors in an assignment written by a Chinese student, whereas another tutor was advised by her supervisor that she needed to correct grammatical errors in the first page only. Some tutors corrected errors when they noticed them, while other tutors believed they were not qualified to correct grammatical errors and that it was not their job to do so.

Giving feedback on grammar proved to be the most flexible aspect of the assessment process because poor grammar could be a reason to mark an assignment down; it could signal to the student that the assignment had been marked; and, it could be regarded as a way to help students. While it was obviously time consuming to correct all a student's errors, ignoring or marking only a selection of grammatical errors could also shorten the marking time if the tutor simply said the assignment was incomprehensible.

When it came to written feedback, some tutors followed a routine operation: It could involve putting just some comments in the written work's margins, or simply giving some encouraging words at the end such as "well done". However, when the tutors received more specific instructions from their supervisors on what kind of feedback was expected, they would take linguistic actions. For example, one tutor struggled to find different words when trying to provide positive comments. Only one of the study participants, a more experienced tutor, took systematic actions in drafting her feedback, using a 'sandwich' genre (i.e., positive comments, aspects to improve and encouraging words). However, no feedback provided suggestions on how to improve the assignment.

The actions tutors took when weighting grades included comparing the grades of the whole cohort or consulting their supervisor when they had to fail an assignment.

However, they were not sure whether they were too lenient or too strict when awarding a grade.

The contradictions among tutors, especially regarding taking actions to deal with grammatical issues and composing written feedback, indicated a lack of consistent rules and practical tools that could help the tutors to achieve the formative goals of the activity. Besides, their lack of confidence in weighting grades reflected the lack of training in assessment.

The Interactions and Regulations of Cognition, Emotion, and Action (ECA)

The context and contradictions were not only sources of cognitive development, but also triggers of emotional reactions that interacted with cognition and action at both the individual and collective level.

At the individual level, the tutors experienced both positive and negative emotions when assessing students' written work. The tutors had positive emotions such as joy and pleasure when marking a well written script. The reasons were perhaps that well written scripts took less time to mark and the tutors did not need to provide negative comments. In this condition, the tutors indicated their positive emotions by placing double ticks in the margins and employing praising words as the overall comment. The tutors felt frustrated and annoyed when marking a script which was full of grammatical errors. They sometimes had to correct the errors or even rewrite the sentences in order to understand the content. However, they did not communicate these negative emotions with students in their overall comments. Instead, they tried to use encouraging words in the summative comment, and they tried not to mark down the grammatical errors in an attempt to reduce students' negative emotional reactions.

At the collective activity level, the ECA interactions were found between the tutors, their colleagues and students. Emotions, especially empathy and confidence, affected the tutors' decision making in assessment. Tutors who were also students were more empathetic towards students while marking. They were more lenient when weighting the grades; for example, they would award a bare pass instead of a fail grade. They avoided negative comments and used encouraging words and emoticons such as smiley faces in their feedback. They believed that these strategies could generate positive emotional reactions and motivate students to make improvement. This belief was based on fresh memories of their own emotional reactions to feedback they had received from their teachers. However, the fact that there was no feedback on how to make improvement indicated that the tutors needed both theoretical and practical guidance on how to regulate students' cognitive and emotional reactions through feedback.

Another emotion—confidence—also played an important role in assessment. The tutors, as novices, occupied a marginal place in the community of practice. They had no professional training in assessing writing; neither had they established themselves in their major area of study. They did not have the same "social-psychological stability" (Russel, 2009, p. 40) as their supervisors who carried out the same assessment activity. As a result, they did not feel sufficiently confident at work. Moreover, students tended to challenge the reliability of the tutor's assessment when the result did not meet their expectations or when they received more positive comments from other teachers. Students' distrust also led to the tutors' lack of confidence. As a result, the tutors tended to be hesitant when deciding on a low, and especially a fail, grade. They sought advice from their supervisors when it was difficult for them to make a decision.

According to Vygotsky (1978), an individual's cognition is first regulated by others and then by the individuals themselves. Individuals internalise and process contextual information and externalise the cognitive products to guide their actions. However, it seemed that Vygotsky (1978) did not explain how emotion interacted with cognition and action in the process of internalisation and externalisation. Rather, the relation between cognition and emotion was explained by Festinger and Carlsmith's (1959) concept of cognitive dissonance. Cognitive dissonance refers to a mental situation where people face conflicting concepts or have to choose between contradictory concepts or behaviours. Cognitive dissonance results in negative emotions. According to Gross (2002, 2008), individuals can regulate their emotional reactions through cognitive reappraisal so that rational actions can be taken to achieve the intended goal. The process of ECA interaction can be illustrated by the following diagram which draws on Engeström's (1987) expanded model:

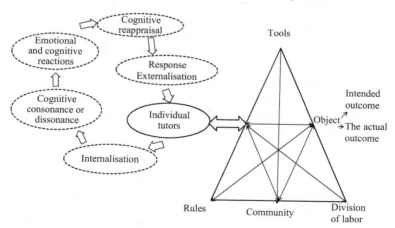

Figure 7.2. Process of ECA interaction in the activity of assessment (Li, 2012, p. 151)

The individual tutors internalised contextual information which resulted in either cognitive dissonance or cognitive consonance which, in turn, triggered emotional and cognitive reactions. The tutors reappraised the contextual information in relation to the intended goal, and then externalised the cognitive product, the assessment feedback.

CONCLUSION

The tutors in this case study were novices in the community of practice, yet they carried out the same important assessment activity as their supervisors. To understand the beliefs and practices of the tutors in the assessment activity, the study applied an Activity Theory based theoretical framework and took a multimethod approach to data collection. The study had three major findings. First, there was a major divergence between the tutors' intended goal of helping students with feedback and the actualised goal which used feedback to justify their grading. Secondly, the tutors intended to focus primarily on the content of students' written work, but shifted their focus to formal issues when there were too many grammatical errors. Thirdly, tutors' emotions interacted with their cognition and actions and played a role in the activity of assessment; here the tutors not only had to regulate their own emotional reactions but also used feedback to regulate their students' emotional reactions to assessment.

According to Engeström (1987), expansive learning begins with questioning and analysing the contradictions in the current model of activity. By revealing the contradictions and difficulties the tutors had in carrying out the assessment activity, the study contributes to the remodelling of the assessment activity. A new model should address both the emotional and the cognitive aspects of assessment feedback in the following areas and ways. It should embrace collaborative efforts between linguistics specialists and subject experts to analyse and construct assessment genres so that novice tutors can be supported by linguistic tools while providing assessment feedback; it should support the professional development of novice tutors within the community of practice through more opportunities to share and learn; and, it should promote dialogue between relevant communities of practice. Identifying contradictions and suggesting new models for the assessment activity that can lead to expansive learning have practical implications for tutor development and the improvement of the assessment activity.

Engeström and Sannino (2010) point out the need for a dimension in the study of expansive learning that addresses "issues of subjectivity, experiencing, personal sense, emotion, embodiment, identity, and moral commitment" (p. 21). By revealing the interactions between emotion, cognition, and action in the process of assessment, this study contributes to the theoretical development of teacher cognitions' studies and Activity Theory.

THE COMMENT ON THE USE OF ACTIVITY THEORY

This case study of tutor beliefs and practices when providing assessment feedback was based on the theoretical framework provided by Engeström's (1987) expanded model of Activity Theory. The application of Activity Theory brought three significant advantages. First, Activity Theory guided the data collection, especially with regard to the definition of the context of the case study. Context is the key to the understanding of cognitive development. However, the relevant literature on teacher cognition lacks a clear definition of context. The expanded model of Activity Theory not only outlines the context of the activity as the activity system, but also specifies the constructs of the context, and in so doing contributes to the study of teacher cognition studies. Secondly, the expanded model of Activity Theory helped my data analysis in terms of categorising contextual factors, and analysing the connections between the contextual factors and the contradictions within and between the contextual elements. Thirdly, through the lens of Activity Theory, I was able to discover the convergences and divergences between tutors' beliefs and practice, reveal the contradictions within the activity system, and answer the research questions. The expanded model of Activity Theory helped me to go beyond the linguistic level of assessing writing and see the complexity of the tutors' cognitive development in relation to its educational contexts. Moreover, the findings of the ECA interaction reveal the complexity of cognitive development and thus contribute to the development of Activity Theory.

In summary, the fundamental research question of the case study is what constitutes tutors' beliefs of assessment feedback and what tension arises when they put their beliefs into practice. The answer to the research question is that the tutors believe that their feedback should help students to make improvement; in practice, however, the tutors mainly use feedback to justify grading. The divergence between tutors' beliefs and practices is due to contextual factors such as assessment policy and division of labour. These contextual factors interact with tutors' beliefs, cause emotional reactions and affect their practices. These contextual factors are able to be examined in depth by using the framework of Activity Theory. Activity Theory, as a systematic and practical approach to the study of the individual's cognitive progress, can strengthen the research design and guide the researcher through the processes of data collection, analysis, and discussion.

REFERENCES

Bailey, R., & Garner, M. (2010). Is the feedback in higher education assessment worth the paper it is written on? Teachers' reflections on their practices. *Teaching in Higher Education, 15*(2), 187–198.

Borg, S. (2006). *Teacher cognition and language education: Research and practice.* London, England: Continuum.

Braun, V., & Clarke, V. (2006). Using thematic analysis in psychology. *Qualitative Research in Psychology, 3*(2), 77–101.

Broad, B. (2003). *What we really value: Beyond rubrics in teaching and assessing writing.* Logan, UT: Utah State University Press.

Burns, A. (1996). Starting all over again. In D. F. J. Richards (Ed.), *Teacher learning in language teaching* (pp. 154–178). New York, NY: Cambridge University Press.

Carless, D. (2006). Differing perceptions in the feedback process. *Studies in Higher Education, 31*(2), 219–233.

Carless, D. (2009). Trust, distrust and their impact on assessment reform. *Assessment & Evaluation in Higher Education, 34*(1), 79–89.

Cohen, L., Manion, L., & Morrison, K. (2000). *Research methods in education* (5th ed.). London, England: Routledge Falmer.

Creswell, J. W. (2007). *Qualitative inquiry and research design: Choosing among five approaches.* Thousand Oaks, CA: Sage.

Crisp, V. (2008). Exploring the nature of examiner thinking during the process of examination marking. *Cambridge Journal of Education, 38*(2), 247–264.

Cross, R. (2010). Language teaching as sociocultural activity: Rethinking language teacher practice. *The Modern Language Journal, 94,* 434–452.

DeLuca, C., & Klinger, D. A. (2010). Assessment literacy development: Identifying gaps in teacher candidates' learning. *Assessment in Education: Principles, Policy and Practice, 17*(4), 419–438.

Engeström, Y. (1987). *Learning by expanding: An activity-theoretical approach to developmental research.* Helsinki, Sweden: Orienta-Konsultit.

Engeström, Y. (1999). Innovative learning in work teams: Analyzing cycles of knowledge creation in practice. In Y. Engeström, R. Miettinen, & R. L. Punamäki (Eds.), *Perspectives on activity theory* (pp. 377–404). Cambridge, England: Cambridge University Press.

Engeström, Y. (2009). The future of activity theory: A rough draft. In A. Sannino, H. Daniels, & K. D. Gutiérrez (Eds.), *Learning and expanding with activity theory* (pp. 303–328). New York, NY: Cambridge University Press.

Engeström, Y. (2001). Expansive learning at work: Toward an activity-theoretical conceptualization. *Journal of Education and Work, 14*(1), 133–156.

Engeström, Y., & Sannino, A. (2010). Studies of expansive learning: Foundations, findings and future challenges. *Educational Research Review, 5*(1), 1–24.

Ericsson, K. A., & Simon, H. A. (1984). *Protocol analysis: Verbal reports as data.* Cambridge, MA: The MIT Press.

Festinger, L., & Carlsmith, J. M. (1959). Cognitive consequences of forced compliance. *Journal of Abnormal and Social Psychology, 58*(2), 203–210.

Glaser, B. G., & Strauss, A. L. (1967). *The discovery of grounded theory: Strategies for qualitative research.* Chicago, IL: Aldine Publishing Co.

Gross, J. J. (2002). Emotion regulation: Affective, cognitive, and social consequences. *Psychophysiology, 39,* 281–291.

Gross, J. J. (2008). Emotion regulation. In M. Lewis, J. M. Haviland-Jones, & L. F. Barrett (Eds.), *Handbook of emotions* (3rd ed., pp. 497–512). New York, NY: Guilford.

Lee, I. (2009). Ten mismatches between teachers' beliefs and written feedback practice. *ELT Journal, 63*(1), 13–22.

Li, J. R. (2012). *University tutors' beliefs about and practices in assessing undergraduates' writing: A New Zealand case study* (Unpublished doctoral dissertation). The University of Waikato, Hamilton, New Zealand.

Lilly, J., Richter, U. M., & Rivera-Macias, B. (2010). Using feedback to promote learning: Student and tutor perspectives. *Practitioner Research in Higher Education, 4*(1), 30–40.

Mutch, A. (2003). Exploring the practice of feedback to students. *Active Learning in Higher Education, 4*(1), 24–38.

Orsmond, P., & Merry, S. (2011). Feedback alignment: Effective and ineffective links between tutors' and students' understanding of coursework feedback. *Assessment & Evaluation in Higher Education, 36*(2), 125–136.

Roth, W. M. (2009). On the inclusion of emotions, identity, and ethico-moral dimensions of action. In A. Sannino, H. Daniels, & K. D. Gutiérrez (Eds.), *Learning and expanding with activity theory* (pp. 53–71). New York, NY: Cambridge University Press.

Russell, D. R. (2009). Uses of activity theory in written communication research. In A. Sannino, H. Daniels, & K. D. Gutiérrez (Eds.), *Learning and expanding with activity theory* (pp. 40–52). New York, NY: Cambridge University Press.

Salomon, G. (1993). *Distributed cognitions: Psychological and educational considerations*. New York, NY: Cambridge University Press.

Scribner, S. (1985). Vygotsky's uses of history. In J. Wertsch (Ed.), *Culture, communication and cognition: Vygotskian perspectives* (pp. 119–145). New York, NY: Cambridge University Press.

Silverman, D. (2006). *Interpreting qualitative data: Methods for analysing talk, text and interaction* (3rd ed.). London, England: Sage.

Sitko, B. (1993). Exploring feedback: Writers meet readers. In A. Penrose & B. Sitko (Eds.), *Hearing ourselves think: Cognitive research in the college writing classroom* (pp. 170–187). New York, NY: Oxford University Press.

Stern, L. A., & Solomon, A. (2006). Effective faculty feedback: The road less traveled. *Assessing Writing, 11*(1), 22–41.

Vygotsky, L. S. (1978). *Mind in society* (M. Cole, Trans.). Cambridge, MA: Harvard University Press.

Vygotsky, L. S. (1986). *Thought and language*. Cambridge, MA: The MIT Press.

Weigle, S. C. (2007). Teaching writing teachers about assessment. *Journal of Second Language Writing, 16*(3), 194–209.

Woods, D. (1996). *Teacher cognition in language teaching: Beliefs, decision-making, and classroom practice*. Melbourne, Australia: Cambridge University Press.

Jinrui Li
University of Waikato
New Zealand

JOSEPH RAMANAIR

8. TURNING CHALLENGES INTO OPPORTUNITIES

Investigating Technology Integration in Tertiary Level English Language Programmes through the Lens of Activity Theory

INTRODUCTION

There is potential in incorporating technology for language learning. Studies investigating the potential that technology offers to English language pedagogy indicated that it supported the learning of vocabulary (Cross, 2011; Prince, 2012; Sydorenko, 2010), stimulated interaction to encourage language output (Acar & Kobayashi, 2011; Franciosi, 2011; Sagae, Kumar, & Johnson, 2009), encouraged collaboration in language learning to share, adapt, and create meaning (Jalkanen & Vaarala, 2013), and enhanced the learning of grammar for writing (Acar, Geluso, & Shiki, 2011).

However, the potential of technology has not always been realised in some educational environments such as in the English language learning environments, as is evident in the educational technology literature (Baker, Bernard, & Dumez-Féroc, 2012; Voogt, Erstad, Dede, & Mishra, 2013). There are contexts where its use has often been described as uneven or limited, with the tendency of technology to be used on the periphery or on an 'ad hoc' basis (Blake, 2013; Kreijns, Vermeulen, Kirschner, van Buuren, & van Acker, 2013). This reality challenges the concept of "normalisation" which was first introduced by Bax (2000) to investigate the integration of technology into tertiary-level English language teaching. As defined by Bax (2003), normalisation involves "the stage when technology becomes invisible, embedded in everyday practice and hence 'normalised'" (p. 23). The state of normalisation is achieved when teachers and students use technology as a learning resource on a daily basis as an integral part of every lesson (Bax, 2003).

Thus, two aspects need to be addressed when investigating technology integration. The first aspect concerns the context in which technology is used which is the classroom learning environment while the second involves the teacher who is using the technology within this context. As both aspects are interrelated, examining this relationship is rather complex. Activity Theory as a framework enables such complex interactions to be described and analysed to provide insights into not only how technology integration occurs through the use of selected tools in classroom learning activities and the challenges involved, but also reveals how such use affects those who are part of this learning environment, and the outcome of the activity.

D. S. P. Gedera & P. J. Williams (Eds.), Activity Theory in Education, 121–138.

Examining technology integration through the lens of Activity Theory, thus informs practice not only within an immediate language learning programme but could also apply more broadly to other similar contexts.

As such, this chapter will discuss how Activity Theory is used as a lens to investigate technology integration based on one empirical study which was conducted as part of a doctoral level research. The study was carried out in the context of a tertiary level English language programme in New Zealand to examine how technology involving one Learning Management System (LMS) known as Moodle was integrated, identify what challenges were experienced, and recommend how these challenges could be addressed within this context.

THE CLASSROOM LANGUAGE LEARNING ENVIRONMENT

English Language Pedagogy

For classroom learning to be effective, conditions that facilitate language learning need to be created. These conditions which can be created through instructional practices include providing learners with extensive and rich personalised language input, sufficient opportunities to produce output (particularly through interaction), and feedback on the learner's comprehension (Ellis, 2005; Franken & Rau, 2009, Nunn, 2006). Creating such conditions can enable both cognitive and social learning to occur and the use of technology can also enhance these learning conditions. Input could be enhanced through the use of technology through the use of multimedia (Cutrim Schmid, 2008; Kessler, 2013; Sydorenko, 2010), video clips with captions (Li, 2013; Perez, Peters, Clarebout, & Desmet, 2014), and video lectures (Yang & Sun, 2013). Providing learners with sufficient opportunities to produce output (particularly through interaction) could be supported through the use of text based Computer Mediated Communication (CMC) (Meskill & Anthony, 2005; Vinagre & Muñoz, 2011; Ware & O'Dowd, 2008). Feedback could be enhanced through the use of CMC as well which involves the use of email and online chats (Guichon, Bétrancourt, & Prié, 2012; Lee, 2006, 2008).

Challenges of Technology Integration

While the use of technology could support to create conditions to facilitate language learning, efforts to incorporate it in the classroom in many educational institutions have not been without their challenges. Various factors have been identified as posing constraints to the use of technology for classroom learning and they have often reflected the same constraints over the years since the inception of technology in classroom learning (Karabulut, 2013; Kopcha, 2012). Some of the constraints concern the limited access to technology (Bacow, Bowen, Guthrie, Lack, & Long, 2012; Johnson et al., 2013), the time required to use technology (Kopcha, 2012;

Laferrière, Hamel, & Searson, 2013), the cost in using technology (Bacow et al., 2012; Liang & Chen, 2012), the limited training for teachers to incorporate technology in the classroom (Johnson et al., 2013; Singh, Schrape, & Kelly, 2012), and the lack of administrative support (Bacow et al., 2012; Karabulut, 2013; Kopcha, 2012). More often many of these constraints are part of the wider sociocultural environment (Bacow et al., 2012; Karabulut, 2013; Laferrière et al., 2013) and are interconnected, related, and emerged from the complexities that occur in this environment (Laferrière et al., 2013).

TEACHERS AND TECHNOLOGY

Teachers play an essential role in the language classroom as they determine the learning needs of the students and how these needs can be approached through instructional activities. With the rapid developments and potential that technology has to offer, teachers are increasingly expected to use it in their classroom teaching (Blake, 2013; Egbert, Huff, McNeil, Preuss, & Sellen, 2009; Gruba & Hinkelman, 2012). However, technology has been largely used to transmit knowledge and information, employed in a disconnected or peripheral way (Bates, 2010; Lai, Khaddage, & Knezek, 2013; Selwyn, 2012), and used because of its novelty factor (Compton, 2009; Toetenel, 2014; Zou, 2013).

Technology is certainly not impartial (Karlström & Lundin, 2013; Steel, 2009) and offers affordances and constraints in the instructional environment. Kaptelinin and Nardi (2012) argue for a need to consider technology affordance from a mediated action perspective as involving a three-way interaction between the person, the mediational means, and the environment. Affordances from the mediated action perspective are considered as "action possibilities offered to the actor by objects in the environment" (Kaptelinin & Nardi, 2012, p. 973). The concept of affordance thus, can be understood as having functional, relational, and cultural aspects (Hutchby, 2001). As such, in considering the teacher factor in investigating technology integration, teachers' knowledge bases need to be explored.

Technological, Pedagogical, Content Knowledge (TPACK) Framework

The TPACK framework informs the integration of technology in classroom teaching and learning. It emphasises the need for teachers to thoughtfully interweave the three main foundations of knowledge: technology, pedagogy, and content to develop good content and strategies for classroom learning activities (Mishra & Koehler, 2006). This form of knowledge is distinct from the knowledge of teachers who are specialists in their subject area or who are experts in using technology. Developing quality learning experiences involves teachers having "a nuanced understanding of the complex relationships between technology, content, and pedagogy, and using this understanding to develop appropriate, context-specific strategies and representations" (Mishra & Koehler, 2006, p. 1029). The TPACK framework is illustrated in Figure 8.1.

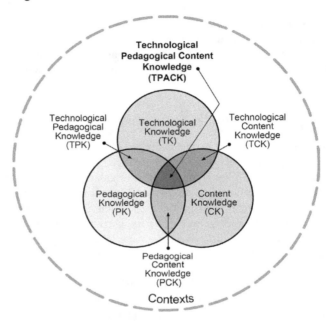

Figure 8.1. Technological Pedagogical Content Knowledge (Reproduced by permission of the publisher, © 2012 by tpack.org)

To explore teachers' conceptions of technology integration, there is a need to consider how teachers think and develop as they interact with the pedagogical and content knowledge. As knowledge is complex, multifaceted, and situated, teachers' conceptions need to be investigated in the context of their practice. In addition, there are social and cultural aspects within an educational environment that can interact with teachers' learning and practices, and can affect their knowledge in integrating technology. As such, there is a need to address how these social and cultural factors interact with teachers' knowledge and affect their learning when integrating technology in their instructional practices. This need is explored from the perspective of sociocultural theory as applied to teacher learning which is explained next.

Sociocultural Theory as Applied to Teacher Learning

A sociocultural theory of learning views learning as involving social interaction and collaboration. It acknowledges mental processing as situated within the cultural, historical, social, and institutional contexts of a broader community. A sociocultural perspective of learning is relevant to this inquiry as it provides a basis for exploring "teachers as learners" as they integrate technology in their instructional practices.

Four interrelated principles of sociocultural theory of learning can be derived from prominent researchers in the area (Barab & Duffy, 2000; Jonassen & Land, 2000; Nasir & Hand, 2006; Salomon & Perkins, 1998). The first principle which is a fundamental concept of sociocultural theory is that the "human mind is *mediated*" (Lantolf, 2000, p. 1, emphasis in original). The second principle concerns the role of context in which the learning takes place (Barab & Duffy, 2000; Lave & Wenger, 1991; Wertsch, 1991) while learning as goal-directed is the third principle of a sociocultural theory of learning. Goals are an important part of activities as they provide the impetus that can promote learning and development (Engeström & Miettinen, 1999). Finally, participation in the practices of a particular community enhances the process of learning and development (Barab & Duffy, 2000; Lave & Wenger, 1991; Sfard, 1998). A sociocultural perspective of learning foreshadows the use of Activity Theory as an explanatory framework for this chapter.

ACTIVITY THEORY

Background

The early model of Activity Theory, which focussed on "activity" consisted of the subject, object, tool, and outcome. The concept of mediation, which is the main focus of early Activity Theory, is reflected in Vygotsky's model of mediated action as shown in Figure 8.2.

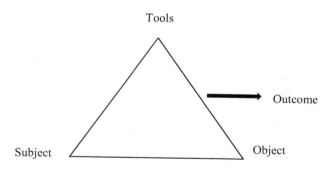

Figure 8.2. Early Activity Theory: Mediated action

Activity concerns a "form of doing directed to an object" (Issroff & Scanlon 2002, p. 78). While the subject concerns an individual or a group, the object involves the product, which the subject acts on during an activity (Keengwe & Kang, 2013). The object thus concerns the motive of the activity. During the activity, the subject typically employs a tool which is simultaneously material such as a computer, a hoe, or a mobile phone, and/or conceptual such as language or mathematical formula, to realise the object. The outcome refers to the overall purpose of the activity system (Keengwe & Kang, 2013). Much later, Vygotsky's model was extended by Leont'ev to explain key differences between an individual action and collective activity (Engeström, 2001). While an action is concerned with an individual or group accomplishing a goal, an activity involves a community with an object and a motive (Bakhurst, 2009). Leont'ev emphasised the significance of the object, which involves the product or the motive which the subject acts on during an activity, suggesting that activities are differentiated by the objects that are pursued (goals) (Barab, Evans, & Baek, 2004). Leont'ev (1974) further distinguished goals as immediate and overall; and described activity as consisting of activities, actions, and operations as hierarchical.

Activity Theory Expanded

Engeström (1987) further expanded on Leont'ev's extended concepts. This new structure emphasised the role of cultural mediation, the social, cultural, and historical context of activity, and the relationship between the individual and the collective. Activity Theory advanced the idea that a natural focus for the study of human behaviour is activity systems, which can be understood as historically conditioned systems of relationships among individuals and their proximal, culturally-organised environments (Cole & Engeström, 1993).

This expanded description of Activity Theory shifted from an emphasis on individual action and processes "to include a minimal meaningful context which is called an activity" (Issroff & Scanlon, 2002, p. 78). In describing this expanded model, Engeström (1987) conceptualised the activity system as comprising of six interacting components, which are the subject, the tool and signs, object, rules, community, and division of labour. Based on this conceptualisation of activity, the action of the individual becomes embedded as part of a system and meaning is derived from a community of people who share the same object (Engeström, 1987, 2001). A diagram of this expanded description of Activity Theory which is also known as second generation Activity Theory is illustrated in Figure 8.3.

The Methodological Implications – Activity Theory

Drawing on Activity Theory as an interpretive framework has particular methodological implications given the descriptive nature of the framework. These implications concern the value of researching human activity in real-life contexts and of employing a variety of data collection methods to provide multiple perspectives of the learning activity. Activity Theory emphasises that research investigating human activities within a particular setting must be in the context of real-life activities. This focus enables research to investigate how people engage in activities that involve goals, objects, and outcomes, which drive that activity and the social and

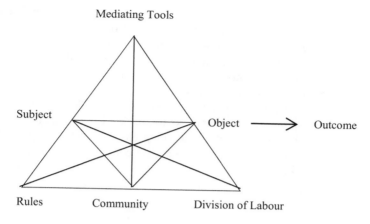

Figure 8.3. Activity Theory: Expanded

cultural relationships among groups of people (Engeström, 2001; Jonassen, 2000; Kaptelinin & Nardi, 2006). As these relationships involve mediation through tool use, research needs to pay close attention to how, when, and where that mediation occurs. In particular, the concept of distributed cognition needs to be considered, as knowledge and understanding are not exclusive but are collectively shared among the community through the use of cultural artefacts. Activity Theory provides a robust interpretive framework for describing the culture of a setting particularly in relation to the cultural artefacts such as tools, the role of the community, and social rules.

A DESCRIPTION OF THE STUDY

The Context

This study which used Activity Theory as a lens to investigate technology integration in one tertiary level English language programme, was aimed at examining how Moodle was used in an English language learning classroom, what challenges were experienced, and how these challenges could be addressed in the English language programme. This study which involved the use of qualitative research with an ethnographic approach was conducted on one 12-week certificate level English language programme offered to international students at the tertiary institution. It involved the voluntary participation of three teachers (T1, T2, T3), the programme administrator, and technology support personnel as key informants, and the students.

Data Collection

Data were collected in two phases, using multiple methods consisting of semi-structured interviews, work-together sessions, and classroom observations. In

Phase One, data were collected from all participants through semi-structured interviews while in Phase Two, data were obtained only from the teachers who participated in Phase One as a follow-up. The teachers and key informants were interviewed individually while the students were interviewed as a focus group. Teacher interviews occurred thrice in Phase One and once in Phase Two while interviews involving others were conducted once. Data were also collected through work-together sessions which involved the researcher working alongside individual teachers at their respective desks to provide verbal guidance on how to create forums and links in the Moodle learning environment as requested. Non-participatory classroom observations were also conducted using a time-based open-ended observation sheet.

Data Analysis

The main data obtained in this study were from the audio-recorded semi-structured interviews involving teachers, students, and key informants. The data from individual teacher interviews at the various stages were also analysed together with the data from the key informant interviews and student focus groups, and notes from classroom observations and work-together sessions. Data from these interviews and the notes complemented the teacher interview data in terms of clarifying and supporting the information each teacher provided and vice versa. All interview transcripts were analysed using a constant comparison approach (Lincoln & Guba, 1985) and a process of inductive reasoning (Goetz & LeCompte, 1984). The overall relationships, patterns, and themes from the categories that were generated were further reconceptualised into new constructs based on the Activity Theory framework.

FINDINGS

The Object of the Activity

The object in this case study concerned preparing the students to speak in the classroom to develop their speaking skills. Moodle was used as a platform to provide the students with opportunities to rehearse ideas to enable them to speak in the classroom.

Technology to Support Classroom Speaking

For the three teacher participants, technology centred on the computer. They considered the computer as having the potential to prepare their students to speak in the classroom especially as the device could connect to the Internet to enable access to the World Wide Web. Thus, the computer provided the students with a different way of learning. The computer was also perceived as replacing face-to-face

128

interaction in the classroom. As such, the presence of the teachers was perceived as unnecessary.

Teacher Perspectives of Moodle

These teacher participants had neither used Moodle for instructional purposes nor attended any training in its use. Nevertheless, they regarded Moodle as a repository for classroom resources, as enabling asynchronous learning, and as saving classroom time. Using Moodle thus, could reduce the time spent in the classroom preparing students for classroom speaking activities and assessments. Their views appeared to have been largely derived from anecdotal accounts of the experiences of others who used it, such as teachers from other departments within the tertiary institution.

Using Moodle to Support Classroom Speaking

The teacher participants used Moodle as a platform to upload a text based speaking exercise every week via the Forum. This strategy was adopted to enable the students who were organised into a number of smaller online groups, to respond to the exercises by sharing and exchanging ideas with one another which could expose them to additional ideas to help them prepare for their classroom based speaking lessons.

Both T1 and T2 were confident that the strategy adopted would achieve the intended object. However, there was no evidence that it did. While T1 was confident that Moodle provided an alternative learning environment and replaced face-to-face classroom interaction, the teacher was unable to provide any observational evidence as to whether students' online written interactions prepared them to speak in the classroom. T2 assumed that as Moodle provided students with opportunities for asynchronous learning, the students would access these online speaking exercises and post their responses on their own. However, this assumption was challenged. The students did not access Moodle unless they were taken to the computer labs and needed to be told repeatedly how to post their responses online.

For T3, boosting the look and feel of the online information to make it appealing to the students was more important. However, it did not encourage more online participation. It was observed during a speaking lesson that the students had to be continuously prompted to speak. During the focus group interview with T3's students, the students reported that many of their classmates did not share their ideas online as many were frequently absent from classroom lessons. They might not be aware of the topics being covered to enable them to contribute their ideas online.

Rules

The teacher participants experienced various challenges that created conflicts and caused tensions as they used Moodle to relate their classroom activities to the object of the activity. These challenges were shaped by the rules existing within the instructional environment.

One challenge concerned the emphasis on assessments in the programme. The requirement to cover the course content so as to prepare the students for the assessments inhibited these teachers' freedom to explore the use of Moodle. There was a conflict between using Moodle, preparing and conducting the assessments, and covering the required course content.

Another constraint concerned the text-based speaking exercises that were used in the Forum. All three teachers expressed the need to revise the content of these exercises as most of the students were not responding to it online. While T2 and T3 felt that the information in these speaking exercises needed to be revised, T1 believed that the format needed to be varied. However, T3 was cautious on the need to review as it might compromise the initial purpose of adopting the exercises, which was to provide the students with opportunities to practise speaking. These exercises were originally available in printed "Task cards" which were used for the past few years as practice for speaking assessments.

Time was another important issue among the teachers in using Moodle to realise the intended object. They believed that using Moodle constrained the time that was available for them to manage their in-class teaching workload. Besides focussing their time on classroom planning and teaching, as well as conducting and evaluating the assessments, the teachers needed to learn how to navigate through Moodle and upload the speaking exercises. Balancing both demands was challenging both at the onset as well as throughout the teaching block.

The lack of training in the use of Moodle was also a constraint. The centralised eLearning unit consisted of a small team of four personnel with two of them providing Moodle support to all staff. A series of hands-on technical training workshops, online tutorial, help desk support via email or telephone were available to support teachers as well as a one-to-one assistance which was available upon request. As the team was small, they had to be careful with the type of support they could deliver. These teachers, however, were not able to attend the Moodle training workshops as the training times clashed with their classroom schedules. All three teachers taught 19 hours per week. This lack of time to access training was also acknowledged by the Programme Manager during a key informant interview. There was, however, no indication that these teachers consulted the online tutorial site for Moodle and the help desk, or requested the one-to-one assistance.

A final constraint was the lack of access to technological infrastructure. There were scheduling issues with the one shared networked computer lab which posed an obstacle to these teachers who wanted more access to enable their students the opportunity to use Moodle. Although the students could access Moodle after class at designated computer spaces, there was limited time and seats. Classes ended at 3.00pm and these spaces were closed by 5.00pm. The students had to compete with one another to access a computer. Also, the classrooms at the new teaching block did not have any computer facilities with the exception of three teaching classrooms which were fitted with interactive whiteboards (IWB). Of the three teacher participants, only T2 used the IWB regularly.

DISCUSSION

The findings from this study revealed three main themes based on an Activity Theory framework – teachers' conceptualisation of the object, mediation of the tool in relation to the object, and the individual teacher in the context of a learning community.

Teachers' Conceptualisation of the Object

Although the teachers in this study were aware of the object, which was to prepare students to speak in the classroom, they lacked a valid conceptualisation of the object. This limitation could be attributed to the absence of a language syllabus in the programme. A syllabus could have provided details on how the programme and classroom learning activities could have been organised and implemented to realise the object programmes (Graves, 2000; Richards & Rodgers, 2001; Yalden, 1987). Another factor contributing to this lack of a valid conceptualisation of the object is the teachers' limited content knowledge in the subject matter which would have affected their classroom pedagogical practices. A teacher-directed approach was clearly evident in their classroom instructional practices as they perceived their role as teachers to transmit knowledge and materials that were mainly content-focussed. They lacked awareness about the role of interaction, language input, and feedback which characterises the nature of language learning – knowledge that only language teachers would possess (Richards, 2008, 2010). As such, these teachers were unable to create conditions that could facilitate the students' classroom language learning and that were important to realise the object.

Further, these teachers lacked a clear conceptualisation of the object. There was a lack of clarity around the object of activity as reflected in the learning materials uploaded on Moodle. Providing the exercises online was insufficient to prepare students to speak in the classroom. Instead, the teachers needed to base the design of the learning materials on the principles of task-based language learning (Ellis, 2003). Task-based language learning promotes negotiation and comprehension of meaning, enables opportunities for teacher feedback, encourages noticing during interaction, and supports reflection and thinking among learners (Albert & Kormos, 2011; Gurzynski-Weiss & Revesz, 2012; Robinson, 2011). Adopting the use of tasks instead of exercises could have helped these teachers to clarify their understanding of the object of their classroom activity.

Teachers' Conceptualisation of Technology to Mediate the Object

The teachers were unable to conceptualise how their use of Moodle could support their students to prepare for the classroom speaking activity. They expected that by

131

uploading the exercises online, the students' responses to them would enhance their classroom learning. This expectation indicated that they lacked awareness of the potential of technology for realising the object and of how to integrate technology meaningfully to serve pedagogical goals. More importantly, they were unaware that they needed to scaffold their students' learning to realise this object. Scaffolding recognises that "the primary process by which learning takes place is *interaction* [emphasis added], more specifically, an engagement with other learners and teachers in joint activities that focus on matters of shared interest and that contain opportunities for learning" (Walqui, 2006, pp. 159–160). The use of Moodle could have supported teachers to scaffold their students' language learning as the LMS enabled the teachers to create links to more online information and design activities that could encourage interaction, particularly through the use of learning tasks, as described earlier.

The teachers also regarded the online and face-to-face classroom environments as interchangeable contexts for learning. They had expected that Moodle could function to replace classroom interaction and as such, uploaded the same learning materials intended for face-to-face classroom learning into the online learning environment. This assumption indicated the teachers' lack of awareness that technology could serve as a valuable pedagogical tool. Assuming that teaching in the online environment is the same as teaching face-to-face in the classroom is a misconception that needs to be addressed (Blake, 2013; Compton, 2009). Teaching online requires that teachers adopt roles and responsibilities that are different from traditional classroom teaching approaches (Compton, 2009). It also requires that teachers not only have knowledge about technology and its functions, but also are able to decide what technological devices are appropriate to serve the identified pedagogical goals (Golonka, Bowles, Frank, Richardson, & Freynik, 2014). Moreover, technology is not neutral (Steel, 2009), as it offers affordances and poses constraints to the learning environment. A learning management system (LMS) for example, does not offer a single comprehensive technological solution for classroom pedagogy as commonly assumed (Hedberg, 2006; Naidu, 2006; Steel, 2009).

The Individual Teacher in the Context of a Learning Community

The findings from this study also concern the individual teacher within the context of a learning community. This community involves teachers' colleagues, programme managers or coordinators, administrators, and also students. The individual teacher's ability to perform is reliant on the members of this community (Leont'ev, 1981).

The teachers demonstrated enthusiasm in adopting Moodle at the outset of this research as it was perceived that the technology could save time and support students' language learning (Blin & Munro, 2008; Christensen, Aaron, & Clarke, 2002). Instead, it did not, as is often the case (Brandau-Brown 2013; Kessler & Plakans, 2008). However, this enthusiasm could be sustained and encouraged if teachers were provided with additional time to explore technology and to discuss its utilisation with colleagues as this strategy could increase their willingness to use it in the classroom (Brandau-Brown, 2013; Haydn & Barton, 2008). Teachers were also reported to be willing to commit their time amidst busy work schedules to share their experiences using technology when they sensed a value in using it and when provided with the opportunities to work as a team to develop and share learning materials (Brandau-Brown, 2013; Johnson et al., 2010). As such, engaging teachers to learn not only *about* technology but also *with* technology might develop positive dispositions to integrate it as part of classroom learning activities (Smith, Moyer, & Schugar, 2011).

Providing Moodle training workshops that mostly focus on technical aspects may not be an effective form of professional development (PD). While such exposure does have the potential to offer some value in terms of exposing teachers to newly acquired technological devices or updated versions of software (Haydn & Barton, 2008), it might not prepare them to effectively integrate technology as part of classroom learning activities (Garrett, 2009; Singh et al., 2012). For PD to be effective, teachers need to be engaged in professional learning, which could consist of formally planned (for example, workshops) and naturally occurring (for example, discussion group) activities (Mitchell, 2013; Singh et al., 2012). Professional learning involves activities that can enable teachers to learn as well as learn *how to learn*, to affect their thinking, knowledge, and skills to change their instructional practices to benefit students' learning (Avalos, 2011; Singh et al., 2012). The teachers in this study could have requested the Moodle training workshops to be provided at times that did not clash with their teaching schedules. During these workshop sessions, the teachers as a collective group could then have collaborated and cooperated as a team to plan and design the use of Moodle for classroom instructional activities to realise the intended object. Their collaboration and cooperation could be continued as they discussed the implementation of their plan and design of using Moodle in the actual classroom.

The uptake of opportunities for professional learning however, needs to be supported and sustained through pedagogical leadership. Although there was a programme manager the focus was on administration. Nevertheless, pedagogical leadership could have been enhanced through an apprenticeship approach that involves teachers participating and collaborating with more experienced others who can provide guidance and demonstration to support the former towards mastery (Dennen & Burner, 2008; Lave & Wenger, 1991). The apprenticeship could involve coaching or mentoring strategies (Beglau et al., 2011; Kopcha, 2012).

CONCLUSION AND IMPLICATIONS

Activity Theory as an interpretive framework served as a suitable lens to observe, explore, and understand how the teachers' conception of the object shaped and was shaped by their use of Moodle in this study. The insights enabled the researcher to interpret human activities as a developmental process interlinking both the level of the individual teachers and the community within the activity system. Through the use of this framework, this research was able to describe, clarify, and analyse the teachers' conceptions and behaviour against a backdrop of patterns and relationships within the context identified (Engeström, 2001; Lantolf & Appel, 1994; Nardi, 1996). Technology integration in any educational context is therefore, not dependent on the potential of a piece of technology alone or any other sole factor such as the teacher, but "a host of social and cultural elements operating together in complex ways" (Bax, 2011, p. 13).

REFERENCES

Acar, A., & Kobayashi, H. (2011). Whys and how's of language exchange meetings. *CALL-EJ, 12*(2), 1–10.

Acar, A., Geluso, J., & Shiki, T. (2011). How can search engines improve your writing? *CALL-EJ, 12*(1), 1–10.

Albert, A., & Kormos, J. (2011). Creativity and narrative task performance: An exploratory study. *Language Learning, 61*(1), 73–99.

Antoniadou, V. (2011). Using activity theory to understand the contradictions in an online transatlantic collaboration between student-teachers of English as a foreign Language. *ReCALL, 23*(3), 233–251.

Avalos, B. (2011). Teacher professional development in teaching and teacher education over ten years. *Teaching and Teacher Education, 27*(1), 10–20.

Bacow, L. S., Bowen, W. G., Guthrie, K. M., Lack, K. A., & Long, M. P. (2012). *Barriers to adoption of online learning systems in U.S. higher education.* Retrieved from http://www.sr.ithaka.org/research-publications/barriers-adoption-online-learning-systems-us-higher-education

Baker, M., Bernard F.-X., & Dumez-Féroc, I. (2012). Integrating computer-supported collaborative learning into the classroom: The anatomy of a failure. *Journal of Computer Assisted Learning, 28*(2), 161–176.

Bakhurst, D. (2009). Reflections on activity theory. *Educational Review, 61*(2), 197–210.

Barab, S. A., & Duffy, T. M. (2000). From practice fields to communities of practice. In D. Jonassen & S. Land (Eds.), *Theoretical foundation of learning environments* (pp. 25–56). Mahwah, NJ: Erlbaum.

Barab, S. A., Evans, M. A., & Baek, E. O. (2004). Activity theory as a lens for characterizing the participatory unit. In D. H. Jonassen (Ed.), *Handbook of research on educational communities and technology* (pp. 199–214). Mahwah, NJ: Lawrence Erlbaum Associates.

Bates, T. (2010). New challenges for universities: Why they must change. In U.-D. Ehlers & D. Schneckenberg (Eds.), *Changing cultures in higher education: Moving ahead to future learning* (pp. 15–25). Heidelberg, Germany: Springer.

Bax, S. (2000). Putting technology in its place: ICT in modern foreign language teaching. In K. Field (Ed.), *Issues in modern foreign languages teaching* (pp. 208–219). London, UK: Routledge Falmer.

Bax, S. (2003). CALL – past, present and future. *System, 31*(1), 13–28.

Bax, S. (2011). Normalisation revisited: The effective use of technology in language education. *International Journal of Computer-Assisted Language Learning and Teaching, 1*(2), 1–15.

Beglau, M., Hare, J. C., Foltos, L., Gann, K., James, J., Jobe, H., ... Smith, B. (2011). *Technology, coaching, and community: Power partners for improved professional development in primary and secondary education.* An International Society for Technology in Education (ISTE) White Paper, Special conference release, Eugene, Oregon. Retrieved from http://www.instructionalcoach.org/images/downloads/ISTE_Whitepaper_June_Final_Edits.pdf

Blake, R. (2013). *Brave new digital classroom: Technology and foreign language learning* (2nd ed.). Washington, DC: Georgetown University Press.

Blin, F., & Munro, M. (2008). Why hasn't technology disrupted academics' teaching practices? Understanding resistance to change through the lens of activity theory. *Computers & Education, 50*(2), 475–490.

Brandau-Brown, F. (2013). Trend becomes tradition: The educational challenges of new communication technologies. *Southern Communication Journal, 78*(1), 1–7.

Christensen, C., Aaron, S., & Clark, W. (2002). Disruption in education. In M. Devlin, R. Larson, & J. Meyerson (Eds.), *The internet and the university: Forum 2001.* Boulder, CO: EDUCAUSE. Retrieved from http://net.educause.edu/ir/library/pdf/ffpiu013.pdf

Cole, M., & Engeström, Y. (1993). A cultural–historical approach to distributed cognition. In G. Salomon (Ed.), *Distributed cognitions: Psychological and educational considerations* (pp. 1–46). New York, NY: Cambridge University Press.

Compton, L. K. (2009). Preparing language teachers to teach language online: A look at skills, roles, and responsibilities. *Computer Assisted Language Learning, 22*(1), 73–99.

Cross, J. (2011). Comprehending news videotexts: The influence of the visual content. *Language Learning & Technology, 15*(2), 44–68.

Cutrim Schmid, E. (2008). Potential pedagogical benefits and drawbacks of multimedia use in the English language classroom equipped with interactive whiteboard technology. *Computers & Education, 51*(4), 1553–1568.

Dennen, V. P., & Burner, K. J. (2008). The cognitive apprenticeship model in educational practice. In J. M. Spector, M. D. Merrill, J. V. Merrienboer, & M. P. Driscoll (Eds.), *Handbook of research on educational communications and technology* (3rd ed., pp. 425–439). New York, NY: Taylor & Francis Group.

Egbert, J., Huff, L., McNeil, L., Preuss, C., & Sellen, J. (2009). Pedagogy, process, and classroom context: Integrating teacher voice and experience into research on technology-enhanced language learning. *The Modern Language Journal, 93*(1), 754–768.

Ellis, R. (2003). *Task-based language learning and teaching.* Oxford, England: Oxford University Press.

Engeström, Y. (1987). *Learning by expanding: An activity–theoretical approach to developmental research.* Helsinki, Finland: Orienta-Konsultit.

Engeström, Y. (2001). Expansive learning at work: Toward an activity-theoretical conceptualization. *Journal of Education and Work, 14*(1), 133–156.

Engeström, Y., & Miettinen, R. (1999). Introduction. In Y. Engeström, R. Miettinen, & R. L. Punamäki (Eds.), *Perspectives on activity theory* (pp. 1–18). Cambridge, England: Cambridge University Press.

Franciosi, S. J. (2011). A comparison of computer game and language-learning task design using flow theory. *CALL-EJ, 12*(1), 11–25.

Franken, M., & Rau, C. (2009). Enabling conditions for professional development of te reo Māori teachers. In S. May (Ed.), *LED 2007: Second International Conference on Language Education and Diversity* [CD-ROM]. Hamilton, New Zealand: The University of Waikato.

Garrett, N. (2009). Computer-assisted language learning trends and issues revisited: Integrating innovation. *The Modern Language Journal, 93*(1), 719–740.

Graves, K. (2000). *Designing language courses: A guide for teachers.* Boston, MA: Heinle & Heinle Publishers.

Golonka, E. M., Bowles, A. R., Frank, V. M., Richardson, D. L., & Freynik, S. (2014). Technologies for foreign language learning: A review of technology types and their effectiveness. *Computer Assisted Language Learning, 27*(1), 70–105.

Gruba, P., & Hinkelman, D. (2012). *Blending technologies in second language classrooms.* Hampshire, England: Plagrave MacMillan.

Guichon, N., Bétrancourt, M., & Prié, Y. (2012). Managing written and oral negative feedback in a synchronous online teaching situation. *Computer Assisted Language Learning, 25*(2), 181–197.

Gurzynski-Weiss, L., & Andrea, R. (2012). Tasks, teacher feedback, and learner modified output in naturally occurring classroom interaction. *Language Learning, 62*(3), 851–879.

Haydn, T., & Barton, R. (2008). 'First do no harm': Factors influencing teachers' ability and willingness to use ICT in their subject teaching. *Computers & Education, 51*, 439–447.

Hedberg, J. G. (2006). E-learning futures? Speculations for a time yet to come. *Studies in Continuing Education, 28*(2), 171–183.

Hutchby, I. (2001). Technologies, texts and affordances. *Sociology, 35*(2), 441–456.

Issroff, K., & Scanlon, E. (2002). Using technology in higher education: An activity theory perspective. *Journal of Computer Assisted Learning, 18*, 77–83.

Jalkanen, J., & Vaarala, H. (2013). Digital texts for learning Finnish: Shared resources and emerging practices. *Language Learning & Technology, 17*(1), 107–124.

Johnson, E. M., Ramanair, J., & Brine, J. (2010). 'It's not necessary to have this board to learn English, but it's helpful': Student and teacher perceptions of interactive whiteboard use. *Innovation in Language Learning and Teaching, 4*(3), 199–212.

Johnson, L., Adams Becker, S., Cummins, M., Estrada, V., Freeman, A., & Ludgate, H. (2013). *NMC Horizon report: 2013 higher education edition.* Austin, TX: The New Media Consortium.

Jonassen, D. H. (2000, October). *Learning as activity.* Paper presented at the Meaning of Learning Project, Learning Development Institute, Presidential Session at AECT, Denver, CO.

Jonassen, D. H., & Land, S. M. (2000). Preface. In D. H. Jonassen & S. M. Land (Eds.), *Theoretical foundations of learning environments* (pp. iii–ix). Mahwah, NJ: Lawrence Erlbaum.

Kaptelinin, V., & Nardi, B. (2006). *Acting with technology: Activity theory and interaction design.* Cambridge, MA: MIT Press. Retrieved from http://www.darrouzet-nardi.net/bonnie/Kaptelinin_Nardi_CHI12_Affordances.pdf

Kaptelinin, V., & Nardi, B. (2012). Affordances in HCI: Toward a mediated action perspective. In *Proceedings of the 2012 ACM Annual Conference on Human Factors in Computing Systems* (pp. 967–976). New York, NY: ACM.

Karabulut, A. (2013). *Factors impacting university-level language teachers' technology use and integration* (Unpublished doctoral dissertation). Iowa State University, Iowa, IA. Retrieved from http://lib.dr.iastate.edu/cgi/viewcontent.cgi?article=4150&context=etd

Karlström, P., & Lundin, E. (2013). CALL in the zone of proximal development: Novelty effects and teacher guidance. *Computer Assisted Language Learning, 26*(5),412–429.

Keengwe, J., & Kang, J-J. (2013). A triangular prism model: Using activity theory to examine online learning communities. *Education and Information Technologies, 18*(1), 85–93.

Kessler, G. (2013). Collaborative language learning in co-constructed participatory culture. *CALICO Journal, 30*(3), 307–322.

Kessler, G., & Plakans, L. (2008). Does teachers' confidence with CALL equal innovative and integrated use? *Computer Assisted Language Learning, 21*(3), 269–282.

Kopcha, T. J. (2012). Teachers' perceptions of the barriers to technology integration and practices with technology under situated professional development. *Computers & Education, 59*, 1109–1121.

Kreijns, K., Vermeulen, M., Kirschner, P. A., van Buuren, H., & van Acker, F. (2013). Adopting the Integrative Model of Behaviour Prediction to explain teachers' willingness to use ICT: A perspective for research on teachers' ICT usage in pedagogical practices. *Technology, Pedagogy and Education, 22*(1), 55–71.

Kuutti, K. (1996). Activity theory as a potential framework for human-computer interaction research. In B. A Nardi (Ed.), *Context and consciousness: Activity theory and human-computer interaction* (pp. 17–44). Cambridge, MA: MIT Press.

Laferrière, T., Hamel, C., & Searson, M. (2013). Barriers to successful implementation of technology integration in educational settings: A case study. *Journal of Computer Assisted Learning, 29*, 463–473.

Lai, K.-W., Khaddage, F., & Knezek, G. (2013). Blending student technology experiences in formal and informal learning. *Journal of Computer Assisted Learning, 29*(5), 414–425.

Lantolf, J. P. (2000). Introducing sociocultural theory. In J. P. Lantolf (Ed.), *Sociocultural theory and second language learning* (pp. 1–27). Oxford, England: Oxford University Press.

Lantolf, J. P., & Appel, G. (Eds.). (1994). *Vygotskyan approaches to second language research.* Norwood, NJ: Ablex.

Lave, J., & Wenger, E. (1991). *Situated learning: Legitimate peripheral participation.* Cambridge, England: Cambridge University Press.

Leont'ev, A. N. (1974). The problem of activity in psychology. *Soviet Psychology, 13*(2), 4–33.

Leont'ev, A. N. (1981). *Problems of the development of mind.* Moscow, Russia: Progress.

Li, Z. (2013). Natural, practical and social contexts of e-Learning: A critical realist account for learning and technology. *Journal of Computer Assisted Learning, 29*(3), 280–291.

136

Liang, R., & Chen, D-T. V. (2012). Online learning: Trends, potential and challenges. *Creative Education, 3*(8), 1332–1335.

Meskill, C., & Anthony, N. (2005). Foreign language learning with CMC: Forms of online instructional discourse in a hybrid Russian class. *System, 33*(1), 89–105.

Mishra, P., & Koehler, M. J. (2006). Technological pedagogical content knowledge: A framework for teacher knowledge. *Teachers College Record, 108*(6), 1017–1054.

Mitchell, R. (2013). What is professional development, how does it occur in individuals, and how may it be used by educational leaders and managers for the purpose of school improvement? *Professional Development in Education, 39*(3), 387–400.

Naidu, S. (2006). *E-Learning: A guidebook of principles, procedures and practices* (2nd ed.). New Delhi, India: Commonwealth Educational Media Center for Asia. Retrieved from http://dspace.col.org/bitstream/123456789/138/1/e-learning_guidebook.pdf

Nardi, B. A. (1996). Studying context: A comparison of activity theory, situated action models, and distributed cognition. In B. A. Nardi (Ed.), *Context and consciousness: Activity theory and human-computer interaction* (pp. 69–102). Cambridge, MA: Massachusetts Institute of Technology.

Nasir, N. S., & Hand, V. M. (2006). Exploring sociocultural perspectives on race, culture, and learning. *Review of Educational Research, 76*(4), 449–475.

Nunn, R. (2006). Designing holistic units for task-based learning. *Asian EFL Journal, 8*(3), 69–93. Retrieved from http://s3.amazonaws.com/academia.edu.documents/30635081/September_2006_Proceedings_final920.pdf?AWSAccessKeyId=AKIAJ56TQJRTWSMTNPEA&Expires=1430852284&Signature=3lX034xCCC%2B0EpgmH45KHkakypw%3D&response-content-disposition=inline#page=122

Perez, M., Peters, E., Clarebout, G., & Desmet, P. (2014). Effects of captioning video comprehension and incidental vocabulary learning. *Language Learning and Technology, 18*(1), 118–141. Retrieved from http://llt.msu.edu/issues/february2014/monteroperezetal.pdf

Prince, P. (2012). Towards an instructional programme for L2 vocabulary: Can a story help. *Language Learning & Technology, 16*(3), 103–120.

Rambe, P. (2012). Activity theory and technology mediated interaction: Cognitive scaffolding using question-based consultation on Facebook. *Australasian Journal of Educational Technology, 28*(8), 1333–1361.

Richards, J. C. (2008). Second language teacher education today. *RELC Journal, 39*(2), 158–177.

Richards, J. C. (2010). Competence and performance in language teaching. *RELC Journal, 41*(2), 101–122.

Richards, J. C., & Rodgers, T. S. (2001). *Approaches and methods in language teaching* (2nd ed.). Cambridge, England: Cambridge University Press.

Robinson, P. (2011). Task-based language learning: A review of issues. *Language Learning, 61*(1), 1–36.

Sagae, A., Kumar, R., & Johnson, W. L. (2009, July). *Scaling up in speaking proficiency by supporting robust learning behaviors*. Paper presented at the AIED 2009 Workshop, Brighton, England.

Salomon, G., & Perkins, D. N. (1998). Individual and social aspects of learning. *Review of Research in Education, 23*(1), 1–24.

Selwyn, N. (2012). Making sense of young people, education and digital technology: The role of sociological theory. *Oxford Review of Education, 38*(1), 81–96.

Sfard, A. (1998). On two metaphors for learning and the dangers of choosing just one. *Educational Researcher, 27*(2), 4–13.

Singh, K., Schrape, J., & Kelly, J. (2012). Emerging strategies for a sustainable approach to professional development. In M. Brown, M. Hartnett, & T. Stewart (Eds.), *Future challenges, sustainable futures. Proceedings Ascilite Wellington* (pp. 833–842). Retrieved from http://www.ascilite.org.au/conferences/wellington12/2012/images/custom/singh,_kuki_-_sustaining_professional.pdf

Smith, C. A., Moyer, C. A., & Schugar, H. R. (2011). Helping teachers develop positive dispositions about technology-based learning: What a brief global learning project revealed. *Journal of Educational Technology Development and Exchange, 4*(1), 1–14.

Steel, C. (2009). Reconciling university teacher beliefs to create learning designs for LMS environments. *Australasian Journal of Educational Technology, 25*(3), 399–420. Retrieved from http://www.ascilite.org.au/ajet/ajet25/steel.html

Sydorenko, T. (2010). Modality of input and vocabulary acquisition. *Language Learning & Technology, 14*(2), 50–73.

Toetenel, L. (2014). Social networking: A collaborative open educational resource. *Computer Assisted Language Learning, 27*(2), 149–162.

van Lier, L. (2004). *The ecology and semiotics of language learning. A sociocultural perspective*. Boston, MA: Kluwer Academic.

Vinagre, M., & Muñoz, B. (2011). Computer-mediated corrective feedback and language accuracy in telecollaborative exchanges. *Language Learning & Technology, 15*(1), 72–103. Retrieved from http://llt.msu.edu/issues/february2011/vinagremunoz.pdf

Voogt, J., Erstad, O., Dede, C., & Mishra, P. (2013). Challenges to learning and schooling in the digital networked world of the 21st century. *Journal of Computer Assisted Learning, 29*(5), 403–413.

Walqui, A. (2006). Scaffolding instruction for English language learners: A conceptual framework. *International Journal of Bilingual Education and Bilingualism, 9*(2), 159–180.

Ware, P., & O'Dowd, R. (2008). Peer feedback on language form in telecollaboration. *Language Learning & Technology, 12*(1), 43–63.

Wertsch, J. V. (1991). A sociocultural approach to socially shared cognition. In L. B. Resnick, J. M. Levine, & S. D. Teasley (Eds.), *Perspectives on socially shared cognition* (pp. 85–100). Washington, DC: American Psychological Association.

Yalden, J. (1987). *Principles of course design for language teaching*. Cambridge, England: Cambridge University Press.

Yang, H. C., & Sun, Y. C. (2013). It is more than knowledge seeking: Examining the effects of OpenCourseWare lectures on vocabulary acquisition in English as a foreign language (EFL) context. *Computer Assisted Language Learning, 26*(1), 1–20.

Zou, B. (2013). Teachers' support in using computers for developing students' listening and speaking skills in pre-sessional English courses. *Computer Assisted Language Learning, 26*(1), 83–99.

Joseph Ramanair
Universiti Malaysia Sarawak
Malaysia

CLAUDIO AGUAYO

9. ACTIVITY THEORY AND ONLINE COMMUNITY EDUCATION FOR SUSTAINABILITY

When Systems Meet Reality

INTRODUCTION

Community Education for Sustainability (EfS) using Information and Communication Technology (ICT) tools and affordances (i.e., possibilities) bring together learning processes occurring within different interconnected dimensions in complex and unpredictable ways. Such complexity calls for the adoption of a systems thinking approach, where the focus is on the existing relationships between the different components composing the learning system.

By adopting a systems thinking approach, the design and implementation of ICT-based online learning systems can account for the ever-changing dynamic complexity that unfolds in multidimensional learning contexts. In this view, learning emerges when learning actors come together in a shared action, or inter-action, which is at the basis of social learning in community EfS using ICT tools. Here the learning process is regarded as an integral outcome of the whole learning system, as properties of systems can only be found as part of the 'whole' and not within its individual 'parts' or components. In this scenario, the role of online learning systems is to act as a facilitator of the learning process by actively promoting meaningful and culturally responsive interaction with community members that can lead to engagement in transformative learning for socio-ecological sustainability.

Although systems thinking can be a useful conceptual framework for the design and implementation of online learning systems for community EfS, it is not a suitable learning theory within a naturalistic approach as it pays little attention to cultural and historical contexts of human activity. It is in this context that Activity Theory can offer useful insights that can be integrated into a systems thinking epistemology, accounting for the overarching multidimensional components of community education for socio-ecological sustainability using ICT tools.

This chapter presents some findings and outcomes from a case study investigating the use of ICT-based online learning systems for community EfS in Chile addressing the socio-ecological sustainability of a lake using Activity Theory as a design guideline an analytical tool.

D. S. P. Gedera & P. J. Williams (Eds.), Activity Theory in Education, 139–151.

THE LANALHUE LAKE IN CHILE

Socio-Ecological Context

The Lanalhue Lake in South Chile is a coastal lake situated in the heart of the Nahuelbuta Range, considered a global biodiversity hotspot due to its high level of endemism (i.e., presence of unique biological species restricted to a particular ecoregion) (Myers, 2005; Smith-Ramírez; 2004; WWF, 1999). The area of the lake covers 3,190 hectares, and is nurtured principally by fluvial waters, in contrast to the majority of Chilean lakes that are nurtured by glaciers and snow waters from the Andes. The Lanalhue Lake is close to two major towns, Cañete and Contulmo, which altogether have around 40,000 inhabitants. There are some other smaller populated areas by the shores of the lake, including some areas with a growing presence of holiday cottages and residential houses. This region of Chile has high levels of poverty and low levels of development, and is considered highly vulnerable in the sense of being at risk of even deeper levels of poverty (MIDEPLAN, 2010). This area of Chile also has a high number of Mapuche people (Chilean indigenous inhabitants) living in the area, including some communities within the catchment of the lake and surrounding valleys.

The main socio-ecological sustainability issue at Lanalhue Lake is the accelerated eutrophication of its waters. This is an increase of the levels of organic nutrients in the lake principally due to factors related to the anthropogenic activity within the catchment of the lake, such as forestry, agriculture, tourism, and the ecological footprint of the local population. This last factor includes an increase of holiday cottages and associated development in some sectors of the lake in the past fifteen years (Etchepare & Furet, 2008). This anthropogenic use of land within the catchment of the lake has contributed to a continuous and significant alteration of the original natural ecological conditions of the Lanalhue Lake. Accumulative deposit of organic nutrients and sedimentation have led to the consequent accelerated process of eutrophication of the lake (Parra et al., 2003; Pauchard et al., 2006).

From a socio-ecological point of view, the most apparent issue worrying local authorities, community members and tourist visitors related to the eutrophication of the lake is the proliferation of the *Egeria densa* (i.e., common name "luchecillo"), an exotic invasive aquatic plant originally from Brazil and the North of Argentina considered an indicator of eutrophication (Lanalhue Sustentable, 2011; Mazzeo, 2005). Besides the profound ecological impacts of the luchecillo in the natural ecosystem of the lake, the proliferation of this invasive plant has created some issues within the local community. These mainly involve negative impacts regarding the recreational use of the lake affecting local members and tourist visitors (i.e., social and economic dimensions), and the practice of indigenous traditions and cultural practices (i.e., cultural dimension) (Etchepare & Furet, 2008; Lanalhue Sustentable, 2011).

Educational Context and Research Intervention

The socio-ecological context at Lanalhue Lake was chosen by Aguayo (2014) as a case study for his doctoral research on the use of ICT tools and affordances for non-formal community education for sustainability. This process included the development of a theoretical model for the design, development and implementation of online learning systems, informed by literature and ideas from education for sustainability, ICT and community education; and framed within a systems thinking and complexity theory in education approach. The main research question to be addressed was *'can the use of ICT assist non-formal education for community understanding and action for sustainability?'*

The research methodology was grounded in a naturalistic research paradigm, principally because the ontological and epistemological standpoints of naturalistic inquiry were appropriate for the purposes of this study. Constructivist and interpretive approaches were adopted to evaluate the learning process occurring among community members, based on their interaction with a socially-constructed and culturally responsive EfS website. Here Activity Theory was used as an analytical framework, in particular for making sense of social and cultural-historical related data.

Following the model for the design and implementation of online learning systems for transformative community education for sustainability (Aguayo, 2014), the EfS website *Lanalhue Sustentable* (http://lanalhuesustentable.cl) was developed to be used as the research instrument. Twenty-four local community members participated in this research process, which included the following four data collection stages: (1) Pre-intervention questionnaire; (2) intervention, i.e., use of the EfS website by participants; (3) post-intervention interview; and (4) a follow-up survey.

Participants were administered a pre-intervention questionnaire aimed to assess some basic demographics, ICT literacy levels, and prior knowledge on the existing local socio-ecological sustainability issues. Immediately after the questionnaire participants were invited to freely browse the EfS website for a period of ten to twenty-five minutes. Following this first visit to the EfS website, a post-intervention interview explored participants' perceptions, change in understanding, and motivations to take action. A final follow-up online survey, five months after their first visit, assessed participants' change in understanding, action taking, and adoption of sustainable living principles and practices over time based on revisits to the EfS website during a period of five weeks.

UNDERSTANDING THE USE OF ONLINE LEARNING SYSTEMS
FOR COMMUNITY SUSTAINABILITY

Online community education for sustainability occurs within larger socio-cultural, educational, technological and ecological dimensions (Aguayo & Eames, in review). As mentioned earlier, from a systems thinking and complexity theory in education perspective both socio-ecological sustainability issues, as well as the design, implementation and use of ICT for community EfS bring together learning in complex and unpredictable ways, which calls for the adoption of a holistic and systems thinking approach (Capra, 2005; Morrison, 2002; Somekh, 2007; Sterling, 2005). This is not only to assist understanding of community EfS phenomena, but also to promote and deliver EfS objectives and goals through the use of online learning systems. In particular, a key consideration here is to approach online learning systems for sustainability as educational facilitators and empowering agents that are capable of self-adapting to the changing conditions of the educational context. Such self-adaptation can be achieved when learning systems are conferred autopoietical (literally 'self-making') properties (Maturana & Varela, 1980), where a dedicated management team can act as the re-configurator of the ICT-based online learning system based on contextuality (Aguayo, 2014; Aguayo & Eames, in review).

From a socio-ecological point of view, communities are social entities embedded within an ecological environment comprising dynamic structures and interactions that are constantly evolving based on their own cultural historicity, which determines them as socio-ecological units in time and space (Aguayo, 2014). Every community is unique, composed of individuals with a range of social and cultural backgrounds, expectations, perspectives, needs, motivations, and conceptions of local socio-ecological issues and challenges (Engeström, 1987; Menzel & Bögeholz, 2008).

Constructivist perspectives emphasise that human experience is socially constructed, where reality is shaped and co-created based on social factors and cultural historicity (Kelly, 1991; Mertens, 2005). Therefore, when community members use and interact with an EfS website, they construct a reality based on the particularities of such experience, as well as on the existing socio-cultural factors and contexts. From a systems thinking perspective, learning emerges from the interaction and coupling process between the components of the learning system, or in this case an EfS website and local community members. The quality of the learning process will be determined by the capacity of the EfS website to facilitate the coupling process (through meaningful interaction), the background that individual learners bring to the process, and the characteristics of the learning context (Jorg, 2000; Sumara & Davis, 1997).

In the context of the research at Lanalhue Lake, systems thinking was easy to accommodate as an epistemological lens to understand phenomena in such a complex socio-technological context, and to a lesser degree, to use as a guideline to develop a research design to study such phenomena. Nonetheless, both systems thinking and complexity theory in education pay little attention to cultural and historical contexts of human activity. As part of the initial research design process, a dilemma arose in how to make sense of data comprising social, cultural, educational, ecological and technological components, while embracing a systems thinking approach. It is in this context that Activity Theory provided conceptual elements in the form of a meta framework that informed and guided data analysis and sense-making.

Using Activity Theory in the Context of Online Community Education for Sustainability

Considering that complex ICT and community EfS phenomena are understood from a systems thinking lens, but learning is approached from interpretivist and constructivist perspectives, Activity Theory as a conceptual framework offered a common ground of inquiry in regard to the use of an EfS website by community members. Conceptual elements from Activity Theory can account for the educational, social, cultural and technological components of human activity, while considering the complexities, change, adaptation and expansion of activity systems (Krasny & Roth, 2010; Yamagata-Lynch, 2007). In this view, people are socially-culturally embedded actors, where cognition is distributed and shaped by the 'technological artefacts' or 'tools' available to the community (Cole & Engeström, 2001).

The basic (first generation) unit of analysis in Activity Theory is a tool-mediated, and goal-oriented, activity system. Here an individual or collective 'subject' engages in an activity through a mediating artefact targeted towards a goal or 'object', producing a resulting 'outcome' (Kaptelinin et al., 1995; Krasny & Roth, 2010). The collective view of an activity system includes the structural, historical, and cultural dimensions, represented by the 'rules', 'community', and 'division of labour' components in Engeström's (1987) second-generation activity system. The third generation activity system involves two or more interacting activity systems, forming a network of activity systems, where 'outcomes' can later become 'subjects' of subsequent activity systems (Engeström, 1999, 2001; Engeström & Sannino, 2010). The novelty here is that this third generation accounts for the dynamism and complexity of human behaviour, characterised by constant transitions, reorganisations, and expansion of activities (Cole & Engeström, 2001). This view of human behaviour aligns closely with ideas from systems thinking and complexity theory in education.

Using an Activity Theory framework in the case of the educational intervention at Lanalhue Lake involved regarding the EfS website as the tool that mediates the learning process for community members towards the expected EfS goals of the system. As represented in Figure 9.1, the expected outcome in the Lanalhue Lake educational activity system is to promote understanding and action regarding existing sustainability issues. According to this representation, individuals (the 'subject') can engage in a learning experience (the 'object') through their interaction with the EfS website (the 'tool' or 'mediating artefact'), which is dependent and influenced by the particularities of the local milieu. Consideration of the educational system underpinned by an EfS website as an activity system is helpful as a guiding principle and theoretical framework for the design of a culturally responsive meaningful EfS website, and for the understanding of its use by local community members.

Through the lens of Activity Theory, the research intervention at Lanalhue Lake was designed considering the activity system from Figure 9.1. In practical terms, this means that the design of the data collection instruments and intervention intended to account for each one of the components of a second-generation activity system, i.e., community structure and historicity, division of labour, social rules, and background of individual learners. Regarding the analytical and interpretive process, other key Activity Theory concepts that were also accounted for included: Object orientedness; internalisation/externalisation processes; hierarchical structure and continuous development of activity systems; multi-voicedness; innovation; expansive transformation; tensions, conflicts and contradictions; environment of the activity system; motivations; dynamics and complexity of real life situations; and networks of interacting activity systems.

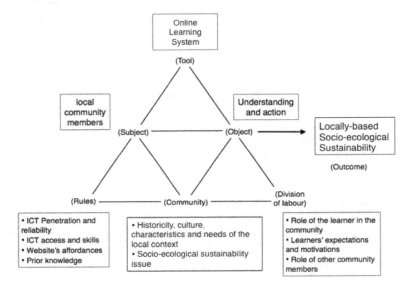

Figure 9.1. Adaptation of Engeström's second-generation model of an activity system in the context of the Lanalhue Lake educational activity system (Source: Aguayo, 2014)

Based on the four data collection phases from the research design, and using the above Activity Theory framework, the use of the EfS website Lanalhue Sustentable by participants was evaluated at three different levels: perceptions towards the EfS website; change in understanding of local socio-ecological issues; and willingness to take action and adopt sustainable living principles and practices. Below are some findings for each one of these evaluative levels that illustrate the application of Activity Theory in the context of the study at Lanalhue Lake.

Participants' Perceptions towards the EfS Website Lanalhue Sustentable

Participants' perceptions regarding the EfS website Lanalhue Sustentable were assessed by means of the post-intervention interview carried out right after participants' first visit to the EfS website. In general, participants reported a good reception and positive perception towards the EfS website. The three most recurrent themes in participants' answers were that the website was locally relevant and meaningful; the website had an attractive and clear message that was easy to understand; and that the website was an evident contribution to the socio-ecological sustainability of Lanalhue Lake. Some participants also stressed that they liked the EfS website 'very much', and that it was 'motivating'.

When asked if they would add or change some of the components and/or sections of the website, the most recurrent feedback was that the website was good and that there was nothing to change. However, some participants indicated that they would add some sections and/or affordances, e.g. activities for kids, extended information on local tourist attractions, or to add graphical prompts such as more photos. For example, from a tourism point of view, Benjamin (i.e., all names reported here are pseudonyms) suggested that the website could include more information on the existing lagoons and waterfalls also existing within the area. Ana stated that she wanted to see the website reaching everywhere, both at the national and international level, and that hopefully the website could one day be translated into other languages. Javiera wanted to see more 'local actors':

> Maybe I would add more local actors, environmental groups that are too passive now and that could be reactivated, authorities and public services... That is something that I would like to see. (Javiera, post-intervention interview)

These answers were later found to be related to the particular socio-cultural backgrounds of participants. Benjamin and Ana were local business people associated with the tourism industry, and Javiera worked in a local government agency, and through her work knew a wide range of relevant institutions and organisations that could have been part of the website (note that the website showcased some local institutions and groups, following design principles from the theoretical model informing its development). From an analytical point of view, the above examples were found to fit the underpinning theory. Community education literature highlights that people pay attention to what is meaningful to them (Brookfield, 1986; Thompson, 2002), and from Activity Theory, what appears to be meaningful to people is shaped by their socio-cultural role and background (Cole & Engeström, 2001; Yamagata-Lynch, 2007).

In another example, many participants reported that the EfS website prompted some motivation such as to re-visit the website, disseminate the website among friends and relatives, and to visit the lake. From an Activity Theory perspective, these motivations from the interaction between the website and participants were taken as *outcomes* of the activity system. Such outcomes could in turn potentially become part of new activity systems from the expansion of the original activity system, where the outcomes of a first activity system are used by other subsequent activity systems to reach other goals (Engeström & Sannino, 2010; Krasny & Roth, 2010). The EfS website was regarded then as being part of a dynamic and expansive activity system nurtured by the EfS website itself, this being one of the expected goals from the design process.

Participants Change in Understanding Regarding Local Socio-Ecological Issues

Following findings from the initial pre-intervention questionnaire, participants were categorised under three typology groups based on their prior level of knowledge, understanding and ecological literacy regarding local socio-ecological issues. This categorisation allowed for the assessment of the change in understanding of participants based on their visits to the website. This was done by comparing initial typologies with data obtained from the post-intervention interviews and follow-up survey, based on an *ecological literacy framework* developed as part of the research for analytical purposes.

Overall, the EfS website promoted change in understanding in the majority of participants regardless their initial typology group. Different types of change in understanding were identified, including 'learning new things', 'deeper understanding', 'thinking shift', 'transformative understanding', and 'acquisition of ecological literacy' (these last three being key EfS goals). Reports also indicated that almost all participants presented some sort of new motivation or interest towards the lake, suggesting that the website was meaningful and relevant to the great majority of participants.

Such positive outcomes regarding the educational role of the EfS website Lanalhue Sustentable can be, in part, traced back to the application of Activity Theory to the design process of the website. A key condition for the design of culturally responsive online learning systems for community education is to achieve a deep understanding of the characteristics and needs of the target audience (Aguayo, 2014). This was achieved in part by following ideas and concepts from Activity Theory during the early stages of this study. A good pre-design understanding of the local conditions and needs of the target community was possible by focusing on those factors highlighted by Activity Theory as crucial in the shaping of socio-cultural activity systems. Understanding the social, cultural, and historical components representing the activity system at Lanalhue Lake (Figure 9.1) contributed to the design of a culturally responsive and meaningful EfS website.

Also, from an analytical point of view based on the activity system, findings from the collective learning process that occurred between the first visit and subsequent re-visits to the EfS website were seen as a process of expansive transformation and continuous development of the activity system (Engeström & Sannino, 2010), while accounting for multi-voicedness, tensions, conflicts, and the dynamics and complexities of real life situations present in the target community. Such representation and interpretation of the socio-ecological context by the target community framed within Activity Theory accommodates and complements well with perspectives from systems thinking and complexity theory in education.

Action Taking for Sustainability

The concepts of action taking and action competence are key in community education for sustainability. In the late 1990s researchers from the Royal Danish School of Educational Studies, Jensen and Schnack (1997), introduced the concept of *action competence* to build learners' ability to act in regard to existing and future sustainability issues and concerns. Within the literature action competence is at the basis of ecologically literate individuals, and a key educational approach to contribute to the real improvement of the natural and socio-ecological environments (Daudi, 2008; Orr, 2004; Sipos et al., 2008). Action competence requires learners to engage with critical thinking, real-life issues, and holistic thinking, as the learner is prompted to make links between inter-related dimensions of sustainability, while considering and actively acting upon the root causes of issues (Jensen, 2002; Jensen & Schnack, 1997).

During the post-intervention interview participants were asked if the EfS website had motivated them to take action towards the sustainability of the lake. The great majority of participants reported a motivation to take action and/or to 'get involved' prompted by the EfS website. For example, Romina, a teacher, stated:

Yes I am motivated, I can teach my students that are under my reach, so they can later educate their parents about it [the luchecillo] at home. (Romina, post-intervention interview)

Rafael indicated that he could educate at the social level by communicating the issue even in a conversation with a friend (Rafael, post-intervention interview).

As mentioned earlier, motivations play a central part in activity systems, as activities contain and are driven by, among other things, motivations directed at a 'goal', or the 'object' of the activity. Findings also indicated that, as expected from Activity Theory, the different types of motivated actions reported by participants were directly related to their individual socio-cultural contexts and reality, making such motivations meaningful to them within their own milieu.

Data from the follow-up survey assessing action taking by participants over time based on their re-visits to the EfS website during the follow-up period indicated that the majority of participants carried out a range of different actions. For example, to disseminate the website among friends, visit the lake, or contact local authorities regarding local socio-ecological sustainability issues. In many cases these actions did not target root causes of sustainability issues, but were considered to be a contribution towards the overall socio-ecological sustainability of the lake. In addition, regarding the adoption of sustainable living principles and practices by participants based on interactions with the EfS website, the majority of them indicated adopting such type of principles and practices at home or at their workplace, with reports being diverse and interpreted based on individual socio-cultural backgrounds.

Considering that during the post-intervention interview the majority of participants reported motivations (as 'outcomes') to take action, and that data from the follow-up survey indicated that the majority of participants did carry out 'actions' of some sort, from Activity Theory it can be said that such early motivations were transformed into precursors ('subjects') of subsequent, or expanded, activity systems, targeted at new 'objects' that were found to be meaningful at the individual level (Engeström, 2001; Engeström & Sannino, 2010). This again refers to the capacity of the EfS website Lanalhue Sustentable to prompt expansive transformation and continuous development of the learning system. More overarching outcomes regarding the role of the EfS website as a mediating artefact capable of facilitating social transformation towards sustainability in an expansive way are further discussed below.

WHEN SYSTEMS MEET REALITY

Community EfS using ICT involves dealing with a wide range of individual learners embedded in a multidimensional, complex and dynamic context, where individuals bring to the learning process their particular backgrounds, motivations, perspectives and needs. This requires online learning systems for sustainability not only to be responsive at the socio-cultural level, but also to satisfy the particularities, whether internal or external, and needs of each individual learner. This can be achieved by offering a wide range and sophistication of content, information and potential affordances (Aguayo, 2014). In this view learning emerges when an individual learner interacts with the online learning system in a process facilitated by the online learning system itself. From an Activity Theory perspective, the different affordances offered by online learning systems, such as an EfS website, are shaped and determined by the individual singularities of the learners, as well as the structure of the learning context.

The EfS website Lanalhue Sustentable was found to promote various types of changes in understanding, action taking, and/or adoption of sustainable living principles and practices grounded in early motivations, which were taken as 'outcomes' of the original activity system prompted by the website. Such initial motivations to get involved, to take action and to adopt sustainable living principles and practices reported during the post-intervention interview were seen as indicators of potential expansive transformation of the EfS website-mediated activity system. As expected from Activity Theory, it appeared that these motivations were related to participants' particular socio-cultural contexts and individual backgrounds, making motivated actions relevant and meaningful within their own particular milieu, linked to their individual historical, socio-cultural, technological, educational and ecological realities. These early motivations, in combination with potential motivations from re-visits to the website, appeared to be at the core of subsequent actions and/or adoptions of sustainable living principles, as inferred from participants' reports.

This collective learning process was seen as the capacity of the educational activity system defined by the EfS website to present characteristics of an expansive learning system, where the outcomes of an initial activity can become precursors of subsequent activities, forming a network of interrelated and successive activity systems (Engeström, 2001; Engeström & Sannino, 2010). Findings also suggested that the key component driving the expansion and continuous development of the original individual activity system defined by the EfS website was its culturally responsive meaningfulness and relevance. There was also indication that the more meaningful and relevant the EfS website was to participants, the more they tended to interact with it and to develop further activities from it. Such levels of meaningfulness and relevance appeared to be dependent on the degree of interest and emotional bond associated with the sustainability issues affecting the wellbeing of the Lanalhue Lake (Aguayo, 2014).

This view of the expansive capacity of the educational activity system based on the EfS website acting as the mediating tool at the core of the learning process accounted for the complexity, unpredictability and dynamism of community-based educational settings. It appeared that the expansion of an initial individual activity system into a network of interrelated activity systems associated with local socio-ecological sustainability issues and challenges was strongly based on the meaningfulness and relevance achieved through the online learning system represented by the EfS website Lanalhue Sustentable.

The representation of the use of the EfS website by community members as an activity system allowed the consideration of complex relationships existing in community-based education for sustainability using ICT. In particular, insights from Activity Theory permitted an account of the influence that the multidimensional context and environment can have on individual learners, influencing the final outcomes of the use of the EfS website. This stresses the importance of understanding the characteristics and needs of the target audience in relation to existing local socio-ecological sustainability issues and challenges, in order to design, develop and implement culturally responsive and meaningful online learning systems for sustainability (Brookfield, 1986; Menzel & Bögeholz, 2008; Thompson, 2002; Tilbury & Wortman, 2008).

In summary, the case study at Lanalhue Lake presented here provided an appropriate case for the use of Activity Theory as a conceptual framework for the design, implementation, understanding and sense-making of longitudinal educational processes occurring at the community level using ICT tools. This approach contributed to linking epistemological views from systems thinking and complexity theory in education with ideas from community education, ICT and EfS within a meta frame of understanding based on socio-cultural, technological, educational and ecological factors. This approach represents a contribution to literature in community EfS as it can provide guidelines to understand, situate and enhance EfS learning processes based on culturally responsive online learning systems for sustainability.

REFERENCES

Aguayo, C., & Eames, C. (in review). A systems thinking approach for the use of ICT tools for community education. *Australian Journal of Environmental Education Research*.

Aguayo, C. (2014). *The use of education for sustainability websites for community education in Chile* (PhD dissertation). University of Waikato, Hamilton, New Zealand.

Brookfield, S. (1986). *Understanding and facilitating adult learning: A comprehensive analysis of principles and effective practices*. Milton Keynes, England: Open University Press.

Capra, F. (2005). Speaking nature's language: Principles for sustainability. In M. Stone & Z. Barlow (Eds.), *Ecological literacy: Educating our children for a sustainable world* (pp. 18–29). San Francisco, CA: Sierra Club Books.

Cole, M., & Engeström, Y. (2001). A cultural-historical approach to distributed cognition. In G. Salomon (Ed.), *Distributed cognitions: Psychological and educational considerations* (pp. 1–46). Cambridge, NY: Cambridge University Press.

Daudi, S. S. (2008). Environmental literacy: A system of best-fit for promoting environmental awareness in low literate communities. *Applied Environmental Education and Communication, 7*(3), 76–82.

Engeström, Y. (1987). *Learning by expanding: An activity-theoretical approach to developmental research*. Helsinki, Finland: Orienta-Konsultit.

Engeström, Y. (1999). *Changing practice through research: Changing research through practice*. Keynote address, 7th Annual International Conference on Post Compulsory Education and Training, Griffith University, Australia.

Engeström, Y. (2001). Expansive learning at work: Toward an activity theoretical reconceptualization. *Journal of Education and Work, 14*(1), 133–156.

Engeström, Y., & Sannino, A. (2010). Studies of expansive learning: Foundations, findings and future challenges. *Educational Research Review, 5*(1), 1–24.

Etchepare, M. S., & Furet, L. R. (2008). *Propuesta de un plan de descontaminación para un lago eutroficado. Caso de estudio: Lago Lanalhue* (Unpublished masters thesis). Universidad del Desarrollo, Santiago, Chile.

Jensen, B. B. (2002). Knowledge, action and pro-environmental behaviour. *Environmental Education Research, 8*(3), 325–334.

Jensen, B. B., & Schnack, K. (1997). The action competence approach in environmental education. *Environmental Education Research, 3*(2), 163–178.

Jorg, T. (2000). About the unexpected: Complexity of learning based on reciprocity and human agency. *Chaos and complexity Theory: Special Interest Newsletter*. Retrieved June 8, 2009, from http://www.udel.edu/aeracc/library/Fall00.htm

Kaptelinin, V., Kuutti, K., & Bannon, L. (1995). *Activity theory: Basic concepts and applications*. Paper presented at the Human-Computer Interaction 5th International Conference, EWHCI, Moscow, Russia.

Kelly, G. (1991). *The psychology of personal constructs*. London, England: Routledge.

Krasny, M. E., & Roth, W.-M. (2010). Environmental education for social ecological system resilience: A perspective from activity theory. *Environmental Education Research, 16*(5), 545–558.

Lanalhue Sustentable. (2011). *Lanalhue sustentable: El luchecillo*. Retrieved from http://lanalhuesustentable.cl/post.php?id=26

Maturana, H. R., & Varela, F. J. (1980). *Autopoiesis and cognition. The realization of the living*. Dordrecht, The Netherlands: D. Reidel Publishing Company.

Mazzeo, N. (2005). *Informe de la visita al lago Lanalhue: Consideraciones para el inicio de un plan de monitoreo y manejo* (Report). Contulmo, Chile: Universidad de la Republica, Montevideo, Uruguay.

Menzel, S., & Bögeholz, S. (2008). The loss of biodiversity as a challenge for sustainable development: How do pupils in Chile and Germany perceive resource dilemmas? *Research in Science Education, 39*, 429–447.

Mertens, D. M. (2005). *Research methods in education and psychology: Integrating diversity with quantitative and qualitative approaches* (2nd ed.). Thousand Oaks, CA: Sage.

Ministerio de Planificación (MIDEPLAN). (2010). *Situación de pobreza a nivel de personas, según provincia.* Pobreza, CASEN 2006. Retrieved November 8, 2010, from http://www.mideplan.cl/casen/Estadisticas/pobreza.html

Morrison, K. (2002). *School leadership and complexity theory.* London, England: RoutledgeFalmer.

Myers, N., & Kent, J. (2005). *The new atlas of planet management.* Berkeley, CA: University of California Press.

Orr, D. (2004). *Earth in mind: On education, environment, and the human prospect* (10th anniversary ed.). Washington, DC: Island Press.

Parra, O., Valdovinos, C., Urrutia, R., Cisternas, M., Habit, E., & Mardones, M. (2003). Caracterización y tendencias tróficas de cinco lagos costeros de Chile central. *Limnetica, 22*(1–2), 51–83.

Pauchard, A., Smith-Ramírez, C., & Ortiz, J. C. (2006). *Informe final estudio de diagnóstico del potencial de conservación de la biodiversidad de la empresa Forestal Mininco en la cordillera de Nahuelbuta.* Concepción, Chile: Universidad de Concepción & Fundación Senda Darwin.

Sipos, Y., Battisti, B., & Grimm, K. (2008). Achieving transformative sustainability learning: Engaging head, hands and heart. *International Journal of Sustainability in Higher Education, 9*(1), 68–86.

Smith-Ramírez, C. (2004). The Chilean coastal range: A vanishing center of biodiversity and endemism in South American temperate rainforests. *Biodiversity and Conservation, 13,* 373–393.

Somekh, B. (2007). *Pedagogy and learning with ICT: Researching the art of innovation.* New York, NY: Routledge.

Sterling, S. (2005). Linking thinking, education and learning: An introduction. In W. Scotland (Ed.), *Linking thinking: New perspectives on thinking and learning for sustainability* (Vol. 1). Surrey, England: WWF-UK, Panda House.

Sumara, D., & Davis, B. (1997). Enactivist theory and community learning: Toward a complexified understanding of action research. *Educational Action Research, 5*(3), 403–422.

Thompson, J. (2002). *Community education and neighbourhood* (Vol. 1). Nottingham, England: NIACE.

Tilbury, D., & Wortman, D. (2008). How is community education contributing to sustainability in practice? *Applied Environmental education and communication, 7*(3), 83–93.

World Wide Fund for Nature (WWF). (1999). *A biodiversity vision for the Valdivian temperate rain forest ecoregion of Chile and Argentina.* Valdivia: WWF Chile.

Yamagata-Lynch, L. C. (2007). Confronting analytical dilemmas for understanding complex human interactions in design-based research from a cultural-historical activity theory (CHAT) framework. *Journal of the Learning Sciences, 16*(4), 451–484.

Claudio Aguayo
AUT University
New Zealand

KAREN POHIO

10. ACTIVITY THEORY TOOLS

What about Organisational Culture?

INTRODUCTION

In an Activity Theory (AT) based study, researchers attend to both the individual elements of the AT model and to perceptions participants have of tensions between elements. Of all the elements analysed, it is arguably the element of tools that plays the most central role in investigations. Engeström (2001) describes tools as the "mediating artifacts" (p. 134) of the AT model. He argues that mediation consistently runs "as the unifying and connecting lifeline" of research based on the principles established by the founders of AT such as Vygotsky, Leontiev and Luria (Engeström, 1999, p. 28). Given the special role of tools, it would seem essential that researchers take time to build a thorough understanding of the complex features that underpin this element. However, there is a predominant focus in AT based studies on one type of tool at the expense of another; and at the expense of the possibilities AT offers education. This suggests the understandings researchers bring to the concept of a tool would benefit from further clarification if notions of what constitutes a 'tool' are to be expanded to incorporate some of the issues that are relevant to education today.

Since the era of Vygotsky, there has been widespread acceptance of many of his findings, notably, his claim that there are two main types of tools: technical (physical) and psychological (conceptual) (Daniels, Cole, & Wertsch, 2007; Engeström, 1999; Kaptelinin & Nardi, 2006; Kozulin, 1998). Vygotsky (1978) maintained each type of tool had different properties, and each provided a focus for human thought and action in different ways. Technical tools he described as being physical in nature (Vygotsky, 1978). They are developed with the aim of supporting humans to bring about change to items in the environment. Psychological tools, on the other hand, have conceptual underpinnings and are aimed at bringing about change in the behaviour and cognitive functioning of humans themselves.

The widespread recognition of Vygotsky's claim that there are two types of tools has been reflected in research. Where research focuses on technical tools, discussion often centres on the conceptual features that underpin the use of the technical tool. Computers, for example, are essentially a technical tool and they are the focus of numerous studies in the field of education (Barab, Barnett, Yamagata-Lynch, Squire, & Keating, 2002; Jonassen, 2004; Kaptelinin & Nardi, 2006; Westberry, 2009). These studies incorporate an analysis of the conceptual features that surround

D. S. P. Gedera & P. J. Williams (Eds.), Activity Theory in Education, 153–165.

the use of computers such as how the knowledge and approach of teachers influences the effectiveness of programmes involving computers. However, it is of concern that psychological tools are seldom the direct focus of studies in their own right. School culture or more broadly, organisational culture, is a tool with few physical features and as such, this chapter argues, is an example of a psychological tool. It is a tool this chapter suggests researchers using AT should take time to consider as a focus of their research on a more regular basis. Organisational culture is, however, a concept relatively new to the literature and one that was not considered at the time of Vygotsky's research (Schein, 1990). Furthermore, the concepts surrounding the features of psychological tools are ones that researchers understandably find difficult to incorporate into their studies without linking them with a technical tool. These issues reinforce the argument that further clarification of the tools concepts would benefit researchers using AT in current studies.

AT AND TOOLS

The notion that human experience and understanding can be shaped through the use of tools is, as noted above, a cornerstone of Vygotskian theory and as such, a foundational principle of AT. It was Vygotsky's interest in tools and their impact on human behaviour and understanding that led to his extensive research in the field of tool mediation. Much of his research focused on the development of psychological tools, a tool Vygotsky (1997) described as one that acts "upon mind and behaviour" (p. 87). In contrast, technical tools, he explained, bring about change in the "object itself" (p. 87). In other words, as Wertsch (1998) clarifies, a psychological tool is inwardly focused while a technical tool has an external orientation. Language, diagrams, maps and signs are examples of psychological tools (Vygotsky, 1978), while hammers, pencils and paper are examples of technical tools. Vygotsky's main thesis was to argue that human consciousness develops through interactions between humans, tools of mediation, and social others. These interactions provide humans with the capacity to develop new meanings of their world, and direct their thoughts and actions. It is the concept of a tool being mainly inwardly focused that many researchers seem to grapple with.

PSYCHOLOGICAL TOOLS

Wertsch (1998), an eminent scholar in the field of Vygotskian theory, helps clarify the concept of a psychological tool. He explains that the function of a psychological tool is not simply to facilitate existing mental functions but to transform mental functions (p. 79). Language, as an example of a psychological tool, does not bring about changes in the human mind in a predetermined manner. Rather, its development is a process where change takes place in the internal tools of the individual in stages unique to each individual; and in ways that are transformational to the manner by which each individual thinks and behaves.

Kozulin (1998), another well recognised scholar in the field of Vygotskian theory, reinforces the power of psychological tools as he describes them as artifacts that "transform the unmediated interaction of the human being with the world into mediated interaction" (p. 4). They are, he goes on to explain, "symbolic" (p. 1) in nature. They are artifacts with symbolic properties that remain meaningless without human input. Maps, for example, contain a set of symbols that require the experience and knowledge of the person using them to bring them meaning. People bring meaning to psychological tools through their cognitive capacities and also through the support they receive from others in their social world.

Psychological tools by their very nature are social in origin or as Wertsch (1985) explains "individuals have access to psychological tools by virtue of being part of a sociocultural milieu" (p. 80). The history, culture and ongoing social interactions people experience as part of living in a society or belonging to an organisation shape the meanings people bring to the psychological tools they encounter. Eventually, their experiences create 'mental maps' which lead them towards acting or thinking in certain ways. People come to understand, for example, that a graph can symbolise a numerical count and that it will include symbols for quantities such as percentages or numbers. They recognise these symbols as having meaning and react to them through the use of the psychological tools they have developed during cognitive transformations and social interactions. In other words, the process of meaning making has both internal and external components.

External resources such as other people support a process of internal comprehension or what Vygotsky referred to as internalisation. Internalisation is a process of mediation but mediation in the head rather than through external means. It is at the stage of internalisation that meaning is created and new thought processes developed, or existing thought processes amended. In the course of studying the concept of internalisation, Vygotsky together with his colleague Leontiev, spent time focusing on how it came to be that individuals are able to master some mental processes more ably than others. Over time some processes require less deliberate mediation and move into a state of unconsciousness or mental maps that guide individuals' behaviours and thoughts. It was during this investigation that Vygotsky's Zone of Proximal Development (ZPD) came to prominence.

The ZPD is a concept with similar meaning to scaffolding in that it relates to the building of knowledge through progressions that extend the learner in manageable steps. Knowledge builds like scaffolding on a building site whereby strong foundations allow ongoing growth or height to be added to the scaffold. Foundational knowledge eventually becomes taken-for-granted ways of doing things and foundations provide a platform that supports further growth. Similarly, when new knowledge is practised often, it becomes taken-for-granted ways of knowing about the world and it can also be added on to. A musician, for example, needs sheets of music to begin with then after time and practice can progress to being able to play pieces of music without visual aids. The key to effective scaffolding, according to Vygotsky (1978), is adult guidance or the support of more capable peers.

What is of interest in is this description of the development of psychological tools is that it has many synergies with descriptions of organisational culture. It too has been described as the acquisition of new knowledge through the support of key personnel who aim to build a team of people who become so familiar with certain ways of working that they become taken-for-granted ways of operating in their organisation (Schein, 2010). However, organisational culture is a tool rarely included in lists of examples of psychological tools and furthermore, it is not a tool often used as a focus of AT based studies. This may in part be because, as with the concept of psychological tools, organisational culture incorporates complex features.

ORGANISATIONAL CULTURE

According to Hofstede (1991), there are three types of culture: national, occupational and organisational. He defines organisational culture as "the collective programming of the mind which distinguishes the members of one organisation from another" (Hofstede, 1991, p. 262). Schein (2010, p. 2), an eminent scholar in the field of organisational culture, also identifies different types of culture. He describes cultures that exist at macro levels, such as national or ethnic cultures and those that exist at micro levels, such as the small groups that develop within organisations. Many years ago, Schein (1992) drafted a definition of organisational culture that has remained prominent in the literature today. He described it as:

A pattern of shared basic assumptions that the group learned as it solved its problems of external adaption and internal integration that has worked well enough to be considered valid, and therefore, to be taught to new members as the correct way to perceive, think and feel in relation to those problems. (p. 12)

Notably, given the previous discussion related to psychological tools and the suggestion that organisational culture could be considered a valid example of a psychological tool, it is of interest that Schein (2010) also defines organisational culture as a "mental map" (p. 29) or a set of "taken for granted" (p. 27) ways of being that guide people's actions and thoughts. Moreover, Schein is not alone in describing organisational culture with these terms. Erickson (1987), another eminent scholar in the field of organisational culture, also describes it as "a system of ordinary, taken-for-granted meanings and symbols with both explicit and implicit content that is, deliberately and non-deliberately, learned and shared among members of a naturally bounded social group" (p. 12).

In essence, these definitions of organisational culture all draw attention to the notion that organisational culture incorporates a range of dimensions; some of them obvious, but many less so. The obvious features include the deliberate actions that are usually undertaken by leaders with the aim of directing members of an organisation towards certain ways of thinking. Deliberate actions may include the development of symbolic artifacts such as vision statements, mottos or displays of achievement. The less obvious features of organisational culture are the taken-for granted ways of being that develop in an organisation. They are behaviours that are often described as 'just the way we do things around here'.

In both the descriptions of psychological tools and those of organisational culture, the existence of two dimensions is regularly noted, hence the suggestion that there is a strong link between the two concepts. However, it is a link many AT researchers are overlooking despite the evidence that culture influences every aspect of an organisation (Fullan, 2010; Ramsey, 2008; Schein, 2010; Schoen & Teddlie, 2008). Culture can affect relationships, goals, outcomes and so forth. It requires attention in research, and given the all encompassing nature of culture, it seems particularly suited to AT based research where the focus is on the organisation as a whole.

There are a number of reasons why organisational culture may not be regularly considered as a focus in AT based studies. Some of these reasons were noted earlier. They relate to descriptions of psychological tools not having significantly changed from the time of Vygotsky's research. In his description of psychological tools, Vygotsky (1978) referred to signs, symbols and text. Kozulin (1998), a well-recognised scholar in the field of psychological tools also refers to items such as signs, symbols, texts, formulae, and graphic-symbolic devices when describing psychological tools. Wertsch (1985), another well recognised AT scholar uses examples that are similar to those of Vygotsky and Kozulin as his examples include language, signs and text. While Vygotsky did make extensive reference to culture in his writings, his references were not specifically to organisational culture; and certainly not as an example of a psychological tool. Vygotsky's focus was on national culture which is understandable given the context of his work which was taking place during a time of turmoil in Soviet Russia. It was a time where cultural divisions were dominating the direction of both research and daily living (Wertsch & Tulviste, 1992). However, it is also not surprising that Vygotsky did not consider organisational culture in his examples of psychological tools given that, as noted previously, organisational culture is a relatively new term to the literature. Schein (1990) explains that although terms such as "group norms" and "climate" have been appearing in the literature since around the middle of last century, the term "organisational culture" only became used with regularity towards the end of the twentieth century (Schein, 1990, p. 109). Given that organisational culture has been a growing phenomenon in more recent years, however, it seems time it became recognised as an example of a psychological tool.

The concern with not including organisational culture as an example of a psychological tool is that it tends not to be a concept current in the minds of researchers using an AT based approach. It is, however, important that this situation changes given that Schein (2010), for example, refers to organisational culture as the key element in the success of an organisation. Fullan (2011), a scholar with vast experience in the field of school improvement also argues that the "right drivers" for change "focus directly on changing the culture of the organisation and that is why they work" (p. 108). Likewise, Deal and Peterson (2009), scholars who have written extensively about school improvement, argue that "the culture of an enterprise plays a dominant role in exemplary performance" (p. 1). The inclusion of culture in AT analysis could illuminate many of the reasons for tensions that are limiting the capacity of an organisation such as a school attaining its goals and bringing forth improvements in critical areas such as student achievement.

Another reason researchers using AT may have for not considering organisational culture in their research design relates to the intangible nature of organisational culture. As with the previous argument related to psychological tools, the lack of a direct item to focus on may limit the understanding researchers have of the features they can focus on during their investigation phase. Breaking organisational culture into a set of identifiable levels, however, is a means of adding clarity to the concept.

LEVELS OF ORGANISATIONAL CULTURE

Following extensive research in the field of organisational culture, Schein (2010) developed a continuum of what he believes are its levels. He suggests organisational culture has three levels: artifacts, espoused values and basic underlying assumptions. His examples of artifacts include an organisation's published list of values, their physical environment, the clothes people wear and their observable rituals. He describes espoused values as the justifications members of the organisation make about their strategies, goals and philosophies. They relate to what ought to be as distinct from how things work in reality. Espoused values exist at a conscious level and according to Schein, can move to the next level or basic assumptions through the work of leaders whose efforts are seen to 'work' by members of the organisation. Ideas or solutions to problems become the norm or accepted way of working when they get to the stage of not being questioned or having to be repeatedly justified. It is when they become just the way things are done in that organisation and they present at more of an unconscious level and they can be referred to as basic assumptions. In a school situation, for example, an espoused value may be to try to build better relationships with the school community. This value may eventually transform into a taken-for-granted way of behaving or a basic assumption when members of the organisation come to accept it as a favoured way of working. Members demonstrate their belief in the value by regularly espousing its virtues and importantly, undertaking practices that reinforce the value of promoting school-community relationships.

The key focus of much of Schein's work has been on the role leaders' play in bringing about change in organisational culture and at which level they should direct their attention. This focus would have implications for AT researchers who are considering adopting organisational culture as a tool in their research framework.

ORGANISATIONAL CULTURE AND AT RESEARCH

Schein (1992) argues for the importance of leaders ensuring they attend not to the first level of culture but to deeper levels. He claims "the essence of culture lies in the pattern of basic underlying assumptions, and once one understands those, one can easily understand the other more surface levels and deal appropriately with them" (p. 26). In other words, Schein is arguing that the focus for leaders who wish to bring change and improvement to their organisation is to understand the underlying assumptions held by stakeholders in the organisation and to focus on change at this deep level. The issue for researchers, however, is to determine whether it is possible to investigate underlying assumptions or whether symbolic artifacts and espoused values provide a key to the interpretation of underlying assumptions. If this is the case, artifacts at levels one and two would be at the heart of their study.

There is a vast amount of research indicating that symbolic artifacts and espoused values can provide a reliable key to understanding underlying assumptions. Deal and Peterson (2009), for example, paid particular attention to the role of symbols in determining and reinforcing the culture of schools. They describe symbols as representing a school's "intangible cultural values and beliefs" (p. 33) and argue that symbols infuse the culture of schools with meaning because they constantly remind staff of the school's cultural values. Deal and Peterson question the depth of understanding people have when they refer to symbols as "fluff" rather than as the "stuff of leadership and culture" (p. 34). They cite mission statements, displays of students' work, banners, displays of past students' achievements and the physical layout and appearance of the school as examples of symbolic artifacts used by schools to promote their culture.

Deal and Peterson (2009), it must also be noted, are clear in their stance that symbols alone do not determine the culture of a school. Symbols require a living presence if they are to be effective in building and reinforcing culture. Meaning is reinforced, they explain, through actions and more so, through the repeated action of members of the organisation. School leaders who wish to spread the cultural values they believe are important to the school community are advised to broadcast the school's values on a regular basis, and through a range of medium such as at assemblies and in school newsletters. These actions are required if symbolic artifacts and espoused values are to have an opportunity to move to a deeper level, or what Schein referred to as shared assumptions.

Prosser (2010), another scholar with extensive experience in the field of school culture, also agrees that culture is represented through the presence of a range of symbolic artifacts. His research led him to analyse features of schools such as their architecture, resources and teaching spaces. He also found that symbolic features provided indicators of the cultural values of the school although he too added that while visual analysis of school culture was enlightening, research also needs to take into account the broader contextual factors that determine the choice of physical artifacts.

The notion that broader contextual factors influence the choice of symbolic artifacts is one that clearly fits with an AT based approach. AT provides a lens that allows researchers to zoom in on specific elements while also withdrawing their lens to consider some of the wider contextual issues that may be creating tensions that are limiting to the success of an organisation. In other words, AT is both specific and widespread in its focus. It examines specific elements but also how these align or create tensions within the organisation as a whole. As an example, tensions may be identified by participants in a research study as being an outcome of their organisation's choice of a computer programme. The researcher is likely to have focused some attention on participants' perspectives of the computer programme during the investigation phase. During analysis, the researcher (possibly together with research participants) could then withdraw their lens of analysis to take into account how wider contextual features of the organisation such as its rules, divisions of labour and perceptions stakeholders have of the goal or vision of the organisation may be impacting on, or being impacted by, the chosen computer programme. This analysis may highlight a broader issue such as that there are differing viewpoints of the organisation's vision. These different viewpoints may have resulted in participants having diverse priorities for a computer programme. This tension would limit the capacity for participants to be using the resources they have available to them in a manner that is fully supportive of the vision of the organisation. It would be restricting their capacity to move towards what Vygotsky described as a level of internalisation of the vision. In other words, a focus on an artifact in an AT based study is not limited to the artifact alone. Studies involve analysis of the deeper levels of the organisation as well.

Where AT is also advantaged is that while a focus on symbolic artifacts fits with understandings related to the tools element, the concept of underlying assumptions fits with the concept of the object of the activity. The researcher together, where possible, with participants from the organisation, is aiming to determine whether symbolic artifacts are supporting subjects to move towards internalisation of the organisation's vision. If, for example, school leaders believe it is important to improve the involvement of the community with the school, as in the case study described below, it would be the aim of the analysis to determine the extent to which symbolic artifacts are supporting the development of this vision, and where tensions exist. The following case study provides an example of AT being used to analyse an activity where symbolic artifacts are the tools of investigation and the development of a caring school community is the object.

CASE STUDY

A research project that aimed to investigate tools of communication used by schools to facilitate communication with their school communities was undertaken by the author of this chapter (Pohio, 2014). The research was based in New Zealand and involved three case studies. At each of the case study sites, schools were using different types of tools to facilitate communication between school and home. One school was using portfolios, another mobile phones, and at the third school, culture was identified as their tool of communication. It is the third school (School H) that is the focus of this section.

School H

School H is located in a low socio-economic region in the northern part of New Zealand. The school was chosen because it was claimed by the Principal and school staff that they had limited need for physical tools to communicate between home and school. Rather, they believed their school culture was their tool of communication. It was a culture the Principal described as one that made people feel "welcome in the school" (Pohio, 2014, p. 233). The Principal's belief that the school had a welcoming culture was reinforced by family members who made comments such as "I've always found the teachers really approachable" and "I find it a family orientated school" (Pohio, 2014, p. 252).

Adding this case study to the research offered an opportunity to investigate school culture as a tool of communication and determine whether there were features of the culture at this school that helped make it a particularly effective tool of communication. Many schools claim they fit into the category of having a caring culture so the researcher aimed to determine whether there were symbolic artifacts or espoused values that were influencing ways of behaving and thinking at the school that were particularly effective, and most importantly, what those artifacts looked like. This made the research focus both broad and specific. The researcher aimed to include specific artifacts in the investigation but also withdraw the lens of analysis to consider how any artifacts described by participants were impacted on and were impacted by wider contextual factors in the school environment. A total of 50 interviews were conducted with a range of participants including school leaders, teachers, school support staff, students, and family members. AT was used to underpin the research framework and data analysis stages.

The first and arguably most significant finding of the research was that at School H they had a simple and effective motto statement. It was a statement that was repeated many times a day by all members of the school community. The motto 'we look after each other' provided a means of reinforcing the caring nature of the school in a very deliberate and overt manner.

Another contributing factor to the development of the school culture was that the school Principal made a deliberate effort to constantly reinforce the caring culture. He was visible in the playground at the start and end of each school day. He had taken the word 'staff' off the tea room door to ensure the community felt comfortable about making themselves a cup of tea and interacting with members of the teaching staff. He built decks to bring classrooms together so the physical spaces created more of what he termed a "village" atmosphere (Pohio, 2014, p. 232). Most importantly, he continually espoused the importance of community involvement and was willing to walk the talk to ensure the vision of a community school could become a reality. His stance was reinforced in his statement that as a staff, they should be giving families "the avenues to get to you rather than the other way around" (Pohio, 2014, p. 233). His leadership was a critical component contributing to the reinforcement of the caring culture.

The teachers and school support staff were also active in promoting the caring school culture. They had identified strengths between them such as an ability in behaviour management or in sports. They used those strengths to support each other and share responsibilities. The students were also very aware of the school motto statement. It was something students from five years of age could understand and put into practice. The caring school culture had many dimensions for the students. They believed they looked after each other by being kind to others, helping peers with their work and looking after students who were unhappy. The dimensions of their culture ranged from social to academic and also emotional in nature.

The example of this school using carefully chosen artifacts such as their school motto statement and a communal like physical environment to scaffold and direct members of their school community towards the understanding that they were a caring school exemplifies the powerful influence that symbolic artifacts and espoused values (Schein's levels one and two) can have on basic assumptions. In the interviews with all stakeholders, there was continual reference to the caring culture of the school and to it being 'just the way we do things around here'. It was a culture that had permeated into the mental maps of the members of the school community, and one that research participants reported had become taken-for-granted ways of thinking and behaving at the school. This suggests the culture was not only an espoused value but it had become an underlying assumption held by members of the school community.

In the analysis of this case study, the symbolic features of the school culture were identified as AT tools. Analysis illuminated many alignments between these tools and all other AT elements. The motto statement, for example, was an unwritten rule and one that was accepted as a guide to thoughts and actions. It was a rule that was being put into practice on a regular basis. Alignments between elements also demonstrated a shared understanding of the object of developing a caring school culture. It was a guiding principle that all members of the school community took some personal responsibility for. They demonstrated an acceptance and alignment with this principle through their espoused values and what they described as their approach to others in their school community. The culture had become an unconscious understanding that was shared between participants. Furthermore, all members of the school community expressed the view that their symbolic artifacts played a significant role in embedding their understanding of their school culture.

IMPLICATIONS FOR USERS OF AT IN EDUCATIONAL CONTEXTS

Both the case study example discussed above and the work of Deal and Peterson (2009), and that of Prosser (2010) demonstrate that by focusing on the symbolic representations of culture together with the values espoused by participants, it may be possible to uncover the basic assumptions held by members of an organisation. Analysis and discussion with research participants can bring the focus towards Schein's third level of organisational culture; a level, we are reminded he believes is an essential factor in understanding how to bring about change and improvement in an organisation.

Not only does this discussion demonstrate that organisational culture can be considered a valid example of a tool for use in AT based research, it highlights that organisational culture may not be as challenging to research as many may assume. If the focus is placed on the observable levels of organisational culture such as a school motto statement or the values espoused by members of the school community, a picture of the basic assumptions held by school personnel can emerge. This can lead to rich and meaningful discussions that may be the source of innovation and change.

An important point that the case study and the work of the scholars discussed above also emphasise is that while leaders play an important role in the development of school culture, it is not their efforts alone that determine the extent to which culture can become embedded in the thoughts and actions of stakeholders. Deal and Peterson (2009) argue that "leaders shape culture" (p. viii) and Fullan (2011) states that it is the leader who is the "key to get things going" (p. 53). While it is regularly accepted that leaders play a central role, AT affords researchers opportunities to analyse and discuss the interpretations of the culture held by other participant groups, and the levels at which various stakeholders appear to have accepted the culture as their way of being. A leader's espoused belief that the school community is a valued resource may be found, for example, to be one that is not shared by members of the community. This could be for reasons such as community members feeling their contributions are not valued, or that they are not being provided with regular opportunities to communicate with school personnel. AT can help school leaders to understand where areas of tension exist and this can lead to efforts that may change practice. It is, however, essential that a range of participants are involved in the research in order to uncover tensions. AT is advantaged in this respect as it offers a framework for managing data collection when a large amount of data is required as would be the case in investigations of organisational culture involving multiple participant groups. Furthermore, the AT diagram provides a visual framework that can support discussions that would otherwise be difficult to conduct given the large amount of data required to be presented to stakeholders.

CONCLUSION

Researchers using AT should aim to develop an understanding of the historical underpinnings of the theory and the various dimensions of the elements of its framework. However, there is a tendency for researchers to overlook some types of tools as the mediating artifact of their AT based study. Organisational culture has been highlighted in this article as a tool that can have a powerful influence on the success of an organisation and yet it is one that is rarely the focus of AT research. Some of the reasons for its exclusion from studies include that although it is a tool with many of the characteristics of a psychological tool, it is not a tool referred to in examples of psychological tools. This is possibly because organisational culture has been a recent addition to literature and not one considered in the era in which AT has its foundations. It is also a tool that may not be considered due to its intangible nature. The intangible features of organisational culture can create challenges for researchers as they try to decide on the focus of their research.

The limited attention being given to organisational culture in AT research is a situation that requires attention given it is argued that organisational culture can be the element that determines a school's readiness to bring about improvement to their ways of working (Schein, 2010). AT offers many advantages for research focusing on organisational culture because its underlying principles can support researchers to account for the different dimensions of culture and furthermore, the element of object provides a means of illuminating whether tensions may be limiting the embedding of culture at a deeper level. It is the determination of the depth of culture that Schein (2010) argues is the key to bringing about lasting change and improvement in an organisation.

A feature of AT research is also that it allows for the inclusion of a range of stakeholders. This is essential in studies where issues of power and communication can impact on the effectiveness of the activity. It is becoming a more commonly used approach by researchers adopting an AT lens to involve participants throughout the research process from design stage to the stage of interpretation of findings (Engeström, 2008; Kaptelinin & Nardi, 2012; Yamagata-Lynch, 2010). This is an approach that would suit research focusing on organisational culture where different perspectives are required to develop a comprehensive understanding of the organisation's context.

Researchers using an AT lens to investigate organisational culture are advised to focus on the more tangible levels of culture such as symbolic artifacts and espoused values as attention to these items can lead to discussions that determine the extent to which participants have embedded the culture of their organisation into their unconscious thoughts and their actions. It is at this level that the extent to which subjects are moving towards achieving the longer term object of their activity can be determined. Such a discussion may lead to school improvement at a deep and lasting level.

REFERENCES

Barab, S., Barnett, M., Yamagata-Lynch, L., Squire, K., & Keating, T. (2002). Using activity theory to understand the systemic tensions characterizing a technology-rich introductory astronomy course. *Mind, Culture, and Activity, 9*(2), 76–107. doi:10.1207/S15327884MCA0902_02

Daniels, H., Cole, M., & Wertsch, J. (Eds.). (2007). *The Cambridge companion to Vygotsky.* New York, NY: Cambridge University Press.

Deal, T. E., & Peterson, K. D. (2009). *Shaping school culture: Pitfalls, paradoxes, and promises* (2nd ed.). San Francisco, CA: Jossey-Bass.

Engeström, Y. (1999). Activity Theory and individual and social transformation. In Y. Engeström, R. Miettinen, & R. Punamaki (Eds.), *Perspectives on activity theory* (pp. 19–38). Cambridge, England: Cambridge University Press.

Engeström, Y. (2001). Expansive learning at work: Toward an activity theoretical reconceptualization. *Journal of Education and Work, 14*(1), 133–156. doi:10.1080/13639080020028747

Engeström, Y. (2008). Enriching Activity Theory without shortcuts. *Interacting with computers, 20*(2), 256–259.

Erickson, F. (1987). Conceptions of school culture: An overview. *Educational Administration Quarterly, 23*(4), 11–24.

Fullan, M. (2010). The awesome power of the principal. *Principal, 89*(4), 10–15.

Fullan, M. (2011). *Change leader: Learning to do what matters most.* San Francisco, CA: Jossey-Bass.

Hofstede, G. (1991). *Cultures and organizations: Software of the mind.* London, England: McGraw-Hill.

Jonassen, D. H. (Ed.). (2004). *Handbook of research on educational communications and technology* (2nd ed.). London, England: Lawrence Erlbaum Associates.

Kaptelinin, V., & Nardi, B. (2006). *Acting with technology: Activity Theory and interaction design.* Cambridge, MA: MIT Press.

Kaptelinin, V., & Nardi, B. (2012). *Activity Theory in Human Computer Interaction (HCI): Fundamentals and reflections.* San Rafael, CA: Morgan and Claypool.

Kozulin, A. (1998). *Psychological tools: A sociocultural approach to education.* Cambridge, MA: Harvard University Press.

Pohio, K. (2014). *An Activity Theory based investigation of communication and connection between families, students, and school* (PhD thesis). University of Waikato, Hamilton, New Zealand. Retrieved from http://researchcommons.waikato.ac.nz/handle/10289/8926

Prosser, J. (2010). Visual methods and the visual culture of schools. *Visual Studies, 22*(1), 13–30.

Ramsey, R. D. (2008). *Don't teach the canaries not to sing: Creating a school culture that boosts achievement.* Thousand Oaks, CA: Corwin Press.

Schein, E. (1990). Organizational culture. *American Psychologist, 45*(2), 109–119.

Schein, E. (1992). *Organizational culture and leadership.* New York, NY: Doubleday.

Schein, E. (2010). *Organizational culture and leadership* (4th ed.). San Francisco, CA: Jossey-Bass.

Schoen, L., & Teddlie, C. (2008). A new model of school culture: A response to a call for conceptual clarity. *School Effectiveness and School Improvement, 19*(2), 129–153.

Vygotsky, L. (1978). Mind in society: The development of higher psychological processes. In M. Cole, V. John Steiner, S. Scribner, & E. Souberman (Eds.), *Mind in society.* Cambridge, MA: Harvard University Press.

Vygotsky, L. (1997). Problems of the theory and history of psychology. In R. W. Rieber & J. Wollock (Eds.), *The collected works of L.S. Vygotsky* (Vol. 3). New York, NY: Plenum Press.

Wertsch, J. (1985). *Vygotsky and the social formation of mind.* Cambridge, MA: Harvard University Press.

Wertsch, J. (1998). *Mind as action.* New York, NY: Oxford University Press.

Wertsch, J., & Tulviste, P. (1992). L. S. Vygotsky and contemporary developmental psychology. *Developmental Psychology, 28*(4), 548–557.

Westberry, N. (2009). *An activity theory analysis of social epistemologies within tertiary-level elearning environments* (PhD thesis). University of Waikato, Hamilton, New Zealand. Retrieved from http://hdl.handle.net/10289/4184

Yamagata-Lynch, L. (2010). *Activity systems analysis methods: Understanding complex learning environments.* New York, NY: Springer.

Karen Pohio
University of Waikato
New Zealand

SECTION IV

APPLICATION OF ACTIVITY THEORY IN UNDERSTANDING TEACHERS' PCK AND CURRICULUM DEVELOPMENT

CHRIS EAMES

11. EXPLORING TEACHER PEDAGOGICAL CONTENT KNOWLEDGE (PCK) DEVELOPMENT USING CORES (CONTENT REPRESENTATIONS)

INTRODUCTION

This chapter describes how Activity Theory (AT) was used as a framework for examining the development of pedagogical content knowledge (PCK) for early career secondary teachers in science and technology. In this study, AT was proposed as a promising lens through which the complexity of the education context and the nature of teacher work could be explored as these beginning teachers built their PCK. PCK is a blend of content knowledge and pedagogical knowledge that is built up over time and experience and is seen to be unique to each teacher (Shulman, 1987).

The academic construct of PCK recognises that teaching is not simply the transmission of concepts and skills from teacher to students but rather a complex and problematic activity that requires many and varied "on the spot" decisions and responses to students' ongoing learning needs. It is this complexity, and the interactional and dialectical nature of PCK, that suggested that AT was a good choice for exploring its development. This can be explained in part by the proposition that PCK is made up of five components that involve a set of knowledges (Magnusson, Krajcik, & Borko, 1999). In these authors' view, an experienced teacher's PCK includes their knowledge of: subject content (and beliefs about it, and how to teach it); curriculum (what and when to teach); assessment (why, what and how to assess); students' understanding of the subject; and instructional strategies.

AT offered the potential to examine how these knowledges can be seen through a process of change such as the development of PCK, as the dialectical tensions which exist within a school/classroom are accounted for by the dynamic nature of AT (Engeström, 2001; Roth, 2004). This permits an examination of how the activities of teaching and learning within a formal school system, and in particular the interactions between these activities may shape, enable or inhibit this PCK development.

PCK Development in Science and Technology

It has been argued (Kind, 2009; Rohaan, Taconis, & Jochems, 2009) that expert teachers are not born with PCK, and that student teachers need to acquire the

D. S. P. Gedera & P. J. Williams (Eds.), Activity Theory in Education, 169–181.

teaching skills and knowledge to become experienced professionals in their fields. Graduates of science and technology entering secondary teacher education courses may be unaware of the learning challenges that lie ahead for them as beginning teachers (Cowie, Moreland, Jones, & Otrel-Cass, 2008; Loughran, Mulhall, & Berry, 2008). Their understanding that effective teaching is a skilled and purposeful activity involving complex processes of pedagogical reasoning and action may be limited (Shulman, 1987). It has been shown that beginning science teachers can also lack a deep conceptual understanding of their subject matter, with disjointed and muddled ideas about particular topics (Loughran et al., 2008), despite these teachers having studied science at undergraduate degree level. The role of PCK development in general design and technology education has also recently been explored (De Miranda, 2008; Jones & Moreland, 2004; Rohaan et al., 2009) as well as in different disciplines of technology such as Information and Communication Technology (Koehler & Mishra, 2005). Significant variations in the content of technology education between countries provides a challenge for understanding the development of PCK for beginning technology teachers, despite some researchers such as McCormack (1997, 2004) having identified the inter-related nature of procedural and technical knowledge in technology education.

One problem in understanding how to develop PCK for these beginning teachers has been the absence of concrete examples of what an expert teacher's PCK might look like, since this highly specialised form of professional knowledge is embedded in individual teachers' classroom practice (Padilla, Ponce-de-León, Rembado, & Garritz, 2008) and not often shared within the teaching community of practice. To address this problem, in the mid-2000s, some science teacher education researchers in Australia devised an approach to help early career teachers to conceptualise their professional learning in order to create a foundation for their own PCK development (Loughran, Berry, & Mullhall, 2006). Loughran et al. explored the PCK of highly regarded science teachers for particular topics in junior secondary science to see if they could identify the pedagogical tools that guided their work as science teachers. They linked these ideas with content knowledge to produce a conceptual tool known as a Content Representation (CoRe), that made explicit the different dimensions of, and links between, knowledge of content, teaching and learning about a particular topic. The CoRe, represented in table form (see Table 11.1), was designed to portray an overview of a teacher's PCK related to the teaching of a particular topic. It contains a set of 5–8 enduring ideas about a particular topic at the head of the columns, and a set of pedagogical questions for each row.

CoRes have since been used in pre-service science teacher education studies with beginning teachers. In a study by Loughran et al. (2008), a pre-service educator provided student teachers with CoRes created by expert teachers and then invited them to construct their own examples. The findings from this study indicated that using CoRes to frame their thinking about the links between science content and pedagogy did help the student teachers to gain a more sophisticated view about learning to teach science. In another study which sought to promote science student

Table 11.1. Sample CoRe matrix

	Enduring idea 1	Enduring idea 2	Enduring idea 3
Why is it important for the students to know this			
Why is it important for students to know about this			
What else you know about this idea (that you do not intend students to know yet)			
Difficulties connected with teaching this idea			
Knowledge about student thinking which influences teaching about this idea			
Other factors that influence your teaching of this idea			
Teaching procedures			
Ways of ascertaining student understanding or confusion about the idea			

teachers' PCK through the process of CoRe design (Hume & Berry, 2010), the student teachers' lack of classroom experience appeared to be a limiting factor in enabling them to construct their own CoRe. In a follow-up study, Hume and Berry (2013) prepared the student teachers to more readily access relevant knowledge prior to their CoRe construction. The teachers' resultant CoRes and comments indicated that with appropriate and timely scaffolding, the process of CoRe construction had the potential for promoting PCK development in these beginning science teachers.

These initial findings led to a study in which scaffolding provided by expert teachers to co-construct CoRes with early career secondary science and technology teachers was examined for its contribution to PCK development (Williams, Eames, Hume, & Lockley, 2012). The question guiding this study was:

How can experts in content and pedagogy work together with early career secondary teachers to develop one science topic CoRe and one technology topic CoRe to support the development of the latter's PCK?

This chapter examines how Activity Theory (AT) was used to explore firstly, how the experts and the early career teachers co-constructed a CoRe in a facilitated workshop situation, and secondly, how the early career teachers then used the CoRe to plan and teach a unit in their classrooms. AT helped to frame the data collection and analysis and held potential for us to focus on the cultural-historical aspects of the activity systems involved. We hoped this AT approach would help illuminate the social and cultural influences on the development of a CoRe, including the nature of the mediating tool (the workshop), the curriculum and assessment imperatives, the nature of the subject, and teacher beliefs. This chapter presents outcomes of the application of Activity Theory in this manner and draws some conclusions regarding the value of using this framework to explore an activity that sought to make explicit the hitherto rather tacit building of PCK by teachers.

RESEARCH DESIGN

This study employed an interpretive methodology using an action research approach (Creswell, 2005). It was based around a cohort of two early career secondary teachers of science and two of technology, acting as practitioner-researchers during their second or third year of teaching. The study took place in the teachers' classrooms in secondary schools in the North Island of New Zealand. This cohort of teachers was chosen because they were beginning to establish themselves in their profession and had some teaching experience to draw upon in planning and delivery. The study comprised three phases (Williams et al., 2012) which lasted five months in total:

Phase 1 of the study involved the design of one CoRe in a science topic and one CoRe in a technology topic. These topics were identified by the early career teachers as topics that they were teaching and within which they would like to enhance their own PCK. The topic in science was organic chemistry to be delivered to a Year 12 (16 year olds) class, and in technology was hard materials to be delivered to a Year 11 (15 year olds) class. Each CoRe was designed with the help of an expert scientist or an expert technologist who provided advice on the key ideas of the subject matter knowledge for the topic of the CoRes, and an expert teacher of science and another of technology at secondary level, who provided appropriate advice on how to address pedagogical aspects related to the key ideas. The experts and the early career teachers co-constructed the CoRe(s) in a facilitated workshop situation at the University of Waikato, New Zealand. A community of learners approach was adopted that encouraged each group member to contribute their ideas drawn from their experiences in distinct socio-historical communities of practice. This connection between different communities of practice was supported by development of an object, the CoRe, which lies at the boundary of each community (Wenger, 1998). Such boundary objects have previously been shown to successfully bring teachers and researchers together in research projects (Otrel-Cass, Cowie, Moreland, & Jones, 2009). The workshop included instruction on the purpose and use of CoRes by members of the research team. Two different researchers observed the process of construction of the CoRe to determine the nature of the contributions made by the expert scientist/technologist, expert teachers, and the early career teachers. Data were gathered using field notes during these observations of the workshop interactions, with a view to understanding how the members interacted in the system. At the conclusion of the workshop, the observing researchers conducted short interviews with each representative group (experts, early career teachers) regarding their experiences in the group and their feelings about the development of the CoRe. This data explored how the groups worked together to share and co-create knowledge of how to teach a science or technology topic.

Phase 2 began an in-school action research process for the teacher in partnership with a researcher. Each early career teacher who was engaged in developing the CoRe undertook a period of planning for delivery of a scheduled unit on the topic using the CoRe as a planning tool. This planning process was reflected upon through an action research partnership with one of the researchers. The researcher respected the planning norms of the teacher and their school, and did not try to unduly influence the planning process in ways that were not consistent with the CoRe. The early career teachers kept a reflective journal as a record of their thoughts about the CoRe collaborative design development process and how they used the CoRe in planning. The early career teachers discussed these reflections about their experiences in using the CoRe for planning with their researcher partner, and the contrast with their classroom experiences from their first years of teaching in general, and within the science or technology topic being planned (Kind, 2009). Data from the reflective journals and discussions addressed the activity of planning mediated by the use of the co-constructed CoRe within the school context.

Phase 3 saw each early career teacher deliver their science or technology unit using the CoRe as a guide and co-researched, with a researcher partner, the outcomes of its use with one class of students. This involved observation of classroom activity by the researcher while the teacher was delivering the unit to promote reflective conversations in an action research process between the teacher and researcher around the teacher's delivery of the subject matter and associated pedagogy, as specified in the CoRe. Three class periods during which one or more of the key ideas from the CoRe was a focus for teaching and learning were observed. Data as field notes from the classroom observations focussed on how the teacher worked with their students and how the students responded. Reflective conversations were held between the researcher and the early career teacher at the conclusion of each of these observations and any changes the teacher planned to make in future lessons in response to their experiences in the unit thus far were noted. A focus group interview of students was conducted by the researcher at the end of the unit to examine how the students' learning experiences may have been influenced by the teacher's implementation of the pedagogical structure in the CoRe. The focus group encouraged the teenage students to share their views and experiences in a supportive manner. To conclude, the researcher held a final reflective conversation with the teacher about their experience using the CoRe as a planning guide during the unit.

Data from the classroom observations, focus group and teacher interviews examined the explicit use of the teacher's developing PCK.

Activity Theory's relationship to sociocultural views of learning and communities of practice (Wenger, 1998) indicated that it could be a useful approach for examining how the CoRe could function as a mediational tool that connects the communities of scientists and technologists to the communities of teachers of science and technology. Additionally, as Hung, Tan and Koh (2006) state, AT can help understand "the activities that teachers and students are engaged in, the types of physical tools/mental models that they use in the activities, the goals and intentions of the activities and the learning outcomes, and/or the artifacts produced within the sociocultural contexts in which they operate" (p. 42). AT could model the interactions between the early career teachers and the experts, the early career teachers and their colleagues, and the early career teachers and their students in this study, and the following diagrams show how this modelling, based on an adaptation of Engeström's second generation (Engeström, 1999) model, was conceived.

In applying the model, the three phases within the study can be understood as follows:

Phase 1 – the CoRe design workshop. In this phase (see Figure 11.1):

- The mediating tool was the workshop, as it provided the means (mediation) for the expert teachers and early career teachers to work together,
- The subjects were the early career teachers who operate within a community of practice,
- The rules under which groups undertook the activity was a community of learners approach in which the early career teachers and the subject specialists interacted,
- The division of labour within the group was seen as the contributions of the content experts (the scientist/technologist) and pedagogy experts (experienced teachers),
- The object of the workshop activity was to design a CoRe.

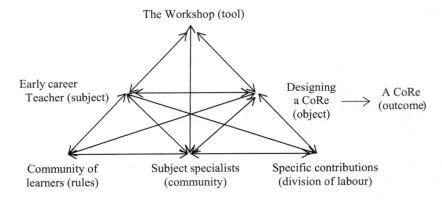

Figure 11.1. An Activity Theory model of the CoRe design workshop

Phase 2 – planning using the CoRe. In this phase (see Figure 11.2):

- The mediating tool was the CoRe developed in Phase 1,
- The subjects were again the early career teachers whose community of practice revolved around planning with the researcher,
- The rules under which the planning activity took place included teacher planning norms influenced both by what the early career teacher typically does and by the school community's expectations for planning,
- The division of labour included the early career teacher's ability and responsibility to plan, and their colleagues' influence on planning through departmental provision of templates, teaching and assessment resources,
- The object of the planning activity was to create a unit plan using the CoRe as a tool in some way.

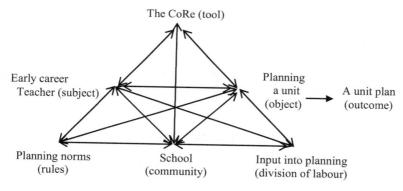

Figure 11.2. An Activity Theory model of planning using the CoRe

Phase 3 – teaching the unit. In this phase (see Figure 11.3):

- The mediating tool was the unit plan developed in Phase 2,
- The subjects were again the early career teachers within a community of practice, in this system it was the classroom,
- The rules were the norms of classroom practice in which the teacher and their students engaged,
- The division of labour recognised the pedagogical approaches that the teacher and their students engaged in, which dictated who did what in the classroom,
- The object was delivering a unit that employed the teachers' enhanced PCK to promote student learning.

These models depict a series of linked activity systems within which the knowledge and expertise of content and pedagogy is shared to create a tool, the CoRe, which mediates learning from the experts through the early career teachers to the students in the classroom. The research was designed to explore this process and the role that

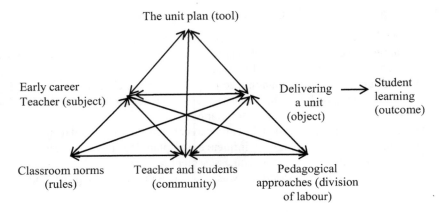

The unit plan (tool)

Early career
Teacher (subject)

Delivering
a unit
(object)

Student
learning
(outcome)

Classroom norms
(rules)

Teacher and students
(community)

Pedagogical
approaches (division
of labour)

Figure 11.3. An Activity Theory model of teaching using the CoRe-influenced unit plan

the CoRe as a mediational tool could play. In this way, the study could contribute to understanding how community members involved together in activity systems around teaching and learning interact, creating multivoicedness and exploring the embedded contradictions (Engeström, 2001) in the activity systems to develop the PCK of these early career teachers.

DATA ANALYSIS

Data analysis was structured around the three phases. In Phase 1, the data gathered as field notes from observations of the workshop interactions, and from the interview transcripts, were content analysed using a framework governed by the interactional elements of the Activity Theory model for this phase (see Figure 11.1). This meant that the system was analysed through who contributed what to the discussions as well as how those contributions were made, all in the context of the subject being discussed.

In Phase 2, the data gathered as teacher reflective journals and conversations with the researchers were content analysed in the same manner as for Phase 1, using the planning activity system as a framework (see Figure 11.2), together with a framework based on the five components of PCK as identified by Magnusson et al. (1999). In this case the system was analysed by examining what the teacher planned and why, who contributed to planning in the school and the systems that impinged on that, including requirements for assessment, and the espoused evidence of PCK components from the teacher.

In Phase 3, the data gathered as classroom observations, teacher reflective conversations, and student focus group and teacher interviews at the end of the unit were content analysed using the teaching activity system as a framework (see Figure 11.3), together with a framework based on the five components of PCK.

In this case, the system was analysed by examining what the teacher did in the classroom and why, how the students responded, and the enacted and espoused evidence of PCK components from the teacher.

APPLICATION OF ACTIVITY THEORY

Activity Theory (AT) was applied to the analysis and interpretation of the data in each phase of the project. In each of these phases, AT was found to be useful to varying extents, with this variation linked to the focus of the theory and the choice of data gathering method. This is now discussed with regards to the three phases.

Phase 1 – this phase was based around a workshop as a mediating tool that would be the focus of the activity system (see Figure 11.1). This workshop was designed to facilitate interactions between the subjects (the early career teachers) and the community (the subject specialists), operating under certain rules (a community of learners approach) with a division of labour (different workshop members were expected to make contributions based on their expertise). The object of the workshop was to co-construct a CoRe and the outcome was indeed a co-constructed CoRe. All members of the CoRe design expressed satisfaction with the outcome and felt that the workshop had helped mediate the production of a useful learning product.

The use of this AT structure for framing and analysis allowed our research teams to both select methods and design research instruments, and then to analyse the interactions within the workshop using this framing. Non-participant observation by a researcher using semi-structured observation and audio-recording enabled the accurate capture of who said what, in response to what, and how this led to further interactions. The complexity of discussion fostered by the activity of designing a CoRe within the workshop brought forth elements of thinking related to the knowledges that Magnusson et al. (1999) had proposed as important in PCK development. These elements of thinking were often influenced by each participant's experience and frame of reference. For example, the early career teachers in science often referred to *The New Zealand Curriculum* (Ministry of Education, 2007) as a basis of their comments, which seemed to reflect both their desire to be seen to be adhering to the policy document guiding their work and their lack of confidence and inexperience in taking a more liberal and nuanced approach to their teaching. On the other hand, the organic chemistry expert often expressed his beliefs about important elements in the subject and why he thought students should know about them, reflecting his orientations towards teaching. The use of an ethnographical style of observation in the workshop appeared important to examining these contributions and their significance. Interviews held with each set of contributors (experts, early career teachers) after the workshop helped to explore the experiences of these contributors within the activity system and the meanings they attributed to these experiences. This served to triangulate the observational data.

The application of AT here also permitted an understanding of some limitations of the AT framework as shown in Figure 11.1. Whilst the element of 'rules' was interpreted in this activity system as the community of learners approach (as these were the rules under which the activity was operating), somewhat hidden within that choice were other 'rules' that appeared to influence how the workshop activity progressed, such as curriculum and assessment 'rules' which the teachers were aware of and seemed to be bound to. This indicates that the process of the activity, and the content or focus of the activity can both influence the framing of the activity system.

Phase 2 – this phase was based around the activity system of planning to teach a unit of work using the co-constructed CoRe from Phase 1 as the mediating tool (see Figure 11.2). The CoRe in this phase was seen to provide the mediation to plan using rules such as planning norms, within the school as a community, and acknowledging the various inputs into planning that represent the division of labour. The outcome in this phase was a unit plan influenced by the CoRe. What was clear from this phase was that neither the CoRe developed in the first activity system, nor the unit plan in this activity system, were static mediational elements. They were seen to evolve through the development process, transforming the systems as they went (Engeström, 2001), a phenomenon that had previously been seen in a similar study (Hume, 2012). The early career teachers used the plan in ways that were influenced by the nature of their class, the planning process they were engaged in, and the particular unit they were to teach with its assessment criteria. There was evidence that the detailed planning process encouraged some refinement of the CoRe for some teachers, indicating how the tensions in the planning activity system could cause the mediational tool itself to evolve.

In this phase participant observation was used by a researcher as they collaboratively designed the unit with the early career teacher. Observational notes and audio-recorded discussions, as well as teacher reflective journals formed the data in this phase. AT in this phase helped the researcher understand how the planning norms of the school influenced the translation of the co-constructed CoRe into a usable unit plan. It was clear that the teachers felt some constraints in their planning due to what they would be allowed to do in their school context, what was expected of them by their colleagues in terms of delivery, and what they understood of their own students. In considering these constraints, the AT lens provided a useful connection to the elements of PCK as discussed above. However, it did again tend to provide more utility when considering the process of planning rather than the focus of planning, and the most insights were gained through the collaborative action research instances where the researcher was working and discussing closely with the teacher. Less insightful were the data gathered from the teacher reflective journals, possibly as they were less interactional in the way they generated data.

Phase 3 – this final phase was based around the activity system of teaching the unit in the classroom to examine how and if the co-construction of the CoRe had developed the PCK of the teacher. In this phase the unit plan was seen as the mediating tool of the activity system for the teaching of the topic to the class. The teaching was seen to be governed by the classroom norms and influenced by the pedagogical approaches which determined who contributed to the teaching and learning and in what ways. The desired outcome was that of any topic that is taught to students, student learning.

It was in this phase that choice of method appeared to render Activity Theory (AT) less useful. In considering the objective of this phase, to explore the development of teacher PCK in response to the co-construction and planning use of a CoRe, the findings were somewhat limited. The teachers' own perspectives were gathered at the end of the unit and these did prove valuable when examined through the PCK knowledges of Magnusson et al. (1999). This self-report data helped provide a view of how the teachers themselves viewed their development, and the process through which the study had been undertaken, with co-construction and reflective practice, appeared to have allowed the teachers to render explicit elements of their PCK that had been developed and those that still needed development. However, the practical constraints of the project, which meant that only three observations were made per class over a period in which 15–20 potential class sessions were available for observation, meant that much interactional evidence was not gathered. This limited findings related to the classroom norms and the pedagogical approaches and how these may have influenced the researcher's access to evidence of development of PCK in relation to the CoRe.

In considering student learning, the focus group with students at the end of the unit revealed little evidence of change that the students had noticed in classroom norms or student-centredness as a pedagogical approach. This perhaps reflects the short duration of the unit which may not have allowed the students to pick up on any cues that illustrated changes in the teacher's PCK. An initial attempt at using pre-test and post-test exploration of the development of student knowledge over the course of the unit was also deemed unsuccessful due to the focus on a short unit delivered to one class. For these reasons, the application of AT in this phase as a framing and analysis lens provided a somewhat limited view of the teachers' PCK development.

What was again evident, however, was the value of being able to focus on the multivoicedness and contradictions in the activity system, and the understanding that the classroom system was evolving through its interaction with both the planning and CoRe design activity systems and not in a linear way. This provides some evidence for how teaching and learning in a classroom, and its connection to an early career teacher's developing PCK, had been transformed through the development of a CoRe co-designed with experts.

CONCLUSION

The study reported here sought to apply an Activity Theory (AT) lens to the development of teacher PCK. It drew on the cultural-historical situatedness of teacher development and practice to examine the role of various activity systems in playing a part in developing teacher PCK. In this way, it examined the multivoicedness, the contradictions and the expansive learning through these activity systems (Engeström, 2001).

The juxtaposition of at least three distinct activity systems, the workshop, the planning of a unit, and the delivery of a unit, each of which exist alongside and in connection with other activity systems, allowed the exploration of how the implicit content and pedagogical knowledge of experts could be shared through the mediation of the CoRe tool. It was found that the tool provided a vehicle for expression and debate around the knowledges required to develop PCK, and that observation of the interactions within the system triangulated with the lived experiences of the participants, analysed through an AT lens, could provide an understanding of how PCK development of early career teachers could occur. The choice of data method and design was found to be important in maximising the potential of AT to provide useful insights in this transformational process, as Hung et al. (2006) also concluded.

What would be of further interest would be to assist teachers to develop their own action research projects using AT as a framework for analysis. This could promote reflection, insightfulness and understanding of the activity systems in which they operate and provide a key support for development of their PCK.

ACKNOWLEDGEMENTS

I am very grateful to my co-researchers, Dr Anne Hume, Professor John Williams and John Lockley, for their contributions to the study reported here and for their feedback on this manuscript.

REFERENCES

Cowie, B., Moreland, J., Jones, A., & Otrel-Cass, K. (2008). *The classroom InSiTE project: Understanding classroom interactions to enhance teaching and learning in science and technology.* Wellington, New Zealand: Teaching and Learning Research Initiative.

De Miranda, M. (2008). Pedagogical content knowledge and engineering and technology teacher education: Issues for thought. *Journal of the Japanese Society of Technology Education, 50*(1), 17–26.

Engeström, Y. (1999). Activity Theory and individual and social transformation. In Y. Engeström, R. Miettinin, & R. Punamaki (Eds.), *Perspectives on Activity Theory* (pp. 19–38). Cambridge, England: Cambridge University Press.

Engeström, Y. (2001). Expansive learning at work: Toward an activity theoretical reconceptulization. *Education and Work, 14*(1), 133–156.

Hume, A. (2012). Primary connections: Stimulating the classroom in initial teacher education. *Research in Science Education, 42,* 551–565.

Hume, A., & Berry, A. (2010). Constructing CoRes – A strategy for building PCK in pre-service science teacher education. *Research in Science Education, 41*(3), 341–355. doi:10.1007/s11165-010-9168-3

Hume, A., & Berry, A. (2013). Enhancing the practicum experience for pre-service chemistry teachers through collaborative CoRe design with mentor teachers. *Research in Science Education, 43*(5), 2107–2136. doi:10.1007/s11165-012-9346-6

Hung, D., Tan, S., & Koh, T. (2006). From traditional to constructivist epistemologies: A proposed theoretical framework based on Activity Theory for learning communities. *Journal of Interactive Learning Research, 17*(1), 37–55.

Jones, A., & Moreland, J. (2004). Enhancing practicing primary teachers' pedagogical content knowledge in technology. *International Journal of Technology and Design Education, 14*(1), 121–140.

Kind, V. (2009). Pedagogical content knowledge in science education: Perspectives and potential for progress. *Studies in Science Education, 45*(2), 169–204. doi:10.1080/03057260903142285

Koehler, M., & Mishra, P. (2005). What happens when teachers design educational technology? The development of technological pedagogical content knowledge. *Journal of Educational Computing Research, 32*(2), 131–152.

Loughran, J., Berry, A., & Mullhall, P. (2006). *Understanding and developing science teachers' pedagogical content knowledge.* Rotterdam, The Netherlands: Sense Publishers.

Loughran, J., Mulhall, P., & Berry, A. (2008). Exploring pedagogical content knowledge in science teacher education. *International Journal of Science Education, 30*(10), 1301–1320.

Magnusson, S., Krajcik, J., & Borko, H. (1999). Nature, sources, and development of pedagogical content knowledge for science teaching. In J. Gess-Newsome & N. G. Lederman (Eds.), *Examining pedagogical content knowledge: The construct and its implications for science education* (pp. 95–132). Boston, MA: Kluwer.

McCormack, R. (1997). Conceptual and procedural knowledge. *International Journal of Design and Technology Education, 7,* 141–159.

McCormack, R. (2004). Issues of learning and knowledge in technology education. *International Journal of Technology and Design Education, 14,* 21–44.

Ministry of Education. (2007). *The New Zealand curriculum.* Wellington, New Zealand: Learning Media.

Padilla, K., Ponce-de-León, A. M., Rembado, F. M., & Garritz, A. (2008). Undergraduate professors' pedagogical content knowledge: The case of 'amount of substance'. *International Journal of Science Education, 30*(10), 1389–1404. doi:10.1080/09500690802187033

Rohaan, E. J., Taconis, R., & Jochems, W. M. G. (2009). Measuring teachers' pedagogical content knowledge in primary technology education. *Research in Science & Technological Education, 27*(3), 327–338. doi:10.1080/02635140903162652

Roth, W.-M. (2004). Activity Theory and education: An introduction. *Mind, Culture and Activity, 11*(1), 1–8.

Shulman, L. (1987). Knowledge and teaching: Foundations of the new reform. *Harvard Educational Review, 57*(1), 1–22.

Wenger, E. (1998). *Communities of practice: Learning, meaning and identity.* Cambridge, MA: Cambridge University Press.

Williams, J., Eames, C., Hume, A., & Lockley, J. (2012). Promoting pedagogical content knowledge (PCK) development for early career secondary teachers in science and technology using Content Representation (CoRes). *Research in Science and Technological Education, 30*(3), 327–343.

Chris Eames
University of Waikato
New Zealand

JOHN LOCKLEY

12. TEACHERS DESIGNING CLASSROOM CURRICULUM THROUGH THE LENS OF CULTURAL-HISTORICAL ACTIVITY THEORY

INTRODUCTION

Teachers in the compulsory education sector interpret curriculum within their school setting to design educational programmes that address intended learning for students. This chapter reports on the use of Cultural-Historical Activity Theory to better understand the influences that guide teachers' planning of school based curriculum and teaching pedagogy. The research, carried out at the University of Waikato, investigated the way a secondary school teacher designed and implemented local curriculum in education for sustainability.

Local curriculum can be defined as the intentional learning and teaching developed by teachers within the school setting, that they plan to deliver to students (Eisner, 1994). This locally enacted curriculum draws on the planned and codified national or state curriculum with teachers making contextual judgements, driven by their pedagogical knowledge, (Magnusson, Krajcik, & Borko, 1999; Shulman, 1987) to design learning experiences they think will best meet the needs of their learners (Marsh, 2009). This locally enacted curriculum is expressed and documented in various forms such as lesson plans, unit plans and overarching schemes of work.

The New Zealand national curriculum is a statement of educational policy in the form of principles, values, competencies, and achievement objectives, setting "the direction for teaching and learning in English-medium New Zealand schools, ... it is a framework rather than a detailed plan" (Ministry of Education, 2007, p. 37). New Zealand teachers are expected to interpret the national curriculum, drawing on a wide range of ideas and resources to arrive at a plan for teaching and learning to suit their particular educational setting. This site based process is called "local curriculum development" (Ministry of Education, 2007, p. 37).

The processes involved in curriculum development have been theorised by various authors over time. Early thoughts by Tyler (1949) for example framed a set of questions from which decisions about the development of curriculum could be made. These fundamental questions, sometimes referred to as 'Tyler's Rationale' include:

What educational purpose should the school seek to attain? What educational experiences can be provided that are likely to attain these purposes? How can

D. S. P. Gedera & P. J. Williams (Eds.), Activity Theory in Education, 183–198.

these educational experiences be effectively organised? How can we determine whether these purposes are being attained? (Tyler, 1949, p. 1)

These questions taken in their barest form imply that educational aims and objectives can be predetermined and separated in space and time from the context of where the learning is meant to occur. If curriculum development is approached entirely from this perspective it negates the role of teachers in the process of curriculum development and under represents the interdependence of the answers to the questions, and how these answers reflect back on each other (Dewey, 1938).

More recent scholarship in curriculum has shown the concept to be far more political in nature (Pinar, Reynolds, Slattery, & Taubman, 1996) with curriculum development a complex process involving teachers making decisions about a number of factors including the learning environment, the students to be taught, their own strengths and experiences, the school situation, and the national/state curriculum (McGee & Taylor, 2008). In this view of local curriculum development, the interplay between the decisions that need to be addressed at the local school level is acknowledged along with the issues of the content to be delivered. It recognises the role of teachers where they make decisions about the interactions between the content knowledge to be addressed, the goals, aims and objectives of the learning programme, an analysis of the situation in which the learning is to take place including recognising the influences of the learning environment, the students, the teachers, and the school. These considerations determine the learning and teaching activities that students will encounter, and influence the evaluation of teaching and learning to be carried out (Nicholls & Nicholls, 1972).

This chapter reports upon the use of Cultural-Historical Activity Theory to add to the understanding of the process of local curriculum development. The chapter reports upon the investigation of the way a secondary school teacher in New Zealand developed local curriculum in education for sustainability within their school setting. The research was qualitative in nature and positioned in an interpretive paradigm. The case reported upon was part of a 2011, yearlong research project investigating local curriculum development in 4 different school situations where education for sustainability was being addressed by teachers in response to changes in the national curriculum. Cultural-Historical Activity Theory was used to frame the investigation into the activity system of local curriculum development. Data, in the form of transcribed teachers' comments were collected from individual teacher guided interviews where the interview questions were designed to probe teachers' understandings and behaviours corresponding to each junction of the Activity Theory system. This data was supplemented and compared with data gathered from collaborative teacher focus group discussions and classroom observations. Data analysis was carried out using an Activity Theory framework.

APPLICATION OF CULTURAL-HISTORICAL ACTIVITY THEORY TO UNDERSTANDING THE DEVELOPMENT OF LOCAL CURRICULUM

The general Activity Theory system as described by Engeström (1999), allows for the investigation of a subject's conception of an object and the development of their outcome to address that object. Moreover it allows for the investigation of the way this process is influenced by the psychological tools, or mediating artefacts, used in the situation; as well as the social interactions within the community of practice; including the composition of the community, the way work is divided and delegated, and the rules that govern those interactions.

Cultural-Historical Activity Theory has been shown to be a useful framework from which to approach questions of education (Dakers, 2011; Hsu, van Eijck, & Roth, 2010; Roth, 2004). In this research it was applied as a theoretical framework addressing the question of how teachers develop local curriculum in education for sustainability. Activity Theory was used in this context as it was perceived to have the potential to elucidate the thinking and valued nature of the decisions being made by the teacher as well as to facilitate an interpretive investigation of the influences upon their curriculum development actions. Furthermore, Activity Theory was perceived as a framework that would allow the identification of the objects that motivated the teacher's activity and the tools they choose to use as well as the way the teacher perceived these influences. The third perceived strength of Cultural-Historical Activity Theory in this context was its ability to identify and describe the interactions occurring in the community of practice within which the teacher participated, identifying the members of the community, their roles, and the understandings that are commonly held within the community (Roth, Tobin, Zimmermann, Bryant, & Davis, 2002).

In the Cultural-Historical Activity Theory system of local curriculum development, shown in Figure 12.1, these nodes of understanding; subject, object, tools, rules, community, and division of labour become defined in context.

In this context the activity system can be theorised as the interaction between teachers (the subject of the system) and their conceptions of education for sustainability as expressed through their local curriculum planning (the object of the system) to address the purpose of their activity, student learning in sustainability (the outcome of the system). The cultural-historical influences on their local curriculum and pedagogy development can be interpreted as the national curriculum (mediating artefact); the culture and operation of the school, expressed through what counts as student success (rules); the extent to which other curriculum shareholders' views, such as students and their parents/caregivers are valued in curriculum development decisions (community); and the way curriculum development is managed in the school (division of labour).

The case study reported in this chapter represents the findings from 'North' School, a decile one,[1] state co-educational secondary school, catering for 400 year 9–13

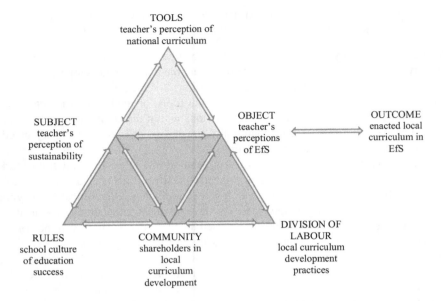

Figure 12.1. The cultural-historical activity system of local curriculum development in education for sustainability

students, which is small for New Zealand standards. The teacher involved, 'Wayne', was an experienced teacher, having taught for over twenty years, who was the head of the technology department (design and graphics, hard materials and food).

Subject: The Teacher's Perception of Sustainability

The subject of the activity system in this study is interpreted as being the perception the teacher had of sustainability. Sustainability, though generally accepted as being the interaction of environmental, social and economic aspects of development (World Commission on Environment and Development, 1987) has been shown to be a values soaked concept that can be interpreted in many different ways (Marien, 1996).

Wayne's perception of sustainability was influenced by a number of factors. The most influential of these was, in Wayne's view, his previous professional experience as an architectural designer. This background, from before he became a teacher, gave him a strong belief in the power of technological development to create more sustainable ways of living. This perspective influenced his view of what sustainability was, and how it could be addressed in his teaching programme where he looked at architecture, building materials and systems.

The second most influential factor affecting Wayne's view of sustainability was, in his view, his personal beliefs and values about sustainability. The first of these was associated with his view of the environment. He described himself as having an affinity for the natural world, commenting, "I have an awareness wherever I go, like fishing or nature; I just have an appreciation. I think I have been programmed to think that way … it is about protecting our planet and avoiding the depletion of resources" (initial interview). The second expression of these beliefs and values was where Wayne acknowledged his cultural-historical understanding of sustainability expressing a belief that people require more than just knowledge to begin to act sustainably, that it is also about attitudes such as caring for others. Wayne commented for example, "For me it is about respect for yourself and respect for the needs of others … It is about trying to persuade people to be more aware and less selfish so that they are taking other people into consideration" (initial interview).

The third major influence on Wayne's perception of sustainability was his ongoing professional learning. In the New Zealand education system there was no opportunity for Wayne to participate in formal collegial teacher professional development so his answer to his felt need for developing his understanding of sustainability at a professional level was to enrol privately in university papers towards a postgraduate diploma. This learning stimulated his thinking about sustainability and prompted him to begin developing his sustainability teaching programme. He explained for example, "When I started studying last year… I was really prompted to start thinking, and everything changed. So I just got my students into it" (initial interview).

Object: The Teacher's Perception of Education for Sustainability

The object of the activity system in this study is interpreted as being the perception that the teacher had of education for sustainability. Though the nature of education for sustainability has been clearly described (Tilbury, 1995) its expression takes different forms. For example, education for sustainability is positioned in many, especially European countries (Wals, 2009), as Education for Sustainable Development (UNESCO, 2014). In the New Zealand context education for sustainability is, however, positioned as 'ecological sustainability' (Ministry of Education, 2007, p. 10) as part of the values of the curriculum, with this positioning focussing on participating and contributing to society, through "understand[ing] the importance of balancing rights, roles, and responsibilities, and of contributing to the quality and sustainability of social, cultural, physical, and economic environments" (Ministry of Education, 2007, p. 13), more than development.

Wayne expressed his understanding of education for sustainability as being primarily about helping students understand the finite nature of resources. For example, when asked about the aim of education for sustainability, Wayne commented, "It is about students understanding the depletion of resources. First and foremost students need to understand that we are limited by our resources" (initial interview). Moreover, Wayne viewed education for sustainability as being holistic in nature, not constrained to any one subject or learning area, and about developing students' attitudes. He described this as switching students on to living curiously and seeing sustainable connections. For example, he recounted the case of a student researching sustainable water use at their home, an aspect of architectural design covered in his classes in preparation for a speech in English, "I loaned him a camera and he took pictures of their water tanks and pumps. That tells me he is switched on" (initial interview).

Wayne expressed his holistic view of education for sustainability through his approach to classroom practice where he wove issues of sustainability into every design brief the students worked on. Students typically encountered sustainability through designing applications of new technologies to create more ecologically sustainable built environments. This approach involved students researching sustainable materials and systems and incorporating these into their building designs, including systems such as voltaic panels and wind turbines, along with landscaping choices such as what trees to plant and the alignment of the building on their site to influence solar heating and cooling.

Wayne's pedagogical approach in education for sustainability was about mixing theory and practice. He explained "It is about having a result from practical things. Just theory is not good enough" (initial interview). He explained that in his view developing students' practical problem solving skills and understandings would empower students to make informed choices leading to living more sustainable lives. Within this approach he did not consider there were any special resources or teaching methods that delineated education for sustainability. In his classroom students worked on individual projects, often at different stages with a variety of learning resources available. Students were exposed to digital media such as "video clips [and] animations" (workshop 2) to capture their imagination and present new knowledge and experiences. Wayne used digital projection to present information to students as well as using a chalkboard and whiteboard. Wayne's students had choices of learning technologies to work with. The room contained computers for students for rendering digital graphics as well as searching information, as well as desks and drawing boards where students could use paper and pencil to communicate their design ideas. Individual learning is celebrated in Wayne's classroom practice.

Tools: The Teacher's Perception of the National Curriculum

The main tool of the activity system in this study is interpreted as being the perception that the teacher had of the national curriculum. The national curriculum in this context is seen as the mediating artefact that guides the design of the local curriculum by the teacher.

Wayne was confident in his view that sustainability was an overarching part of the national curriculum and something he should be focussing on with his students in design and technology, though was less confident identifying where sustainability was actually positioned in the curriculum as part of the values and competencies to be developed. Wayne's curriculum knowledge mainly focused on the achievement objectives of his learning area where he exhibited an in depth knowledge. This achievement objective knowledge was, however, mediated and actualised through two other operational representations of curriculum. The first of these was Wayne's knowledge of the way curriculum achievement objectives were re-presented as national assessment standards. This assessment standards knowledge in many ways became the operational 'national curriculum' that Wayne reflected upon when making local curriculum development decisions, particularly on a lesson-by-lesson, day-to-day basis.

The second alternate representation of curriculum that operated upon Wayne's local curriculum development was pre-prepared units of work supplied by industry training organisations, such as the Building and Carpentry Industry Training Organisation (BCITO). Wayne explained that in his school, these pre-prepared and moderated units of work were used by teachers as starting points for developing local and authentic contexts for student learning. He explained his use of these units commenting, "I look at the curriculum but am guided largely by the pre-moderated unit of work from the industry training organisation. It has already included all those curriculum objectives" (workshop 3).

Rules: The Educational Culture of the School

The rules governing the activity system in this study is interpreted as being the perception the teacher had of what counts as educational success for students within the school setting. 'Educational success' is a valued concept which can be interpreted in different ways. For example, it may be measured by students gaining success through achieving competency credentials on a national qualifications framework. In the New Zealand context this success is expressed through the National Certificate of Educational Achievement (NCEA) which is administered by the New Zealand Qualifications Authority (NZQA) (New Zealand Qualifications Authority, 2011). Alternately educational success may be perceived more holistically and indicated by students' appreciation of their humanity, the society they live in and their relationship with the world around them. Students who are successfully educated in this view of educational success become more civilised.

Wayne's local curriculum development activities took place within the educational culture of North School. Here the Board of Trustees[2] has articulated the vision for the school through the school prospectus and mission statement. The stated strategic priority for the school was to raise student achievement with a particular focus on Māori and Pacifica student achievement as measured by results on the NZQA framework. In Wayne's mind, this priority played out through the way he considered student learning, and his own teaching success. He acknowledged that the system was results driven, with the results that matter being success against national qualifications standards. He explained his thinking:

The principal puts the sheet on the table and looks at his graphs. He has his objectives that the Board of Trustees have set. He shows this to the parents and

189

to the staff in the staffroom and it shows how many students have achieved level one and compares that to the previous four years. It is very results focussed. We need to keep students in school and get them qualifications, and we compare that with the rest of New Zealand schools at our decile level. (workshop 3)

Wayne felt a tension between this focus on improving student qualifications and his desire to innovate in his teaching practice. He appreciated the need for focus and direction with curriculum development at the school level accepting the need for strong leadership. He explained his view reflected that "While we could have these lovely themes and inquiry learning happening, when teachers have the option to say no, it will never happen. When there is too much choice people won't do it, it is an issue of leadership" (workshop 2). Wayne balanced this strong school wide curriculum leadership structure by innovating in his own classroom curriculum in education for sustainability in response to the perceived needs of his students. He argued that he could do anything as long as his students got their NCEA credits.

Community: The Shareholders in Local Curriculum Development

The community of the activity system in this study is interpreted as being the groups of people that the teacher allowed to influence the development of the local curriculum. These groups had a vested interest in the success of the local curriculum being developed, hence the term shareholder is applied.

In North School a number of shareholder groups were identified as having influence on Wayne's local curriculum development in education for sustainability. Within the school structure these included, at the governance level, the Board of Trustees which had set clear expectations of teachers to improve student achievement as measured against national achievement standards. At the department / middle management level Wayne worked with a team of colleagues acting at one level as a member of the team even though he was in effect the team manager. As a team member Wayne's programmes of work needed to be consistent with the programmes and curriculum norms of others so that all students received equivalent teaching and curriculum coverage. This influence by his peers reduced his opportunity to innovate within in his local curriculum.

Outside of the school the parent/caregiver community was also identified by Wayne as being influential in his local curriculum development decisions. For example, he saw this group as a potential source of support for his teaching programme commenting, "In our community you have to identify the parents in business, and in those strategic positions which could assist in a project" (workshop 2).

The most influential shareholder group that acted upon Wayne's local curriculum development decisions however was his students. His students influenced his curriculum planning in two ways. Firstly, he understood his students as a cohort of learners. This understanding was expressed for example through acknowledgement of the issues that his students faced living in a low socioeconomic community. For example, he was aware that many of the families of his students lived on less than the average wage for New Zealand, and many relied on social welfare benefits. He felt that for many of his students, learning was not their immediate need, commenting "in my experience, in a decile one school, it is about survival. Economic survival [where] food comes first. Just to go through the day, to have sandwiches is important. It is about understanding their parents and their households" (initial interview). Another way he appreciated his students as a cohort was when he considered the difference between teaching junior and senior students. For example, when thinking about his education for sustainability programme he commented:

> I find that my seniors become more interested in sustainability where I teach a unit on sustainable architecture. The juniors like to design houses and put furniture inside and that sort of thing, but it is the seniors that really get into it. I think it has a lot to do with the amount of time I have spent teaching them. A different culture is created and they really think differently. (workshop 2)

The second way Wayne considered his students in his local curriculum development was as individuals. This was evidenced in the way Wayne made allowances for students with differential learning needs, explaining that "You have some students at the head and some in the middle and some at the tail. You can't give them the same project, so we plan to have different projects for students of different ability" (workshop 3). Wayne's knowledge of his individual students was also expressed through his understanding of students' individual interests. He explained this, saying "you might walk up to a student and say well, we are going to make a loud speaker box because you know that his brother has got a car and he likes sounds. Immediately you have got his attention" (workshop 3).

This knowledge of students as individuals was critical in Wayne's view of local curriculum development and something he worked hard at achieving, "I know about 90% of my students well, as I work with them year after year. You always get new students, and that is a challenge, but when they arrive I spend two or three extra hours working with them" (workshop 2). This knowledge of individual students was also valued by other teachers and enhanced by the teachers from different technology classes; graphics, automotive, engineering, building construction; talking together and sharing their understanding of individual students. Wayne commented that "we talk with each other or email one another. You need to know the hobbies and the interests of the students, if you know that, you are in a very good position" (workshop 3).

Wayne's classroom practice reflected this view that knowing his students as individuals is key to creating successful learning experiences for them. The way Wayne constructed the classroom environment, the choice of learning materials and the roles he adopted in the classroom allowed him to work one on one with his students and make adjustments to his local curriculum in response to feedback from his students, for example:

191

I have the advantage of sitting next to individual students as they are working on their computers and asking a couple of questions. Like, explain how this photovoltaic panel gets the power to this battery? Or explain why you have your windows oriented here on this side of the building? I have a building mock-up in my classroom and I talk with students; we connect up all the systems and talk about them. I know exactly where the student is going, what I should do and where I should concentrate. So it is in real time, next to the student. (workshop 2)

This detailed and current knowledge of his students was critical in Wayne's approach to local curriculum development where he had learnt the importance of capturing his students' imagination and interest quickly and structuring student learning in meaningful contexts, for example:

When I do a lesson, say designing a backpack to harvest human energy, I may have about 5 different things going on in my classroom. I will have some of my Westside[3] friends starting out creating a backpack with tagging on it, starting with the artwork. Some of the girls will be doing girl friendly stuff and some of the more advanced kids will be doing the real backpack thing, magnets and copper wire and that. Then there may be another student that says they don't want to use the computer so they will use the drawing board and use pencil and paper and coloured pencils. Then you maybe have one girl that you know who is into handbags so they can design a sustainable handbag instead. So I have to have things prepared and be able to just go 'click' and it is there for them. It works because they feel valued. (workshop 2)

An implication of Wayne's approach to local curriculum planning, focussing on individual students, is that the planning process is ongoing and time consuming and not just something that is done at the beginning of the unit. Wayne expressed that the process for him was more of an iterative, design-based process where he considered his students in an ongoing way, continually acknowledging and actualising their input into the planning process. He explained, "I think a lot [about planning], even at home, or when I am on the computer at home, I always think about those students" (initial interview).

Division of Labour: Local Curriculum Development Practices

The division of labour within the activity system in this study is interpreted as being the perception that the teacher had of the way local curriculum is developed within the school and the social structures that exist to frame and direct that development. For example, Wayne described his personal approach to local curriculum development as "the typical secondary scenario where teachers all create their own units of work" (initial interview). When pressed to describe this in more detail he acknowledged, however, that there was an active collegial relationship between members of his department and that they often shared ideas by visiting each other's classrooms and talking about particular learners. Wayne explained that in North School teachers didn't work together in a shared workroom so communication among teachers wasn't facilitated in that way. Instead teachers worked informally making time to talk in breaks or visiting each other's classrooms when they had non-contact periods. Wayne valued these opportunities to clarify ideas about potential projects and to talk about students and their learning.

This informal way of working together to develop local curriculum was effective in Wayne's view in North School because staffing had been very stable for a number of years. He explained that all the staff he worked with were, "very experienced, making small changes all the time to be more successful" (workshop 3). Moreover, he explained that the staff had been teaching the same courses for a long time and knew the material and progressions of learning expected for their students.

As the head of the technology learning area, Wayne also interacted with the teachers in his department in a more formal way. Interaction at this level linked back to the whole school focus on student achievement as measured by assessment success on the NZQA framework. Wayne described these typical departmental interactions with his staff in terms of:

> I look at [the teachers work and how] it should build towards the graph[4] and the result. How are they going to do that? I visit them about once a week and we spend time together. I comment on the projects, sometimes give them my ideas and ask questions about how and why they are doing things. I ask about student engagement. Are the students really engaged? Are they interested? That is a big thing for us. If we achieve that, everybody is happy. We are all working towards those students passing those standards and walking out with specific skills and a certificate.[5] (workshop 3)

Outcome: Enacted Local Curriculum in Education for Sustainability

The outcome of the activity system in this study is interpreted as being the local curriculum in education for sustainability that was enacted by the teacher. In Wayne's case this local curriculum in education for sustainability was infused within the normal course work in his design and graphics programme at all levels. This approach was consistent with his view of sustainability as being about practical problem solving which can be applied to sustainability issues to create more sustainable technical solutions. In this approach issues of sustainability are infused seamlessly into the learning area alongside other planned learning outcomes, a pattern that began for students in year 9 and became part of the normal approach to the subject. For example Wayne explained:

> In year 9 and 10 we talk about sustainability and include it in a subtle way, but we do incorporate that into our curriculum. I think in [design and graphics] we do the most sustainability, it is a huge chunk. It connects with design all the

time. For example in sustainable architecture you have to plan how to include sustainability with aesthetics and function. So, the student has to consider; the architect, the style, the design era, the art, the colours, the shape, shadows, and also sustainability, the systems and materials in there. (Wayne, initial interview)

In Wayne's enacted local curriculum in education for sustainability the choice of topic, or as is referred to in technology – project, became less important than identifying the opportunities to address sustainability within any topic. Issues of sustainability were seen to be important in all projects and therefore education for sustainability could be incorporated across the whole year's work. This approach was exemplified in his year 11 programme where his students designed a sleep-out[6] for someone else, a stakeholder. The students considered concepts of sustainability while researching and designing their response to the design brief. This work was scaffolded for students with handout material that showed clearly how the project addressed the eight NCEA achievement standards in design and graphics. This scaffolding was achieved by Wayne using a series of Power Point presentations that contained the content that students should cover which included a section on relevant sustainability concepts and key words including: earth building (cobb/ adobe/straw bales/rammed earth); water systems including rain, grey and black water; bio-filtration; energy flow and conservation principles including solar energy, photovoltaic panels, L.E.D. lighting, wind turbines, inverter, deciduous planting to increase insolation in the winter, insulation including double glazing and green (vegetative) roofing, passive heating e.g., thermal mass walls, cooling towers and heat recovery ventilation. All of these sustainable architecture concepts were linked seamlessly with contemporary aesthetic design considerations such as pattern, rhythm, balance, colour and style. This yearlong project was punctuated by different aspects of sustainability being focused upon in a number of connected units of work. Students learned about, and then responded to these ideas in the context of their sleep-out designs.

In Wayne's EfS classroom practice, students worked on individual designs preparing a portfolio of work to explain and justify their design decisions showing how they had addressed concepts of sustainability within their designs. The pedagogy was student centred with student work individualised and varied. Though students worked on individual portfolios, Wayne valued students being involved in "collaboration and group work" as well as "practical work and experimentation" (workshop 1). Observation of these portfolios showed how students understood and used the concepts of sustainability they had been introduced to within their designs. The evidence of their understanding was shown through annotated graphical representations of their individually planned sleep-outs through statements such as "harvesting the sun and wind energy means I will have free power available to use. I can send power back to the grid and get a rebate or credit from the power company" (Student 1, classroom observation). As well as design annotations, student learning in sustainability was evidenced through student written self-evaluation of their design decisions as part of their design portfolios. Students justified their decisions acknowledging advantages and disadvantages of their designs for example, "In this design I combine horizontal and vertical louvers to maximise the screening effect. One of the advantages of louvers is that it creates turbulence and enhances the air flow" (Student 1, classroom observation).

SUMMARY AND CONCLUSIONS

The use of Cultural-Historical Activity Theory in this research, to theorise the activity system of local curriculum and pedagogy development in education for sustainability, adds to the successful application of Activity Theory to understanding issues of education in many contexts (Dakers, 2011; Hsu et al., 2010; Pearson, 2009; Said et al., 2014). The use of Activity Theory as a theoretical framework in this context has allowed an investigation and clear articulation of the sociocultural and historical influences at work upon a teacher as they develop local curriculum and pedagogy at the school level. This articulation of local curriculum development, a part of the sociocultural practice of teaching (Bell, 2010), has been shown to be a complex design process, influenced by the teacher's sociocultural and historical identity as well as the norms of the community of practice within the school setting. The use of Activity Theory in this way has not only facilitated a rich description of the enacted curriculum, in this case addressing education for sustainability, but identified the influences that guide the development of that curriculum and the way these influences are perceived and acted upon by the teacher.

The influence of the sociocultural historical identity of the teacher (Leibowitz, Garraway, & Farmer, 2015) has been shown in this research to be a significant factor in the way that local curriculum is perceived and developed. In this case study the teacher's perception of the concept to be taught (sustainability) and the way this should be taught (education for sustainability) are shown to be influenced strongly by his past personal and professional experiences. His chosen pedagogical approach focussing on technological problem solving and design of new built environments flows from these experiences.

The sociocultural-historical influences of the community of practice the teacher works within is also clearly articulated through the use of the Activity Theory framework. Teaching can be viewed as working within an established community of practice (Korthagen, 2010; Lave, 1996; Lave & Wenger, 1991) where activity is mediated by the social norms of that community. In this case study the use of Activity Theory aided an articulation and analysis of the social norms of that community. For example, curriculum, a fundamental organising concept for teachers was shown in this context to be operationalised via alternate intermediary objects; pre-prepared units of work and assessment frameworks. The use of these objects and the acceptance of innovation were shown to be mediated by the social norms and practices of the community of teachers.

The sociocultural-historical setting of the school and the culture expressed within that setting were also shown to be influential in the process of local curriculum development. The constraints of community culture (Cobb, McClain, de Silva Lamberg, & Dean, 2003) in this case created a tension within which the teacher operated where they balanced school cultural expectations against personal views of teaching and learning. This tension was exemplified by the question of what counted as educational success. From the perspective of school governance, perhaps in response to political pressure to be seen as an effective school, educational success equated to national assessment 'pass' rates. This definition of educational success was in tension with the teacher's own internal definition of educational success, which was to have students aware and critical of their lives, in the context of education for sustainability, making sustainable decisions.

The application of Cultural-Historical Activity Theory in this setting has produced a rich description of the influences that affect the development of local curriculum, which can be interpreted in the context of the school setting. Moreover, the data obtained through the use of the Activity Theory framework have allowed the interpretation of the data to show the way the subject, in this case the teacher, made sense of, and valued the different components of the activity system to inform their decision making process. Cultural-Historical Activity Theory applied in this way has the potential to add to our understanding of how teachers act professionally to develop local curriculum balancing their personal and professional influences within the cultural influences of their school setting.

NOTES

[1] Low socioeconomic.
[2] Governance body comprising members of the local community.
[3] Students with affiliation to a local gang.
[4] Assessment results showing student pass rates over the last 4 years.
[5] National Certificate of Educational Achievement.
[6] Small self-contained habitable building as defined by local building planning authorities.

REFERENCES

Bell, B. (2010). Theorising teaching. *Waikato Journal of Education*, 15(2), 21–40. Retrieved from http://doi.org/10.15663/wje.v15i2.111

Cobb, P., McClain, K., de Silva Lamberg, T., & Dean, C. (2003). Situating teachers' instructional practices in the institutional setting of the school and district. *Educational Researcher*, 32(6), 13–24. Retrieved from http://doi.org/3699898

Dakers, J. (2011). Activity Theory as a pedagogical framework for the delivery of technology education. In M. Barak & M. Hacker (Eds.), *Fostering human development through engineering and technology education* (Vol. 6, pp. 19–34). Rotterdam, The Netherlands: Sense Publishers.

Dewey, J. (1938). *Experience and education*. New York, NY: Macmillan.

Eisner, E. W. (1994). *The educational imagination* (3rd ed.). New York, NY: Macmillan.

Engeström, Y. (1999). Activity Theory and individual and social transformation. In Y. Engeström, R.-L. Punamaki, & R. Miettinen (Eds.), *Perspectives on Activity Theory* (pp. 19–38). Cambridge, England: Cambridge University Press.

Hsu, P.-L., van Eijck, M., & Roth, W.-M. (2010). Students' representations of scientific practice during a science internship: Reflections from an activity-theoretic perspective. *International Journal of Science Education, 32*(9), 1243–1266.

Korthagen, F. A. J. (2010). Situated learning theory and the pedagogy of teacher education: Towards an integrative view of teacher behavior and teacher learning. *Teaching and Teacher Education, 26*(1), 98–106. Retrieved from http://doi.org/10.1016/j.tate.2009.05.001

Lave, J. (1996). Teaching, as learning, in practice. *Mind, Culture and Activity, 3*(3), 149–164. Retrieved from http://doi.org/10.1207/s15327884mca0303_2

Lave, J., & Wenger, E. (1991). *Situated learning: Legitimate peripheral participation.* Cambridge, England: Cambridge University Press.

Leibowitz, B., Garraway, J., & Farmer, J. (2015). Influence of the past on professional lives: A collective summary. *Mind, Culture and Activity, 22*(1), 23–36. Retrieved from http://doi.org/10.1080/1074903 9.2014.979949

Magnusson, S., Krajcik, J., & Borko, H. (1999). Nature, sources, and development of pedagogical content knowledge for science teaching. In J. Gess-Newsome & N. G. Lederman (Eds.), *Examining pedagogical content knowledge: The construct and its implications for science education* (1st ed., pp. 95–132). Dordrecht, The Netherlands: Kluwer Academic.

Marien, M. (Ed.). (1996). *Environmental issues and sustainable futures: A critical guide to recent books, reports and periodicals.* Bethesda, MD: World Future Society.

Marsh, C. (2009). *Key concepts for understanding curriculum* (4th ed.). New York, NY: Routledge.

McGee, J., & Taylor, M. (2008). Planning for effective teaching and learning. In C. McGee & D. Fraser (Eds.), *The professional practice of teaching* (3rd ed., pp. 116–135). Melbourne, Victoria: Cengage Learning Australia.

Ministry of Education. (2007). *New Zealand curriculum for English-medium teaching and learning in years 1–13.* Wellington, New zealand: Learning Media Ltd.

New Zealand Qualifications Authority. (2011). *Home NZQA.* Retrieved May 2, 2011, from http://www.nzqa.govt.nz.ezproxy.waikato.ac.nz/

Nicholls, A., & Nicholls, H. (1972). *Developing a curriculum: A practical guide.* London, England: George Allen & Unwin.

Pearson, S. (2009). Using Activity Theory to understand prospective teachers' attitudes to and construction of special educational needs and / or disabilities. *Teacher and Teacher Education, 25*(2009), 559–568. Retrieved from http://doi.org/10.1016/j.tate.2009.02.011

Pinar, W., Reynolds, W., Slattery, P., & Taubman, P. (1996). *Understanding curriculum: An introduction to the study of historical and contemporary curriculum discourses* (Vol. 17). New York, NY: Peter Lang.

Roth. (2004). Activity Theory and education: An introduction. *Mind, Culture and Activity, 11*(1), 1–8. Retrieved from http://doi.org/10.1207/s15327884mca1101_1

Roth, W., Tobin, K., Zimmermann, A., Bryant, N., & Davis, C. (2002). Lessons on and from the dihybrid cross: An activity–theoretical study of learning in coteaching. *Journal of Research in Science Teaching, 39*(3), 253–282. Retrieved from http://doi.org/10.1002/tea.10018

Said, M. N. H. M., Tahir, L. M., Ali, M. F., Noor, N. M., Atan, N. A., & Zaleha, A. (2014). Using Activity Theory as analytical framework for evaluating contextual online collaborative learning. *International Journal of Emerging Technologies in Learning, 9*(5), 54–59. Retrieved from http://doi.org/10.3991/ ijet.v9i5.3972

Shulman, L. (1987). Knowledge and teaching: Foundations of the new reform. *Harvard Educational Review, 57*(1), 1–22.

Tilbury, D. (1995). Environmental education for sustainability: Defining the new focus of environmental education in the 1990s. *Environmental Education Research, 1*(2), 195–212. Retrieved from http://doi.org/10.1080/1350462950010206

Tyler, R. (1949). *Basic principles of instruction.* Chicago, IL: University of Chicago Press.

UNESCO. (2014). *Education for sustainable development: United Nations decade (2005–2014).* Retrieved December 4, 2014, from http://www.unesco.org/new/en/education/themes/leading-the-international-agenda/education-for-sustainable-development/education-for-sustainable-development/

Wals, A. (2009). *Review of contexts and structures for education for sustainable development*. Paris, France: UNESCO.

World Commission on Environment and Development. (1987). *Our common future*. Oxford, England: Oxford University Press.

John Lockley
University of Waikato
New Zealand

CPSIA information can be obtained
at www.ICGtesting.com
Printed in the USA
BVHW04s1922130418
513222BV00003B/46/P

9 789463 003858